Nachmanides
An Unusual Thinker

NACHMANIDES

An Unusual Thinker

Israel Drazin

Copyright © Israel Drazin
Jerusalem 2018/5778

All rights reserved. No part of this publication may be translated, reproduced, stored in a retrieval system or transmitted, in any form or by any means, electronic, mechanical, photocopying, recording or otherwise, without express written permission from the publishers.

A version of chapter 2 appeared in *Journal of Jewish Studies* 50, no. 2 (autumn 1999), and a portion of chapter 4 was delivered as a lecture at the World Congress of Jewish Studies in Jerusalem in 2001. They are reprinted here with permission.

Cover design: Leah Ben Avraham/ Noonim Graphics
Typesetting: Raphaël Freeman, Renana Typesetting

ISBN: 978-965-229-887-4

1 3 5 7 9 8 6 4 2

Gefen Publishing House Ltd.
6 Hatzvi Street
Jerusalem 94386, Israel
+972-2-538-0247

Gefen Books
140 Fieldcrest Ave.
Edison NJ, 07081
516-593-1234

orders@gefenpublishing.com
www.gefenpublishing.com

Printed in Israel

Library of Congress Cataloging-in-Publication Data

Names: Drazin, Israel, 1935- author.
Title: Nachmanides : an unusual thinker / by Israel Drazin.
Description: Jerusalem : Gefen Publishing House Ltd., [2017] | Includes index.
Identifiers: LCCN 2017003780 | ISBN 9789652298874
Subjects: LCSH: Nachmanides, approximately 1195-approximately 1270. | Rabbis--Spain--Biography.
Classification: LCC BM755.M62 D73 2017 | DDC 296.3/96092 [B]
--dc23 LC record available at https://lccn.loc.gov/2017003780

*Dedicated
in love and in gratitude
to my dear wife*

Dina Drazin

~ Thirty-eight books by Israel Drazin

MAIMONIDES AND RATIONAL SERIES:

Mysteries of Judaism

Mysteries of Judaism II: How the Rabbis and Others Changed Judaism

Maimonides: Reason Above All

Maimonides and the Biblical Prophets

Maimonides: The Extraordinary Mind

A Rational Approach to Judaism and Torah Commentary

Nachmanides: An Unusual Thinker

UNUSUAL BIBLE INTERPRETATION SERIES

Five Books of Moses

Joshua

Judges

Ruth, Esther, and Judith

Jonah and Amos

Hosea

Who Was the Biblical Samuel?

The Authentic King Solomon

Who Really Was the Biblical David?

The Tragedies of King David

SCHOLARLY TARGUM BOOKS:

Targumic Studies

Targum Onkelos to Exodus

Targum Onkelos to Leviticus

Targum Onkelos to Numbers

Targum Onkelos to Deuteronomy

EDITOR OF:

Living Legends

WITH CECIL B. CURREY:

For God and Country

WITH STANLEY WAGNER:

Understanding the Bible Text: Onkelos on the Torah: Genesis
Understanding the Bible Text: Onkelos on the Torah: Exodus
Understanding the Bible Text: Onkelos on the Torah: Leviticus
Understanding the Bible Text: Onkelos on the Torah: Numbers
Understanding the Bible Text: Onkelos on the Torah: Deuteronomy
Understanding Onkelos
Beyond the Bible Text
Iyunim Betargum (Hebrew)

WITH LEBA LIEDER

Can't Start Passover without the Bread
Sailing on Moti's Ark on Succoth

AS DANIEL A. DIAMOND

Around The World in 123 Days
Chaos on the Victoria: Around the World in 78 Days, Almost
Rational Religion

NOVEL

She Wanted to Be Jewish

Contents

Introduction xvii

Part one
Nachmanides

Chapter 1: Nachmanides' View of Himself 3
    Nachmanides' Goal 3

Chapter 2: Reasonable Nachmanidean interpretations of the Torah 6
    Biblical Laws Change 6
    Why Does the Torah Begin with the Story of Creation? 8
    Scripture Frequently Uses the Third Person in Reference to God 8
    Do Animals Sin? 8
    Why Tell Us That Aaron Acted Properly? 8
    Why State Both "Created" and "Made"? 8
    Maimonides and Nachmanides on the Obligation to Pray 9
    What Does Tzitzit Recall? 9
    Scripture Should Not Always Be Taken Literally 10
    Why Only Three Cities of Refuge Are in Canaan 11
    Summary 11

Chapter 3: Nachmanides' View of God 12
    Questions Raised by Nachmanides' Approach 12
    Reading Mystic Ideas into Halakhah 12
    God's Involvement in Human Affairs 13
    God Physically Descended to Earth to Investigate a Matter 14
    Miracles Occur Daily 15
    Doctors Are Unnecessary 16
    The Human Duty to Influence God 16
    God Needs Sacrifices 17
    The Duty to Help God 17
    Belief in an Anthropomorphic God 17

Reasons for God's Commands ... 18
God Does not Allow an Injustice to Occur ... 18
Faith and Reliance on God's Help ... 19
Compassion to Animals ... 19
Summary ... 20

Chapter 4: Demons, Hell, Souls, and Other Subjects ... 22
Midrashic Legends are Historical Truths ... 21
His Belief in Midrashim Led to Difficult Conclusions ... 22
Superstition ... 23
Life After Death ... 24
Hell ... 24
Transmigration of Souls ... 24
Women ... 25
Raped Women are Defiled and Prohibited to Their Husbands ... 27
Bible Predicts Future Events ... 28
The Sanctity of the Land of Israel ... 28
Idolatry, Magic, and Divination ... 30
Astrology ... 31
Angels and Demons ... 32
Attitude to Ancient and Contemporary Scholars ... 33
Dating Targum Onkelos ... 33
Mystical Interpretations ... 34

Chapter 5: Difficult Nachmanidean Interpretations of the Torah ... 35
Inventing a Narrative ... 35
Another Invented Narrative ... 36
What is the Blessing of the Sabbath? ... 37
Does the Torah Speak About Rewards After Death? ... 37
The Duty to Have Faith ... 37
The Noahide Commandments ... 38
Family Relations ... 38
Noah's Flood ... 39
Evil Inclination ... 39
The Biblical Use of the Singular ... 39
The Israelite Population ... 40
Mystical Value of Seventy ... 41
The Torah Is Speaking of a Heavenly Sanctuary ... 41
Does Pakad Mean All That Nachmanides Reads into It? ... 42

Why Couldn't God Perform a Miracle?	42
Single and Plural Words	43
Another Example of Singular and Plural Words	43
When Did the Levites Begin Working in the Tabernacle?	44
Why Was a Shofar Blown in the Desert?	45
Inventing History	45
Another Instance of Inventing a Narrative	45
Does the Torah Mandate Living in Israel?	46
Should We Explain a Biblical Event by Stating It Was a Miracle?	47
Were the Edomites Circumcised?	48
Reading More into a Word Than Is Warranted	48
Does God Manipulate Humans Against Their Will?	48
Did Moses and the Israelites Receive Different Versions of the Decalogue (the Ten Commandments)?	49
Did the Israelites Ever Have a Dispensation to Eat non-Kosher Foods?	49
Did God Miraculously Keep the Israelites Clothes from Wearing Out for Forty Years?	50
Why Did Moses Break the Two Tablets of the Decalogue?	50
Did God Write the Second Tablets?	51
Summary	51

Part two
Targum Onkelos

Chapter 6: The Notion that Targum Onkelos Contains Derash	55
The Law	55
What is Targum Onkelos?	56
The Significance of Onkelos	56
Why Did the Rabbis Require Jews to Read Targum Onkelos?	57
The Earliest Understanding of Targum Onkelos	57
Midrash and Talmud	58
Die Masorah Zum Targum Onkelos	59
Saadiah Gaon	59
Menachem ibn Saruq	60
Samuel ben Hofni Gaon	60
Rashi (Rabbi Shlomo Yitzchaki)	60
Rashbam (Rabbi Samuel ben Meir)	61
Abraham ibn Ezra	62
Maimonides	62

Joseph Bechor Shor	63
Radak (Rabbi David Kimchi)	63
Conclusions from Reading the Ancient Commentators	64
Nachmanides Was the First Bible Commentator to Read Derash into Onkelos	64

Chapter 7: Differences between Onkelos and the Hebrew Bible — 66

Clarity	66
Respectful Concept of God	67
Honoring Israel's Ancestors	71
Alternative Translations	71
Onkelos and Halakhah	72
Summary	73

Part Three
Nachmanides Misunderstands Onkelos

Chapter 8: Reasonable Interpretations in Genesis — 77

Some Statistics	77
The Following Are Nachmanidean Interpretations That Seem Reasonable	78

Chapter 9: Genesis Problematical Interpretations — 89

Bachya is Troubled by Nachmanidean Interpretations	89
The Problematical Interpretations Found in Nachmanides' Commentary To Genesis	90

Chapter 10: Exodus — 118

Nachmanides Discovers Mysticism in Onkelos	118
The Thirty-four Problematical Nachmanides Interpretations in Exodus	118

Chapter 11: Leviticus — 136

Problematical Interpretations	136
The Twenty-Three Problematical Nachmanides Interpretations in Leviticus	136

Chapter 12: Numbers — 156

The Thirteen Difficult Comments by Nachmanides in Numbers	156

Chapter 13: Difficult Interpretations — 166

Eighteen Difficult Nachmanidean Comments on Onkelos in Deuteronomy	166

Appendix: **Bachya ben Asher**	177
Who was Bachya?	177
Some Statistics	177
Bachya Misuses Onkelos	178
Bibliography	180
Index	188
About the Author	192

Acknowledgments

I want to thank Darlene Jospe who has helped me by doing the first editing job on my works since we worked together with Stanley M. Wagner on the "Onkelos on the Torah" series. She also composed the index and list of sources. I also want to thank Ruth Pepperman of Gefen who did the final editing of this book.

Introduction

Nachmanides was also known as Rabbi Moshe ben Nachman; Ramban, the Hebrew acrostic of this name; Rabbenu Moshe Geronde; and Bonastru da Parta. He was born into a prominent family in Gerona in northern Spain in 1194 or 1195 and died around 1270 in the land of Israel where he had traveled in 1267 to escape persecution following a public religious debate before King James I.

The debate took place in 1263 in Barcelona and concerned the validity of Judaism versus Christianity. The apostate Jew Pablo Christiani contended that some of the midrashic stories that Nachmanides had insisted were true occurrences foreshadowed the birth and mission of Jesus.[1] Nachmanides sidestepped Pablo's trap by disclaiming his belief in the truthfulness and the authority of *Midrashim*, and said that they were only legends.[2]

Nachmanides is recognized by many scholars as a great Jewish Bible and Talmud commentator.[3] About fifty scholarly works authored by him have been

---

1. Charles B. Chavel, *The Disputation at Barcelona* (New York: Shilo Publication House, 1983). B. Septimus, "Open Rebuke and Concealed Love," in *Rabbi Moses Nahmanides (Ramban): Explorations in his Religious and Literary Virtuosity*, Isadore Twersky, ed. (Cambridge, MA: Harvard University Press, 1983), 15–22. Pablo used Nachmanides' method in which the latter tried to show the truth of mystical teachings.
2. Commenting upon *Genesis* 12:11, where Abram instructs his wife Sarai to state she is his sister, ibn Kaspi states that Aristotle contended that a lie is permissible under certain dire circumstances such as a threat of death. Plato called it a "noble lie" and Maimonides "an essential truth."
3. Solomon Schechter, *Studies in Judaism, First Series* (Philadelphia: Jewish Publication Society of America, 1896), 99–141; Isaac Unna, *R. Moses Ben Nahman: His Life and Activities* (Jerusalem, 1942); C.B. Chavel, *Ramban, Commentary on the Torah, Genesis* (New York: Shilo Publishing House, 1971–1976); Yaacov David Shulman, *The Ramban* (New York: CIS, 1993); David Novak, *The Theology of Nahmanides Systematically Presented* (Atlanta: Scholars Press, 1992); C.J. Henoch, *Ramban, Philosopher and Kabbalist* (Jerusalem: Torah Lamm Publications, 1998); H. Pedaya, *Nachmanides, Cyclical Time and Holy Text* [Hebrew] (Tel Aviv, 2003).

preserved and show that he was without doubt, one of the most brilliant Bible commentators of his generation. Although frequently called a philosopher, a more apt description of him would be kabbalist. Unlike his predecessor Moses Maimonides (1138–1204), whose philosophical ideas were based on systematic logic and a conviction that humans are endowed with intelligence that they are obligated to use to orient and control their lives, Nachmanides downplayed the efficacy of the intellect and stressed the pervasive impact that the kabbalistic *sefirot* (the ten divine emanations) have upon humans.[4]

Maimonides was a rationalist and his philosophy was "expressed systematically and explicitly, open to thinkers in every generation, whereas the majority of Ramban's basic ideas are rooted in the metalogical realm of the *Kabbalah*. Their manner of expression is the allusion, which only a select few were able to fathom throughout the generations."[5]

As a mystic, Nachmanides was the first person to introduce the idea that the Torah contains mystical notions, and the first to offer a mystical interpretation of the Bible. He was also the first to state that the Aramaic translation of the Pentateuch, *Targum Onkelos*, contains imaginative *aggadic* material and mysticism. It was as if he were arguing that if the Torah is true, and mysticism is true, and *Targum Onkelos* is true, then it follows that the Torah and *Targum Onkelos* must contain mysticism.

Needless to say, not all of Nachmanides' Bible interpretations are difficult. Nachmanides wrote his monumental commentary to the Torah when he was about seventy years old after his flight to Israel, a country that had considerable difficulties at that time.

Many people who have high respect for Nachmanides respect him because they feel that unlike Maimonides who relied on non-Jewish philosophers, even

---

4. The rationalist Maimonides did not accept the mystical notion of *sefirot*. People preferred to use Nachmanides' books for kabbalistic teachings instead of the *Zohar* until 1325.
5. Henoch, *Ramban, Philosopher and Kabbalist*, x. Contrary to Maimonides, but like Abraham ibn Ezra and most people of his time, Nachmanides believed in astrology and the impact that the heavenly bodies have upon people. Joseph Stern, *Problems and Parables of Law: Maimonides and Nachmanides on the reasons for the Commandments* (Albany: State of New York University Press, 1998). Nachmanides presented his mystical interpretations of the Bible in a very brief form, which is expanded upon in such commentaries as Bachya ben Asher, *Torah Commentary* (Jerusalem: Urim Publications, 1998).

the pagan Aristotle, Nachmanides only used Jewish sources. However, they are mistaken. Many Nachmanidean ideas are not founded on Torah teachings, but instead they are sometimes based on the superstitious notions of his time.

Maimonides included non-Jewish ideas because he taught that "the truth is the truth no matter what its source." Baruch Epstein pointed out that the *siddur* begins with *ma tovu*,[6] the words of the pagan Balaam who was determined to curse the Israelites during the days of Moses, to emphasize the Maimonidean lesson that we should seek truth from every possible source.[7]

Without criticizing Nachmanides, I intend to show that despite his brilliance and broad knowledge of Jewish sources, many of his biblical commentaries and the majority of his *Targum Onkelos* interpretations are puzzling.

I will reveal some unusual and generally unknown facts, including:

- Contrary to the thinking of most people, neither Rashi, ibn Ezra nor Nachmanides felt obligated to offer only ancient rabbinical views of biblical passages. They felt free to present their own novel never-before-heard interpretations.
- Nachmanides stated that he would reveal the true plain meaning of the biblical text, but this is not his real goal.
- Nachmanides used the commentaries of Rashi and Abraham ibn Ezra, and less frequently Maimonides as a springboard with which to contrast his own original mystical biblical interpretation.
- He generally disagrees with these sages, often with strong disparaging words.
- He also cites the Aramaic translation of the Pentateuch, *Targum Onkelos*, but always with admiration, deference, and respect.[8] Yet, although he mentions *Onkelos* 230 times in his commentary to the Pentateuch, generally to support

---

6. Numbers 24:5.
7. See Rabbi Dr. Israel Drazin, *Maimonides and the Biblical Prophets* (Jerusalem: Gefen Publishing House, 2009) chapter 1, where this subject is discussed in detail with the citation of many rabbinic sources.
8. Rashi, Tosaphot (on the Babylonian Talmud, *Kiddushin* 49a), and Maharsha (on *Nedarim* 27b) contend that the *Onkelos* translation was so significant that God handed it to the Israelites through Moses at Mount Sinai. While Nachmanides does not state this view explicitly, he treats *Targum Onkelos* as a near sacred document. It was this very respectful attitude to the *Targum* that prompted him to seek its support for his biblical interpretations.

his own understanding of the scriptural text, more than half of his interpretations present problems.
- Nachmanides' biblical interpretations are very frequently based on his own translation of words, non sequiturs, and the reading of elaborately invented events into a single word that the word itself does not imply.

I will describe many things about Nachmanides and his views on:

- Kabbalistic notions, his stand on *aggadah*, medicine, magic, astrology, divination, life after death, the land of Israel, angels, and demons.
- Examples of commentaries that most people consider reasonable, perhaps even capturing the original biblical intent better than those of Rashi and ibn Ezra, but I will also offer examples of his rather difficult comments and suggests reasons for the difficulty.

I will introduce the reader to the *Targum*, "translation," of *Onkelos* in part two. I will show that this rabbinically authorized translation, called *Targum didan*, "our *Targum*," by the talmudic sages, was composed about 400 CE by an unknown translator or translators. I will explain how I came to this date of "about 400 CE."

I will acquaint the reader with the fact that the *Onkelos* Aramaic translation differs from the original Hebrew biblical text in over ten thousand instances, and will categorize and explain what motivated the Babylonian translator to make these changes in his rendering of scripture.

I will address several misconceptions about *Onkelos*, including the notion that *Onkelos* contains *derash*, fanciful, indeed imaginative interpretations. I will examine ancient Bible commentaries, showing that all of them used the *Targum*, and treated it with enormous esteem as the foremost source for the simple Torah meaning, *peshat* not *derash*.

After introducing Nachmanides in part one and *Onkelos* in part two, part three contains an analysis of Nachmanides' comments about the Aramaic translation of *Targum Onkelos*. This analysis reveals the extent of Nachmanides' error and its nature. Every instance where Nachmanides mentions *Onkelos* is analyzed. The analysis shows that the Gerona sage commented upon *Onkelos* 230 times in his commentary to the five books of the Pentateuch. Fifty-five of the 230 comments mention the *Targum* without any analysis. In the remaining 175 instances, where

Nachmanides analyzes *Onkelos*'s Aramaic rendering of the original biblical Hebrew, 129, or about seventy-five percent, of his comments are problematical.

In these instances, Nachmanides seems to be reading more into an Aramaic word than the word means either standing alone, or in context. He appears to be trying to find support for his own worldview and his own kabbalistic understanding of the Torah in the wording of the esteemed *Targum*, even when a simple reading of the *Targum* indicates otherwise.

The Gerona sage seems to have ignored the words of his countryman Maimonides, and thereby created the difficulties that we will be encountering:

> Now you must concentrate and understand what I am about to say. Know that one is not permitted to detach a statement from its context and use it as proof. One should rather ascertain meaning by the context so as to know the speaker's intention. Then it may be used as proof. If one may adduce proof from discourse taken out of context, then one might say that God (may He be blessed and exalted) has forbidden us in the Torah to obey any prophet, as He says: "Do not heed the words of that prophet" (*Deuteronomy* 13:4). And similarly, we might say that God commanded us to practice idolatry, for He says "There you will serve man-made gods" (*Deuteronomy* 4:28), and so on. And many similar examples could be cited in every discourse, but this is obviously false. For one ought never to bring a proof from a text until its contextual meaning is determined. Only then will its intention be understood.[9]

No one can read the mind of another person, especially an individual who lived in a culture so radically different than our own. Yet it may be helpful to consider the impact that cognitive dissonance could have had on Nachmanides.

Cognitive dissonance is a normal psychological process, described by Leon Festinger (1919–1989) in 1957.[10] Festinger explained that people generally feel distressed (dissonance) when they "find themselves doing things that don't fit with what they know, or having opinions that do not fit with the opinions they hold." Stated differently, people are usually unable to deal with two ideas that conflict

---

9. Ralph Lerner, "Epistle to Yemen," in *Maimonides' Empire of Light* (Chicago: University of Chicago Press, 2000), 114.
10. See, for example, Leon Festinger, *The Theory of Cognitive Dissonance* (California: Stanford University Press, 1973).

with one another. Festinger states that people deal with stress, which is usually only subconscious, by changing their ideas. They subconsciously decide which of the two ideas is more important to them and then change the other idea to fit the first to avoid any tension. It is possible that our Gerona sage faced such a dilemma.

PART ONE
Nachmanides

– CHAPTER 1 –

Nachmanides' View of Himself

> Rabbi Dr. Charles B. Chavel made a comprehensive study of Nachmanides, wrote books in Hebrew and English containing the correct text of Nachmanides' works, and included his analysis of Nachmanides and Nachmanides' introduction to his Bible commentary. His books are significant because they aid readers in understanding how Nachmanides understood his commentary. The following is a summary of what they say.

NACHMANIDES' GOAL

Nachmanides describes his goal in his introduction. He states that he wants to reveal or at least hint about the mystical ideas that are in the Torah, what he calls "the hidden matters of the Torah."[1]

He tells readers in his introduction to *Genesis* that Moses wrote the entire Torah "from the mouth of the Holy One, blessed be He." When Moses descended from Mount Sinai, he "wrote the Torah from the beginning of *Genesis* to the end of the account of the Tabernacle. He wrote the conclusion of the Torah at the end of the fortieth year of wandering in the desert."

God, Nachmanides continues, informed Moses about the creation of "all things, high and low. Likewise, [God informed him of] everything that had been said concerning the esoterics of the Divine Chariot," meaning everything about *Kabbalah*, Jewish mysticism. Moses included all of this information in the Torah, although much of it is hidden in the "implication in words, in the numerical value of letters, or the form of letters.... [E]verything may be learned from the Torah."

Nachmanides maintains that the Torah includes the secrets of divination, enchantments, sorcery, and secrets King Solomon knew and used. The Torah is

---

[1]. All the quotes in this chapter are from Chavel's books.

also "comprised of the Names of the Holy One, blessed be He, and...the letters of the words separate themselves into divine names when divided in a different manner." That is why if a "mistake has been made in one letter [of the Torah] being added or subtracted [the Torah scroll] is disqualified." The "masters of the *Kabbalah*," he insists, know how to read the Torah and see the divine names.

Rabbi Dr. Chavel comments upon this Nachmanidean introduction and commentary in his preface. He writes that Nachmanides' commentary is filled with "*Kabbalah* – the mystic teachings of the Torah – which Ramban [the Hebrew equivalent of Nachmanides] was the first to introduce into Biblical commentary."[2]

Chavel states that the "great kabbalist of the sixteenth century Rabbi Yitzchak Luria spoke of Ramban's presentation of kabbalistic principles of thought in the highest terms: 'Deep they lie, exceptionally deep; who can grasp them?'" The wide extent of kabbalistic influence on the coming generation can be traced to Ramban.

Chavel writes that Nachmanides focused on "two prior works which had already gained wide acceptance," by Rashi and Abraham ibn Ezra. Chavel explains that Nachmanides differed with Rashi's approach in three ways: (1) He disagreed with Rashi's approach of explaining the biblical texts in an aggadic, homiletical manner. He preferred to seek the plain meaning of the passages. (2) He rejected Rashi's view that the Torah was not written chronologically. He felt that the "whole Torah is written in chronological order except where Scripture itself tells us differently." He also insisted that when these exceptional situations occurred they must have occurred for a special reason. (3) While Rashi explained obscure Hebrew words by relating them to foreign, non-Hebrew terms such as Aramaic, Nachmanides insisted that the divine Torah only contained pure Hebrew terms.

Nachmanides' view of ibn Ezra, according to Chavel, is as Nachmanides wrote "open rebuke and hidden love," because ibn Ezra, as Chavel explains, frequently articulated "independent views [that] brought him into conflict with traditional authority."

Chavel states that Nachmanides had enormous respect for Maimonides but

---

2. Chavel was the first commentator to say that Nachmanides originated the notion that the Torah contains mysticism. I believe that I am the first to say that Nachmanides originated the notion that *Onkelos* contains mysticism.

disagreed with him strongly concerning Maimonides' view that prophecy is a natural event, a higher level of intelligence, and that God is not anthropomorphic.[3]

Although not mentioned by Chavel, Nachmanides also had immense respect for the Aramaic translation of the Pentateuch called *Targum Onkelos*. Since the Torah is true and *Onkelos* is stating the truth, Nachmanides maintained that just as the Torah contains mystical teachings, so too does *Onkelos*. We will see that this position caused the sage to read matters into the Aramaic translation that are not present.

---

3. We will see Nachmanides' view that God has a body when we discuss his view of *Genesis* 46:1.

– CHAPTER 2 –

Reasonable Nachmanidean interpretations of the Torah

> When Nachmanides does not insert a mystical interpretation into his commentary and attempts, instead, to show the plain meaning of the scriptural text, a fair reading of his commentary discloses that he frequently gives a better understanding of the Torah's plain meaning than Rashi, since Rashi focuses on midrashic interpretation of the Torah passages.[1] However, even in these instances there are many times where Nachmanides' commentary seems unreasonable.
>
> Although I will be discussing Nachmanides' difficult interpretations, it would help set the stage here to first show some reasonable examples of his thinking.

BIBLICAL LAWS CHANGE

Nachmanides mentions Rashi's interpretation of *Numbers* 8:2, critiques it, and offers a substitute explanation.[2] Rashi notes that the Torah places the section dealing with Aaron lighting the Sanctuary's menorah after the section dealing with the offerings that the Israelite princes brought to the recently built Sanctuary when they participated its dedication. This, according to Rashi, was to console the disheartened Aaron because neither he nor his tribe participated, as the Israelite princes did, in the dedication of the Sanctuary. Rashi understood that God was

---

[1]. Rashi states several times that he is presenting the plain meaning of the text, but frequently this means that he is offering the midrashic understanding that fits best with the plain meaning, but not the plain meaning itself. See Sarah Kamin, *The Bible in the Light of its Interpreters: Sarah Kamin Memorial Volume*, ed. Sara Japhet (Jerusalem: The Magnes Press, 1994).

[2]. I thank Professor Raphi Jospe for reminding me of this interpretation.

saying to Aaron: Your contribution to the Sanctuary is greater than the sacrifices of the princes, for you will kindle and trim the lamp every morning and evening.[3]

Nachmanides saw no sense in consoling Aaron by mentioning the lighting of the lamp; there were far more significant things that Aaron did in the sanctuary such as the daily sacrifices. Additionally, why should Aaron have been bothered? He had offered many sacrifices during the preceding seven days of the initiation of the Sanctuary, far more sacrifices than those brought by the princes.

Nachmanides wrote that the midrashic statement cited by Rashi was not saying what Rashi understood it to say. The *Midrash* was a homily that was alluding to the Chanukah rededication lights that occurred during the period of the Second Temple in 165 BCE when Aaron's descendants, the priests called the Hasmoneans, rededicated the Temple after the Syrian Greeks defiled it.[4] It was by lighting the Chanukah dedication lights that Aaron's descendants performed more for the Sanctuary than the Israelite princes.

Nachmanides also states that he saw this idea that focuses on the Hasmoneans in *Tanchuma Beha'alotkha* 5 and *Numbers Rabbah* 15:5 in more detail. These *Midrashim* state that sacrifices are only "brought as long as the Sanctuary is in existence, but the lamps will give light in front of the candelabrum forever." The "sages of the *Midrash* were alluding to the rededication lights of the Hasmoneans [the candles of Chanukah which were lit] after the destruction of the Sanctuary." This reference to Chanukah is how "the rabbis interpreted the proximity [of the laws of the menorah] to the dedication offerings of the princes."

Significantly, Nachmanides is recognizing that the midrashic "explanation" is a sermon, not a fact. But the sermon is highlighting that (1) biblical laws will change in the future, even sacrosanct laws such as sacrifices, and (2) the future laws, such as those of Chanukah, can be more significant than the biblical law – for this is exactly what the *Midrash* has God saying to Aaron: the act of your descendants will be superior to the offerings brought by the princes.

---

3. Rashi's source is *Tanchuma Beha'alotkha* 5.
4. Nachmanides states he found this idea in *Megillat Setarim* of Rabbeinu Nissim of the first half of the eleventh century CE.

WHY DOES THE TORAH BEGIN WITH THE STORY OF CREATION?

Nachmanides' commentary to *Genesis* 1:1 is closer to the plain meaning of scripture than Rashi's homiletical interpretation. Nachmanides dismisses Rashi's contention that the Torah begins with a recital of God's creation of the world to teach that everything belongs to God and God has the right to give the land of Israel to the Jews. Nachmanides correctly calls this "a homiletic exposition." It is not the plain meaning of the verse.

SCRIPTURE FREQUENTLY USES THE THIRD PERSON IN REFERENCE TO GOD

Numbers 19:2, like many other biblical passages, states "The Lord commanded." Nachmanides asks: Since God is speaking directly to Moses and Aaron, why is the third person being used? It should have said "I commanded." Nachmanides explains that this is the biblical style; therefore, the verse can be read as if it states that "This is the statute of the law that the Lord commanded, saying: 'Speak with the Israelites and tell them.'"

DO ANIMALS SIN?

Similarly, *Genesis* 6:12 states, "all flesh corrupted their ways." Rashi argues that "all flesh" means that animals and birds also sinned. Nachmanides recognizes that animals do not sin and states that "all flesh" denotes "all people."

WHY TELL US THAT AARON ACTED PROPERLY?

Numbers 8:3 states: "Aaron did so. He lit the lamps in front of the menorah as the Lord commanded Moses." Why was it necessary for the Torah to inform us that Aaron fulfilled God's command? Rashi seemingly complicates the question when he cites *Sifrei*, which states that Aaron is being commended because he made no changes in the procedure. But who would have imagined that Aaron would take it upon himself to do so? Nachmanides understands that Scripture is saying that although Aaron could have delegated this responsibility to his sons, he chose to kindle the menorah himself all of his life.

WHY STATE BOTH "CREATED" AND "MADE"?

Genesis 2:3 seems to have a duplication, "which God created, had made." Ibn Ezra states that "had made" means that God gave the items the power to reproduce.

Rashi opines that it suggests that God did double work on the sixth day. Nachmanides understands "had made" as suggesting, "that which He had made out of nothing."

MAIMONIDES AND NACHMANIDES ON THE OBLIGATION TO PRAY

The Five Books of Moses portray a close relationship between humans and God. People in the Pentateuch do not pray to God; instead, they speak to God, call upon God, complain, cry out, and beg. Today, we think of these activities as forms of prayer.

Despite the absence of the word "prayer" in the Bible, there is a dispute between Maimonides and Nachmanides as to whether the duty to pray is biblical or rabbinical in origin. Maimonides seems to say that the command is biblical.

> It is a positive Torah commandment to pray daily, for it states: "You should serve the Lord your God" (*Exodus* 23:25). Tradition [meaning the rabbinical interpretation] teaches that "service" means "prayer." It [the Bible also] states: "Serve Him with your entire heart" (*Deuteronomy* 11:13), and our sages said, "What is service of the heart? This is prayer."[5]

Nachmanides disagrees. He insists that the Torah is silent on the matter of prayer and that the commandment to pray, therefore, must be a post-biblical rabbinical enactment.[6]

Nachmanides is certainly correct that the Bible does not command Jews to pray, but he apparently did not understand that Maimonides categorized laws that are not explicitly mentioned in the Torah as biblical commandments if the rabbis felt that they were deriving the law from a biblical verse.[7]

WHAT DOES *TZITZIT* RECALL?

Rashi to *Numbers* 15:38 derives the meaning of the noun *tzitzit*, the fringes that the Torah states should be placed on four-cornered garments, from the verb *metzitz*

---

5. Moshe ben Maimon (Maimonides), *Mishneh Torah, Hilkhot Tefillah* 1:1–3; also Maimonides, *The Book of Divine Commandments* (New York: The Soncino Press, 1967).
6. Moshe ben Nachman (Nachmanides), *Hasagot Haramban on Maimonides' Sefer Hamitzvot*, Positive Command 5.
7. Drazin, *Maimonides and the Biblical Prophets*, chapter 29 on the 613 biblical commandments.

"to stare keenly [as in *Song of Songs* 2:9]." How do the *tzitzit* remind people of the divine commands? A simple answer is that any unusual item, such as a ribbon on a finger, could prompt people seeing it to unconsciously ask why it is there, and then remember that it was placed there to remind the person of a particular thing. Thus, one could think that the details of how the *tzitzit* is made is of little significance. However, Rashi (based on *Tanchuma*) states that the numerical value of the letters in *tzitzit* equals 600, plus the eight fringes and five knots equals 613, the number of all the Torah commandments.[8]

Nachmanides questions this interpretation. He notes that the biblical spelling of *tzitzit* is without the second *yud* and only equals 590. Additionally, according to the academy of Hillel (Babylonian Talmud, *Menachot* 41b) there should be only six, not eight fringes. Hence, the count is short of the 613. Therefore, he concludes, the *tzitzit* is worn to remember the divine commandments, but not because of the numerical value of its letters. People remember the duty to observe the commandments by looking at the blue thread of the *tzitzit* (called *tekheilet* in *Numbers* 15:38) because the letters of *tekheilet* contain the letters *kh-l*, which could be understood as "all" and remind the person seeing the *tekheilet* of the all-inclusive attribute of God.

While Nachmanides may present a somewhat more realistic explanation than Rashi, the Talmud is even more realistic than both commentators. The Babylonian Talmud, *Menachot* 43b, states that the blue color of the *tekheilet* is what reminds the Jew of the duty to observe the divine commands: the "blue resembles the color of the sea, the color of the sea is similar to the color of the heaven, and heaven reminds us of the blue of God's throne of glory."

SCRIPTURE SHOULD NOT ALWAYS BE TAKEN LITERALLY

Numbers 23:5 states: "The Lord put the word in the mouth of [the Midianite prophet who sought to curse the Israelites] Balaam and said: 'Return to [the king] Balak and speak thus.'" Nachmanides recognizes that some Bible commentators suppose that God actually placed words in his mouth, and whatever he uttered came out against his will. He also cites an opinion that it was an angel that spoke through Balaam. He rejects both notions and says that the phrase "put the word" is a figure of speech meaning that God instructed Balaam what to say.

---

8. Rashi on *Numbers* 15:39.

WHY ONLY THREE CITIES OF REFUGE ARE IN CANAAN

Numbers 35:12 contains a law that apparently attempts to stop the vigilante justice of the time, which allowed a relative of a murdered person to kill the murderer. Verse 14 mandates that three cities were to be placed in Transjordan, the settlement of two-and-a-half tribes, and three in Canaan, where the remaining nine-and-a-half tribes settled. The murderer could escape to the refuge city and could remain there if he killed another by accident; the blood avenger was not permitted to kill the murderer as long as he was in the city. This law did not apply to an intentional killing.

Why were an identical number of cities placed in both areas when it is clear that Transjordan had a much smaller population?

Rashi (based on Babylonian Talmud, *Makkot* 9b) suggests that there were many more murders committed in Transjordan, as attested hundreds of years later in *Hosea* 6:8, and Transjordan needed more cities per capita to house the murderers.

Nachmanides seems to have disliked this traditional explanation: it assumes that the Torah is legislating for a situation that would not arise until hundreds of years after Moses' death. Nachmanides offers what he thinks is the plain meaning of the text. The same number of cities, three, were necessary on both sides of the Jordan because although only two-and-a-half tribes settled in Transjordan, the land was very large, about the size of Canaan, and it would have been difficult for a murderer to escape to a refuge city if there were only one or two such cities there.

SUMMARY

Nachmanides often begins his commentary by contrasting it with the explanation of biblical verses by Rashi, Abraham ibn Ezra, and occasionally Maimonides. He chose these sources because they differ greatly from his approach to the Torah. He says in effect, "so-and-so says *x*; now let me show you why *y* is correct." It is easy to show the passage's plain meaning in contrast to Rashi who generally seeks the midrashic or homiletical explanation of scripture. This is clear from the examples in this chapter. However, as we will see, Nachmanides frequently ignores the text's plain meaning and selects a mystical interpretation, and the logic he uses to prove his analysis does not appear to be reasonable.

– CHAPTER 3 –

Nachmanides' View of God

> Nachmanides' views of the world and the Bible are often different than those of many people in the modern world. Modern readers may consider some of his thirteenth-century thoughts superstitious notions. But fairness requires that readers should recognize that Nachmanides' beliefs were held by most of his contemporaries, Maimonides being a startling exception. Even today, many Jews and non-Jews would champion quite a few of the Gerona rabbi's opinions.

QUESTIONS RAISED BY NACHMANIDES' APPROACH

Nachmanides' Bible commentary raises many questions, such as those addressed in this chapter. Was Nachmanides convinced that God is involved in *everything* that occurs on earth? Did he suppose that miracles occur daily, most of them unseen? Did he consider God as the healer of people and on whom people should rely? Was he convinced that people have a duty to influence God? Is it his view that God needs sacrifices? Did he believe that people must help God who needs their help? Was he certain that God has physical parts? Why did he think that God gave humans commands? Is faith that God will aid people an integral part of his belief system? Did he feel that God assures that injustice will not occur? Did he say that God does not care about the feelings of animals?

READING MYSTIC IDEAS INTO *HALAKHAH*

Nachmanides inserted his version of mysticism into his conception of *halakhah* (Jewish law). For example, he insisted that white wine is unacceptable for the Shabbat *Kiddush* (the blessing over wine that introduces the Shabbat meal). Rabbinic non-mystical sources state just the opposite: if people have white wine that is superior to their red wine, the white wine should be used. Even the mystic Joseph Karo allowed white wine for *Kiddush* in his *Beit Yosef*.[1]

GOD'S INVOLVEMENT IN HUMAN AFFAIRS

Nachmanides states in *Genesis* 17:1, 46:15, *Exodus* 13:16, and *Leviticus* 26:11 that this world does not function through the laws of nature. God is constantly and directly involved in every human act and thought and frequently interferes and even controls them. He calls these divine manipulations "hidden miracles." Thus, he contends that when the *Midrash* relates that the patriarch Abraham was saved when King Nimrod threatened to kill him, this happened because God interfered with nature and changed Nimrod's intention; He "put it in the heart of that king to save him." He used this principle of divine intervention to explain various other *Midrashim*, which he considered facts, such as the unusual length of the lives of Moses's mother, Aaron's grandson Pinchas, and King David's ancestress Ruth.

Since he was certain of the truthfulness of the story of Abraham's father being an idol worshiper and that Abraham was saved by God when Nimrod tried to kill him, he wondered how it was possible that *Midrash Genesis Rabbah* interpreted *Genesis* 15:15, "And you will come to your father in peace," to say that Abraham would join his father, an idolater, in the world-to-come.[2] He answers his question with the view of some rabbis in the Babylonian Talmud, *Sanhedrin* 104a, that the merit of a son's good deeds has the power to affect and benefit his father even though the father was evil during his lifetime, committed idol worship, despised his son's behavior, and is now dead.[3]

Nachmanides' theory of war is another example of his view that God is involved in human affairs. He asserts that God manages the outcome of all wars,

---

[1]. Joseph Karo, *Shulchan Aruch, Orach Chayim*, 272, s.v. *garsenan*. Nachmanides' approach to *halakhah*, reading material into texts that is not present and which can only be seen by an adept in mysticism, helped in the development of the charismatic leader, the pious rabbi who understood and who alone could pass on truth.
[2]. The conflict between *Midrashim* does not exist when one realizes that each *Midrash* is not recounting a truthful event, but is only telling a tale as a parable to teach a lesson.
[3]. This concept of *zekhut avot* and *zekhut banim* is in the Targums *Pseudo-Jonathan* and *Neophyti*, but is absent from *Targum Onkelos*. See Rabbi Dr. Israel Drazin, *Targumic Studies* (Ann Arbor: University Microfilm International, 1980), 77–103.

irrespective of human power.⁴ Still another illustration is his notion that God chooses every person who serves in every community function, from kings to "even a superintendent of the well is appointed in heaven."⁵

GOD PHYSICALLY DESCENDED TO EARTH TO INVESTIGATE A MATTER

Genesis 18:20 and 21, as well as the narrative that follows, contains a rather remarkable story that raises fundamental and disturbing questions about how to interpret the Bible. "God said, 'the cry of Sodom and Gomorrah is great, and their misdeeds are very grievous. *I will go down now and see* whether they acted as [indicated in] the cry that has come up to me, then I will destroy them, if not I will know.'"⁶

Leaving aside the many difficulties that the original Hebrew presents to the translator (such as the one previously footnoted), these two verses, as well as the subsequent story of Abraham's attempt to change God's mind,⁷ raise quite a few theological and philosophical questions. One of the questions is whether the episode narrated in *Genesis* 18 actually occurred or whether it was only a dream.

Nachmanides insists that the Bible means what it says and the episode actually happened. God needed to descend to discover the truth about the people's behavior.⁸

Maimonides disagrees. He states in his *Guide of the Perplexed* 2:45 that all biblical prophecies, with the exception of Moses' prophecy, were dreams. He states in 1:10 that Scripture's divine descent is only a figure of speech indicating a divine decision to render punishment. Thus, according to Maimonides, the

---

4. Nachmanides, *Commentary to Deuteronomy* 8:18.
5. Ibid. 17:15. Nachmanides seems to recognize that people can sometimes choose a community official whom God does not want, but he is unclear as to when and how this occurs. The issue is discussed in the Babylonian Talmud, *Berakhot* 58a.
6. This last phrase is obscure in both Hebrew and English and has been the subject of various attempts at clarification. The simple meaning is that God does not know if what he is hearing is correct, and he needs to descend to the earth to investigate what is really happening. In the prior phrase, he states that if he discovers that people have been acting improperly, he will "destroy them." He then concludes "if not," meaning that if they are not doing wrong, "I will know" this and not harm them.
7. The idea that humans can change God's mind is problematic because it assumes that God is not altogether wise and that humans have, at least sometimes, a better understanding of a situation than does God.
8. Nachmanides, *Commentary to Genesis* 18:1 and 32:33, where the question of dreams reappears.

story in chapter 18 never took place. It was a dream that Abraham experienced; Abraham dreamed of a conversation with God and thought of God in his dream in anthropomorphic terms.

MIRACLES OCCUR DAILY

Nachmanides writes: "And now I shall declare to you a general principle in the reason of many commandments."[9] He identifies several groups of individuals with wrong-headed convictions. The first denies the basic principle that God created the world. The second refuses to recognize that God knows what occurs to humans. The third may think that God knows about people, but denies that God pays attention to them. They assert that God cares for humans as much as humans care for a bowl of goldfish. They look, admire and delight in them, but do not care for their individual lives. These people say that just as it is ridiculous to imagine people rewarding and punishing fish for their behavior, so too, God neither rewards nor punishes.

Many scholars are convinced that Maimonides denies the existence of miracles. All agree that he at least minimizes them. But Nachmanides was convinced, strongly and unyieldingly, that God is constantly involved in the world, as in the saying that no leaf falls from a tree unless God wills it to do so.

Nachmanides was persuaded that there are two kinds of miracles. The first, like the exodus from Egypt and the plagues that preceded it, are open and evident to all. Others are hidden and do not show God's involvement, like the falling leaf, winter snow, and summer rain, even the shining sun. This belief in miracles was so significant and fundamental to Nachmanides that he proclaimed, "From [belief in] large perceptible miracles one [comes to believe] in hidden miracles, which are the very foundation of the entire Torah. A person has no share in the Torah of Moses our teacher until he believes that all that occurs is the result of miracles, not the laws of nature.... Everything happens by divine decree."

He states that many Jewish practices were instituted for no other purpose than to teach or remind Jews that miracles occur daily. This, for example, is the reason that the Passover Seder is celebrated.

---

9. Nachmanides, *Commentary to Exodus* 13:16.

DOCTORS ARE UNNECESSARY

Nachmanides' conviction of the involvement of God in human affairs impacted his view of medicine. Although some scholars believe that he was a physician, he felt that the physician's role in medicine was misunderstood. He believed that only God can heal people. He insisted that religious people have no need for medical treatment for God will care for them. He interpreted *Exodus* 21:19, "He will surely heal," as a God-given dispensation to doctors to assist those who are *not* righteous, as long as "the physician is aware of the source and limit of his healing power and sees them as a participation in God's work."[10] He emphasized that Rachel's conception, following years of barrenness, was "through prayer and not by way of human cures."[11]

THE HUMAN DUTY TO INFLUENCE GOD

While humans are extremely limited in exercising control over themselves and other matters of this world, Nachmanides was convinced that people, especially Jews, can, and indeed are obligated to participate in supernatural matters and influence God. Thus, the concept of "sympathetic magic," a human act forcing a similar one from God,[12] was a cornerstone of his theology. God and Israel need each other. Israel, according to Nachmanides, "cannot be conceived without its intimate connection to God [and God] ... cannot be conceived apart from Israel."[13] Nachmanides stated that the Torah is composed of God's names.[14] "In other words, in the Torah, God is ultimately speaking of himself *and his own needs*, needs that Jews can help God achieve." The Torah, according to Nachmanides, is directed not merely to the human situation, but is the Jews' *"opportunity to participate in the divine life."*[15]

---

10. *Emphasis added.* Novak, *The Theology of Systematically Presented*, 84. See David Margolith, "Ramban as Doctor" *Sinai*, year 2, Vol. 40, Booklet 3, (Kislev, 1957), 147–57. See also Nachmanides' *Commentary to Exodus* 15–26.
11. Nachmanides, *Commentary to Genesis* 30:14.
12. An example would be: when a person pours water on the ground as part of a rain ceremony, such as in a dance by Native Americans, the heavens must produce rain.
13. Nachmanides, *Commentary to Exodus*, 23:21 and *Numbers* 14:4; Novak, *The Theology of Nachmanides Systematically Presented*, 122–23.
14. *Genesis Introduction on the Commentaries.*
15. Novak, *The Theology of Nachmanides Systematically Presented*, 123.

GOD NEEDS SACRIFICES

Maimonides and Nachmanides differed over whether God wanted and needed sacrifices. Maimonides contended that God did not want or need them. He maintained that the Torah allowed sacrifices only because the Israelites, like their contemporaries, were so accustomed to them that it would have been psychologically impossible to wean them away from sacrifices at that time. Maimonides cited the views of the prophets to support his contention.[16] Nachmanides, as we noted above, felt that humans have a duty to help God who needs them to do so. He insisted that God wants and needs sacrifices to bring about harmony between the ten *sefirot*.[17]

THE DUTY TO HELP GOD

As strange as this concept of God needing human help is, it is quite prevalent in Nachmanides' thoughts and in that of mysticism generally. This notion influenced Nachmanides' understanding of the Joseph story. In his commentary to *Genesis* 42:9, he raises the question of how Joseph could disregard the feelings of his old father Jacob by putting his brothers and their father through a charade and not revealing his identity to his father who was mourning his apparent death and was in great distress. Nachmanides states that Joseph felt that it was more important to aid God and make sure that the divine predictions in his two dreams[18] came true in all their details than to care for his father.[19]

BELIEF IN AN ANTHROPOMORPHIC GOD

Like many mystics, Nachmanides thought of God in an anthropomorphic manner. This idea will be discussed in some detail in my analysis of his commentary to *Genesis* 46:1. It should be noted here that Nachmanides was convinced that if a husband and wife concentrated on the ten parts of God's anthropomorphic image

---

16. ben Maimon, Moshe (Maimonides), *Guide of the Perplexed*, trans. M. Friedlander. (New York: Dover, 1956). 3:32.
17. Ibid., 3:32, 46; Nachmanides, *Commentary on the Torah, Leviticus* 1:9; Isaiah Tishby, *Mishnat Hazohar*, 2 volumes (Jerusalem, 1957), 194–206.
18. *Genesis* 37.
19. "Nachmanides seems to be of the opinion that *helping Providence* is the right thing to do, though we may doubt the theology of this." Jacob Licht, *Story Telling in the Bible* (Jerusalem: Hebrew University Magnes Press, 1986), 81. *Emphasis added.*

during their sexual intercourse they could produce a son that fits the holy form that they pictured.[20] As Arthur Green wrote:

> Both partners are to concentrate on the divine anthropic form during intercourse, the beauty of the union [of God's parts] above... and the child of their union will be that beautiful form they have gazed upon during lovemaking.[21]

REASONS FOR GOD'S COMMANDS

Nachmanides' view regarding the observance of the Torah commandments differed radically from those of Maimonides. Whereas his predecessor gave reasons for all the commands and enumerated the human individual and societal benefits,[22] Nachmanides wrote, "You should not serve God in order to receive a reward but because of His simple will. [Because God said so, not because there is a rational basis for the command.] This is what obligates us to serve Him."[23]

GOD DOES NOT ALLOW AN INJUSTICE TO OCCUR

Nachmanides' position that God is involved daily in human affairs and that God manipulates human behavior, has led, as we have seen, to positions that many rationalists would find hard to accept. We see it again in his interpretation of *Deuteronomy* 19:19. The section discusses the law of the *ed zomeim* (the false witness who gave his testimony as part of a plot to harm the person he is testifying against). The *halakhah* states that the plotting witness is punished with the same punishment he attempted to inflict upon the person he is testifying against. An exception to this rule is the situation where, in a murder case, the witness is found to be false only after the person he was testifying against has been executed. The law is that the false witness is not executed.[24] Nachmanides states that the witness is not killed because it is obvious that, despite all evidence proving that the witness

---

20. Moshe Ben Nachman, (Nachmanides), *Kitvei Ramban*, ed. Charles Ber Chavel (Jerusalem: Mossad Harav Kook, 1964), volume 2, 331.
21. Arthur Green, "Shekhinah, the Virgin Mary and the Song of Songs," *AJS Review*, 26:1 (2002), 35, note 141.
22. Maimonides, *Guide of the Perplexed* 3:25–49; Yeshayahu Leibowitz, *Conversations with Yeshayahu Leibowitz on the Moreh Nevukhim of Maimonides* [Hebrew] (Jerusalem: Mira Ofran, 2003).
23. Nachmanides, *Commentary to Leviticus* 19:2.
24. *Midrash Sifrei*; Babylonian Talmud, *Makkot* 5a; Rashi; Malbim; and others.

lied, he must have been telling the truth. God, he insists, would never allow an innocent person to be killed.[25]

FAITH AND RELIANCE ON GOD'S HELP

Nachmanides, as we have seen, felt strongly that one must rely on God and act with a certainty that when he encounters trouble, God will assist him. Thus, in his commentary to *Genesis* 12:11, he does not hesitate to criticize the patriarch Abram for what he considers his great sin of faithlessness when he lied and claimed that Sarai was his sister. Abram should not have resorted to a stratagem; he should have understood that God would protect him.

COMPASSION TO ANIMALS

Nachmanides and Maimonides are markedly different in their attitude to animals. *Deuteronomy* 22:6 commands: "If you chance upon a bird's nest along the road, in any tree or on the ground, with fledglings or eggs, and the mother is sitting over the fledglings or the eggs, do not take the mother together with her young." *Leviticus* 22:28 is similar: "No animal from the herd or from the flock should be slaughtered on the same day with its young."

In the *Guide of the Perplexed*,[26] Maimonides explains that animals, like humans, have feelings and the Torah prohibits people from tormenting them.

> [Regarding the slaughtering of animals] the Law enjoins that the death of the animal should be the easiest. It is not allowed to torment the animal by cutting the throat in a clumsy manner, by poleaxing, or by cutting off a limb whilst the animal is alive. It is also prohibited to kill an animal with its young on the same day, in order that people should be restrained and prevented from killing the two together in such a manner that the young is slain in the sight of the mother; for the pain of the animals under such circumstances is very great. There is no difference in this case between the pain of man and the pain of other living beings, since the love and tenderness of the mother for her young ones is not produced by reasoning, but by imagination, and this faculty exists not only in man but in most living beings.

---

25. C. Crescas, Y. Arama, and Sforno to *Leviticus* 4:3 give a contrary view.
26. 3:48. Translation of M. Friedlander, 371.

Maimonides gives three reasons for the prohibition against taking the dam and its young: (1) the animal's feelings, (2) assuring that humans eat healthy food, and (3) training people to be similarly sensitive to the feelings of other humans.

> The same reason applies to the law which enjoins that we should let the mother fly away when we take the young. The eggs over which the bird sits, and the young that are in need of their mother, are generally unfit for food, and when the mother is sent away she does not see the taking of her young ones, and does not feel any pain. In most cases, however, this commandment will cause man to leave the whole nest untouched, because [the young or the eggs], which he is allowed to take, are, as a rule, unfit for food. If the Law provides that such grief should not be caused to cattle or birds, how much more careful must we be to not cause grief to our fellow men.

Nachmanides disagrees. He contends:

> …that it was not a matter of God's mercy extending to the bird's nest or the dam and its young, since His mercies did not extend so far with them, for, if so, He would have forbidden slaughter altogether. But the reason for the prohibition [against taking the dam with its nest, or against killing the dam with its young in one day] is [only] to teach *us* the trait of compassion and that we should not be cruel, for cruelty proliferates in man's soul.[27]

Nachmanides concludes by stating that there is also a mystical reason for the command, but he does not elaborate, and his commentators differ in suggesting interpretations of his intention.

SUMMARY

Nachmanides' mystical views of God, the Torah, the universe, and natural law were very different than those of the rational Maimonides. It is important to note that his mystical preconceptions led him to his conclusions. He read his own views into the biblical writings, views never intended by, indeed alien to the Bible. We will see this occurring many times in our discussions on his interpretations of *Targum Onkelos*.

---

27. Moshe ben Nachman (Nachmanides), *Commentary to Deuteronomy* 22:6, translation by Chavel, in *Ramban, Commentary on the Torah, Deuteronomy*, 271.

– CHAPTER 4 –

Demons, Hell, Souls, and Other Subjects

> The prior chapter examined Nachmanides' mystical view of God and God's relationship with humans. This chapter looks at his approach to other subjects. Did Nachmanides insist that midrashic tales are not parables, but true facts? Did this insistence lead to difficult and unscientific conclusions? Was superstition an integral part of his life and thinking? What was his understanding of "life after death"? What were his opinions about hell? Did he believe in the transmigration of souls? Was he convinced that women are evil? Did he decide that a woman who was raped is polluted and that the innocently raped woman may no longer live with her husband? Did he say that people could read future events in biblical passages? What were his unique feelings about the land of Israel? Did he teach that idols exist and can help people? Was he certain that magic and divination work but Jews are forbidden to use them? Did he imagine that astrology influences people? What were his views about angels and demons? How did he appraise his rabbinic predecessors and contemporaries and *Targum Onkelos*? How did he use mysticism?

MIDRASHIC LEGENDS ARE HISTORICAL TRUTHS

Nachmanides insisted that the midrashic tales are true accounts of past events. His commentary to *Genesis* 11:32 is an excellent example of his manner of thinking. He retells the imaginative non-biblical talmudic legend of Abram destroying his father's idols,[1] and expands upon the story, giving his original details. He insists

---

1. Babylonian Talmud, *Bava Batra* 91a.

that the episode is true and warns us not to be misled by ibn Ezra who argues that the story is a parable that was invented to teach a moral lesson.[2]

His commentary to *Exodus* 33:6 is another illustration of Nachmanides accepting *Midrash* literally. *Midrash Exodus Rabbah* 45:1 states that God gave the Israelites armor when they stood at Mount Sinai and received the Decalogue. The *Midrash* states that the gift protected the people from dangers, including the angel of death, and gave them immortality. However, the Israelites later rejected the gift. They saw that some of the people worshipped the golden calf and felt unworthy of the divine present; they returned the protective armor and were again subject to death.

Still another example is his acceptance of the truthfulness of the midrashic tale of the first human creation being a single body with both male and female parts that were later divided.[3] He writes that the two sexes were an *eizer* (helpmate) to one another while being combined, but the Bible calls the female part *eizer k'negdo*, "a helpmate next to him," after the separation.

HIS BELIEF IN *MIDRASHIM* LED TO DIFFICULT CONCLUSIONS

Nachmanides' commentary on *Exodus* 19:13 was influenced by his belief in the truthfulness of midrashic stories, God's daily involvement in human affairs, miracles occurring daily, the patriarchs observing the Torah before it was given to Moses generations after their death, and an anthropomorphic deity. *Exodus* 19:13 reads, "when the *yovel* [ram's horn] sounds, they [the Israelites who were told not to approach Mount Sinai while the Decalogue was being revealed] shall come up the mount." Nachmanides notes that Rashi quotes a *Midrash* that states that the ram's horn used here was that of Isaac's ram.[4] Nachmanides accepts the truthfulness of the midrashic tale, but asks how this is possible since the ram was offered as an *olah*, a burnt offering, and the law in *Leviticus* 1:9 and 13 states that

---

2. Nachmanides does not mention Maimonides' view in his introduction to the tenth chapter of the tractate *Sanhedrin*, Chelek, that people who accept unnatural and illogical statements of the ancient sages literally instead of realizing that they are parables are pathetic and foolish people.
3. The tale is told in the Greek philosopher Plato's *Symposium* as a humorous anecdote by the comic playwright Aristophanes, and the *Midrash* may have been drawn from this source. Nachmanides' commentary is in *Genesis* 2:18.
4. The ram substituted as a sacrifice in place of Isaac whom his father Abraham was about to sacrifice in *Genesis* 22:13.

the entire animal, including its horn must be burnt.[5] "Perhaps," he replies, "the Holy One, blessed be He, shaped the ashes of the horn and restored it to what it was originally." Since Rashi and Nachmanides were convinced that the sound was not a noise created by God, but that a physical horn was blown, who blew it if not an anthropomorphic God?

SUPERSTITION

Nachmanides was very superstitious. *Numbers* 14:9 relates that when the Israelites murmured against Moses and said that they wanted to return to Egypt rather than battle against the Canaanites, Joshua and Caleb attempted to calm them by saying, "Only rebel not against the Lord, neither fear ye the people of the land, for they are bread for us, their defense is removed from over them, and the Lord is with us; fear them not." Nachmanides read into this verse a superstitious notion that did not at all fit the context of the passage, "the well-known fact that there will be no shadow over the head of a person [on the night of Hoshanah Rabbah, the seventh day of Succoth, when some believe that God decides the future of people] who will die that year." The earliest Jewish reference to this widespread Christian notion is found in the writings of Eleazar of Worms, a short time before Nachmanides.[6]

The people believed, like Nachmanides, that if they could not see their head, they would die during the year. If their right hand was not visible, their son would die, and if it was their left, their daughter would perish. Some of these people felt they could save themselves from the omen predicted by the shadow of the moon by giving charity.[7] The *Zohar* also has this belief. It tells a tale of a person who was no longer able to see his shadow, and writes: "So long as a person's shadow has not left him, his spirit is sustained within him. But as soon as the shadow departs and cannot be seen, that person is already in the process of departing from the world."[8]

---

5. Even if one accepts the story as real, a simple answer is that Abraham did not observe a law that was not issued until long after his death. However, Nachmanides could not accept this solution.
6. Joshua Trachtenberg. *Jewish Magic and Superstition* (New York: Behrman's Jewish Book House, 1939), 215.
7. See Daniel Sperber, *Minhagei Yisrael*, (Jerusalem: Mossad Harav Kook, 1989), vol. 6, 173–81.
8. Maurice Simon, ed. *The Zohar* (London: The Soncino Press, 1984), 1:217–18.

LIFE AFTER DEATH

There are many apparent inconsistencies in the logic of Nachmanides. One would expect, for example, that he, as a mystic, would conceive of life after death, the world to come, as a bodiless period of mystical union with the divine, but Nachmanides contended that, "the world to come is not a world of disembodied souls.... Those who are resurrected there will exist in body and soul."[9]

HELL

Contrary to Maimonides,[10] Nachmanides was convinced that a *Gehenna* (physical hell) exists where bodies of certain sinners are punished for as long as twelve months. At the end of the year, their bodies are destroyed, but their souls continue to live. Sinners with heinous crimes have their souls destroyed.[11] He also wrote of the existence of a physical paradise (Gan Eden), which, like *Gehenna*, he described at great length.[12]

TRANSMIGRATION OF SOULS

Relying on *Genesis* 3:8 and especially on *Leviticus* 18:6, Nachmanides believed in the transmigration of souls, the passing of a person's soul after death into another newly born body. He used this notion to explain why righteous people are punished. People suffer because of their sins and for no other reason. Righteous people suffer because of the sins their soul committed in a prior life.[13] Conversely, wicked individuals may prosper because of righteous deeds they performed in

---

9. Rosner, Fred, *Maimonides' Commentary on the Mishnah, Tractate Sanhedrin* (New York: Sepher-Hermon Press, Inc., 1981). In the introduction to chapter 10 we see that in contrast, Maimonides systematically emphasizing the importance of the intellect, stated that only the intellect exists after death.
10. Ibid.
11. C.B. Chavel, *Ramban, His Life and Teachings* (New York: Feldheim, 1960), 473–95. See also the Babylonian Talmud, *Rosh Hashanah* 17a, which Nachmanides understood literally, and upon which he drew his belief.
12. Chavel, ibid., 504–18.
13. C.B. Chavel, "The Gate of Reward," in *Ramban, Writings and Discourses* (New York: Shilo Publishing House, 1978) vol. 2, 454, 464, 467, and 468. For the rationalist's view, see Maimonides, *Guide of the Perplexed* 3:12. For a full treatment of the Jewish view toward metempsychosis, see David B. Ruderman, *A Valley of Vision: The Heavenly Journey of Abraham ben Hananiah Yagel* (University of Pennsylvania Press, 1990), 199–202, and the many books cited by him.

their prior life. He also used this idea to explain the biblical command that one should marry the wife of his deceased brother when the deceased left no child: the living brother was making it possible for the transmigration of his brother's soul within the family.[14]

His belief in the transmigration of souls affected his understanding of many other subjects. He wrote that when people eat or drink animal blood, their souls change and absorb the animal's characteristics (*Leviticus* 17:11), and this must not happen since their souls will be transmigrated and their wrongful acts will change the lives of many future people. He felt that certain sexual relationships were biblically forbidden, such as homosexuality, sex during menstruation, with near relatives, and bestiality because such sex hinders the transmigration of souls and because these unions would produce unhealthy offspring (*Leviticus* 18:6, 21). This lesson is contained in the scriptural prohibition against grafting certain fruits and vegetables together and mixing wool and linen. These laws teach people that human joining must be done properly (*Leviticus* 19:19) for the "Torah permitted sexual intercourse only for the sake of raising children" (*Leviticus* 18:19).[15]

Nachmanides' pupil's pupil Bachya ben Asher wrote that the patriarch Abraham was the reincarnation of Adam, the first human creation. He said, "He resembled Adam spiritually in that he spent the early years of his life as an idolater whereas he became a penitent like his ancestor Adam."[16] He also contended that the soul of Abel, who was killed by his brother Cain, was reincarnated in Moses.[17]

WOMEN

The ancient attitude of many men to women, in Greece and Rome, and in Judaism from at least the Greek and Roman period, if not earlier, was poor. The conception

---

14. Nachmanides, *Commentary to Genesis* 38:8. See also his *Commentary to Genesis* 4:1, 46:2, *Leviticus* 18:6, 26:11, and *Deuteronomy* 25:6, introduction to his commentary to *Job* and *Job* 33, and his discourse on *Kohelet*. The idea is also in *Zohar* 1, 187.
15. Rabbenu Bachya, questions Nachmanides' restrictive attitude toward sex. Additionally, Chavel, *Ramban*, 255, note 298, states that since Nachmanides mentions ibn Ezra's view in *Leviticus* 18:20, that there are three purposes for sex, it is possible that he agrees with ibn Ezra. Ibn Ezra states that the purpose of sex is to beget children, relieve the body of fluids, and for the satisfactions of one's passion. Ibn Ezra considers the latter purpose animalistic.
16. Bachya, *Torah Commentary to Genesis*, 2.
17. Ibid. 4:3.

by men of women was on the whole based upon the observation that women, who were uneducated, act in unsophisticated ways. However, as poor as this attitude was, the idea of many mystics was worse, for they saw the female as the source of evil.

Nachmanides and other mystics, such as Bachya ben Asher thought that the world derived its power from the two sides of the *sefirot*, the ten parts of God, according to mystics. They believed that the right side of God, the male side, is the source of good, and the left side, the female side of God, is evil. As Bachya put it, "This explains why Eve's soul received input from the serpent [why she was seduced by the serpent to eat of the fruit of the tree of good and evil in the Garden of Eden], since she was produced by the left emanations [of the *sefirot*], the female ones." Thus, he continues, "it was entirely natural that the serpent had sex with her and not with Adam. The affinity between the origin of the soul of Eve and the origin of the serpent, made it likely that she would be a victim to instant seduction."[18]

The mystics viewed menstruation as a punishment inflicted upon all women because Eve ate a fruit from the tree of good and evil in violation of God's explicit prohibition. They thought of the blood flow as effusion of evil, an ebullition of disgust. Nachmanides states that he agrees with people who have decided to distance themselves as much as possible from menstruating women.[19] "She contaminates even the earth upon which she steps. One should take no benefit from her. Even otherwise innocuous speech from such a woman is impure. A proper person does not even speak about such a woman or even ask about her health. Her contamination radiates from her: if she looks in a mirror for some time, red blood-like spots appear on the glass."[20]

Bachya ben Asher reflected the view of Nachmanides when he wrote "as soon as Eve was created Satan was created along with her."[21] He wrote, "Women may be perceived as the body, the personification of the evil urge."[22] He contended that

---

18. Ibid. 5:2.
19. Ibid. 31:35.
20. Leviticus 18:19. See also Charles Ber Chavel, "The Law of the Eternal is Perfect" *Kitvei Haramban* (Jerusalem: Mossad Harav Kook, 1983), 112.
21. Bachya, *Torah Commentary to Genesis* 2:21, referring to the *Midrash Genesis Rabbah* 17:6.
22. Ibid. 3:1.

women could be easily seduced and even Abraham took advantage of their weak nature: "When Abram wanted to get Sarai's agreement to tell the lie [that she was his sister, so that the Egyptians would not kill him when they would kidnap her] he introduced his request by complimenting her on her beauty ['now I know that you are a beautiful woman']."[23]

Maimonides disagreed: "The prohibition of eating [food prepared by a menstruating woman] or [touching] a garment handled by the menstruating woman is a Karaitic practice. He who distances himself [from a menstruating woman] because of this prohibition has removed himself from rabbinic Judaism and has denied the oral Torah!"[24]

RAPED WOMEN ARE DEFILED AND PROHIBITED TO THEIR HUSBANDS

Nachmanides felt that raped women are polluted and can no longer have sex with their husbands.[25] He explains that Reuben slept with his father's concubine for mercenary reasons. He imagines that Bilhah was the only woman left with whom Jacob could have children. The Bible states that Rachel died and he supposes that Leah was too old to give birth and her servant Zilpah was also too old or had died. If Bilhah gave birth, Nachmanides argued, Jacob would have had another child and his share of the inheritance would be reduced. So he slept with Bilhah, defiled her, and made it impossible for Jacob to sleep with her again.[26]

Maimonides' view of the Jewish law is contrary to that of Nachmanides. In his *Mishneh Torah, Hilkhot Ishut* 24:6, 17 and 19, he states:

> When a woman commits adultery...he is obligated to divorce her and is forbidden to have sex with her. [However] a woman who committed adultery unknowingly or who was raped is permitted to [have sex with] her husband... [whether] a non-Jew or a Jew raped her.[27]

---

23. Ibid. 12:11
24. Y. Blau, ed., *Responsa Haramban* (Jerusalem, 1960), 588.
25. Nachmanides, *Commentary to Genesis* 35:22.
26. Radak (David Kimchi), 1160–1235, and Joseph Bechor Schor (born around 1080) share his view. They write that when Jacob heard what Reuben did, he separated from his wife, and this is hinted at in the end of the verse that states that Jacob had [only] twelve children.
27. This reflects the conclusion of the Babylonian Talmud, *Yevamot* 33b, *Sotah* 28a, and *Ketubot* 3b and 51b.

BIBLE PREDICTS FUTURE EVENTS

Nachmanides saw the curses in *Leviticus* 26 and *Deuteronomy* 27 as an oracle forecasting what would occur during and after the destruction of the First and Second Temples, respectively. He does not discuss the difficulty, raised by this view that this understanding appears to deny the concept of free will.[28] The *Zohar*, Sforno, and Bachya agree with Nachmanides. Rashi and Rashbam appear to do so as well, but not as explicitly. Abravanel states that both sections foretell the destruction of the First Temple and its aftermath. *Midrash Pesikta* states that *Deuteronomy* predicts the occurrences of the First Temple and *Leviticus* the Second. In view of these differences, the possibility for various, even contrary interpretations, is clear in that the chapters are not as explicit as commentators suppose. Ibn Ezra and Maimonides reject the idea that the Bible is relating future events. They understand the verses to warn of dire consequences *if* the Israelites refuse to obey God's laws, but not a promise that the misfortunes will occur.[29]

THE SANCTITY OF THE LAND OF ISRAEL

Nachmanides had a profound love of the land of Israel, which he considered sacred ground, and contrary to Maimonides, he insisted that settlement in Israel is a divine commandment.[30] His feeling that Israel was holy was so intense that he stated that God killed Jacob's beloved second wife Rachel just prior to the family entering the land of Israel so that the patriarch Jacob, who was allowed to marry two sisters outside of Israel, would not violate the Torah's command forbidding matrimony with two sisters in Israel, thereby desecrating the holy earth.[31]

---

28. Nachmanides believed in free will. See also Nachmanides' commentary to *Exodus* 4:25, *Leviticus* 26:12 and *Deuteronomy* 30:1. Nachmanides states that the latter oracle did not yet occur, but that it will happen in the future.
29. Ibn Ezra's view can be seen in his commentary to these chapters and in his general approach to prophecy. Similarly, the Maimonidean concept is apparent in his statements about prophecy and in his comments on these chapters, such as *Guide of the Perplexed* 3:36.
30. C.B. Chavel, *Sefer Hamitzvot La'Rambam im Hasagot Haramban* (Jerusalem: Mossad Harav Kook, 1981).
31. Nachmanides maintained that the patriarchs learnt the Torah by divine inspiration and the observance of the commands applied only in the land of Israel. *Commentary to Genesis* 26:5 and *Leviticus* 18:25. See Joseph Bonfils, *Tzafanat Pane'ach*, ed. D. Herzog (Heidelberg, 1930), vol. 2; and ibn Shaprut, *Tzafanat Pane'ach*, Ms. (Oxford: Bodley Opp. Add. 40–107, Neubauer 2350, beginning on 53b.

Nachmanides was convinced that God only exercises divine power in Israel for only Israel is a holy land. God set other divine-like powers to control other lands.[32] "There is in this matter a secret relating to that which the rabbis have said [in the above-quoted talmudic statement]: 'He who dwells outside of the land of Israel is like one who has no God.'"[33] He understands that the Talmud is stating that people who live outside of Israel are under the influence and power of these other supernatural beings and even if they try to worship God it is as if they have no God. Maimonides rejected this notion out of hand. When he escaped the persecution of Jews in Spain and Morocco and came to Israel and saw the terrible conditions facing Jews in the land, he left and settled in Egypt where he was a fully practicing Jew.

This love of the land of Israel also led Nachmanides to the doctrine that all the Torah commandments are only divinely obligated upon those who are dwelling in Israel. Outside of the land, Jews observe the laws only so that they will not be "new to us" when we return to the land of Israel.[34]

Nachmanides' view that the Bible requires Jews to conquer the land of Israel and dwell in it does not appear to be reasonable. He derived this command from *Numbers* 33:53, which states: "You should take the land as a possession and dwell in it, because I gave it to you as a possession." In his glosses to Maimonides' *Sefer Hamitzvot*, he cites the Babylonian Talmud, *Sotah* 44b, which calls Joshua's war against the Canaanite nations an "obligatory war."

> Do not assume erroneously that the obligatory war applies only to the seven [Canaanite] nations. This is untrue. We will not abandon this land to idolatrous nations throughout the [subsequent] generations. Even if these nations will run from us and leave the land, we are still commanded [today] to come to the land, conquer it and settle it with our people.... Hence, this is a command for all generations and is an obligation for every individual.

This gloss places an obligation on Jews to act to conquer Israel, but Nachmanides' biblical comments seem to be contradictory: it is God, not human beings, who

---

32. Nachmanides, *Commentary to Genesis* 28:21.
33. Chavel, *Ramban, Commentary on the Torah, Genesis*, 359.
34. Nachmanides, *Commentary to Leviticus* 18:25, *Deuteronomy* 11:18, and "Sermon on the Words of Kohelet" in *Kitvei Ramban*, ed. Charles Ber Chavel (Jerusalem: Mossad Harav Kook, 1964).

will give Jews the land of Israel. He cites *Psalms* 44:4, "For not by their sword will they inherit the land, nor through their strength will they be helped, but by Your right arm, Your strength."[35]

Furthermore, his reliance on *Numbers* 33:53 to support his view that Jews have a perpetual obligation to conquer Israel whenever it is not in Jewish possession is difficult. Verses 50–56 concern Joshua's entry into Canaan, as *Sotah* 44b also saw it. God gave directions to the Israelites as they stood near Jericho, ready to cross the Jordan and conquer Canaan. The verses state explicitly that what is mentioned is what the Israelites should do when they cross the Jordan. The verses speak of the Israelite duty to also destroy the Canaanite idols and altars as they enter the land. They also tell how the conquered land is to be divided among the tribes. There is no command in *Numbers* or anywhere else in the Bible, requiring Jews to conquer and settle the land in future years.

Although Nachmanides stressed the importance of settlement in Israel and his belief that one does not observe biblical *mitzvot* outside Israel, he did not leave Spain to settle in Israel until his old age, several years before his death, and even then only to escape the threat of assassination due to his involvement in the religious debate of 1263.

Nachmanides' student's student Bachya ben Asher held a similar view about the sanctity and power of Israel. In his commentary to *Genesis* 11:30, he writes that when Abram and Sarai saw that she was barren, they "decided to leave their home and move to Canaan with the hope that because of the merit of the holy land they would be able to have children." In his commentary to 12:6, he writes that in addition to holiness, Canaan has the perfect climate, better than every other land.

IDOLATRY, MAGIC, AND DIVINATION

Nachmanides' view of life and his contention that the world is dependent on the metaphysical, is exemplified in his view of idolatry, magic, and divination. Idolatry, he maintains, is not prohibited because it is based on a false belief in the existence of nonexistent gods. The opposite is true. Jews are forbidden to worship idols because although they exist and are powerful, Jews may not have any dealings with them because Jews are God's people and must not reject God by

---

35. Nachmanides, *Commentary to Genesis* 48:22; see also *Genesis* 15:18.

seeking efficacious help from the idols.[36] The *Zohar* also contends that the "gods of the nations" that are mentioned in the Bible are not useless material but actual celestial beings with real, but limited powers to influence the world and people.[37]

ASTROLOGY

Similarly, although he was convinced that the sun, moon, stars, and constellations have power over people and influence them for good and bad, Jews are forbidden to worship these objects.[38] The same applies to magic and divination, which works as is "well-known to the eyes of all viewers."[39] Unlike Maimonides, who strongly criticized those who believed in the foolishness of astrology, Nachmanides was convinced that it worked.[40]

Nachmanides used his belief in astrology to explain that Moses did not include the tribe of Simeon in his blessings because, among other reasons, Moses needed to divide the tribe of Joseph into two and this would have resulted in thirteen blessings.[41] Simeon had to be excluded to bring the count back to twelve to correspond to the number of constellations.[42]

Bachya ben Asher refers to an opinion in the Babylonian Talmud, *Shabbat* 75, that those who know how to use astrology and fail to do so are like the people mentioned in *Psalms* 82:5, "they neither knew nor understood, but make themselves walk in darkness." He states that the Jewish people are not affected as a nation by astrological forces because God protects the nation; however, "the fate of individual Jews is subject to the influences of the horoscope."[43]

---

36. See the notes in the next two sections on astrology and angels and demons.
37. *Zohar* 2:7, 2:67, and 2:237.
38. Bachya, *Torah Commentary to Genesis* 5:23 states that the Bible said that Enoch "walked with God" because although he recognized the power of astrology, he also realized the source of this power is God.
39. Nachmanides, *Commentary to Deuteronomy* 18:9, 21:12, 13.
40. As did ibn Ezra and most other sages of Nachmanides' generation. In contrast, see Maimonides' *Letter on Astrology*, written in 1194, about when Nachmanides was born, and an analysis in Lerner, *Maimonides' Empire of Light* 56–64 and 178–87.
41. In *Deuteronomy* 33:6
42. Compare *Numbers Rabbah* 14–29.
43. Bachya, *Torah Commentary to Genesis* 15:5.

ANGELS AND DEMONS

Maimonides rejected the notion that demons exist,[44] defined angels as all things that do the will of God, including the elements of nature,[45] and held that "Satan" and "the angel of death" are metaphors for the powers that exist in nature. Nachmanides and his near contemporaries Rashi, Judah Halevi, Rabad of Posquieres, and many others disagreed. They believed in the existence of angels and demons, both of which are corporeal and can have powerful positive and negative impacts upon humans, but God told Jews not to seek their assistance.[46] Chasdai Crescas based his belief in demons in what he saw as explicit biblical verses, rabbinical statements in the Talmuds and *Midrashim*, in the acceptance of the notion even by many non-Jews, and because he felt that they could be sensed by the five human senses.[47] God created angels on the fifth day of creation, according to Bachya ben Asher, who understood the biblical reference to flying creatures, not as birds, but angels.[48] Angels and demons, according to others, can be seen with special perspicuity of vision.[49]

"Satan," according to Nachmanides is an angel that causes evil and the "angel of death" is an angel that causes death.[50] In his commentary to *Leviticus* 16:8, which I will discuss in my analysis of his understandings of *Targum Onkelos*, he states that God instructed Jews to bribe the chief demon every year on the holiday of Yom Hakippurim. Rashi states that Noah rescued the demons from extinction in the flood by taking them aboard his ark.[51]

Bachya ben Asher reflects Nachmanides view of angels when he writes that even "good" angels can sin.[52] "One example is found in *Genesis* 19:13 where the

---

44. Maimonides, *Guide of the Perplexed* 3:46.
45. Ibid. 2:6 and 7.
46. *Leviticus* 17:7.
47. Chasdai ben Judah Creskas, *Sefer Or Adonai* (South Carolina: Nabu Press, 2010), 4:6.
48. Bachya, *Torah Commentary to Genesis* 1:21.
49. Ibid. 18:1; Judah Halevi, *Kuzari* (New York: Schocken Books, 1987), 3, 11; Trachtenberg, *Jewish Magic and Superstition*, 73; Isidore Twersky, *Rabad of Posquieres*, (Philadelphia: Jewish Publication Society, 1980). Nachmanides discusses Maimonides contrary view in *Genesis* 18:1.
50. See Nachmanides' commentary to the book of *Job* and Chavel, *Kitvei Haramban*, 24–25 and 381.
51. *Genesis* 9:10.
52. Bachya, *Torah Commentary to Genesis* 3:6.

angels [sent to Abraham's nephew Lot] who had been commanded to destroy Sodom and to save Lot describe themselves as if it were they who were destroying Sodom and not God." Bachya states that God sometimes sends angels to fight for Israel.[53] Both Bachya and Nachmanides were convinced that four women – Lilith, Naamah, Igrat, and Machalat – became mothers of demons.[54]

ATTITUDE TO ANCIENT AND CONTEMPORARY SCHOLARS

Nachmanides revered the authority of the ancients and wrote: "We bow before them, and even when the reason for their words is not quite evident to us, we submit to them."[55] Nevertheless, he frequently treated the opinions of his near contemporaries ibn Ezra and Rashi with seeming disrespect.

He called ibn Ezra's comments to *Exodus* 24:12 and 28:30, for example, "a comment of no value." He stated more strongly in *Leviticus* 2:13 that "there is no sense to his words." His treatment of Rashi was similar. The following are two examples. He said that Rashi's explanation of *Esther* 31:10 "avails me nothing" and the commentary to *Exodus* 24:14 "is impossible."

In contrast, he avoids such language when he mentions Maimonides, with whom he also disagreed, and refers to him respectfully as "the rabbi." He quotes *Targum Onkelos* on many occasions, as we will see, and does so with near reverence, usually to support his own understanding of the biblical verse, although his understanding of the *Targum*, as we will come to understand, raises questions.

DATING TARGUM ONKELOS

Since we will be discussing Nachmanides' understandings of *Targum Onkelos*, it is interesting to note that the rabbi uniquely contended that Onkelos became a proselyte to Judaism because he was attracted to the study of mysticism. He dated the *Targum* to the time just after the Greek philosopher Aristotle, 384–322 BCE, and misses the date recorded in the Talmud of about 130 CE by about 400 years, and the date I established by comparing the *Targum* to the *Midrashim* of about 400 CE, which is approximately 700 years.[56]

---

53. Ibid. 6:6.
54. Ibid. 4:22.
55. Moshe ben Nachman (Nachmanides), *Asifat Zekenim to Ketubot* (Warsaw, 1861).
56. Chavel, *Writings of Nachmanides, The Law of the Eternal is Perfect*, 75–76; Rabbi Dr. Israel

MYSTICAL INTERPRETATIONS

Mysticism was important to Nachmanides. Therefore it is not surprising that he was the first person who contended that the Bible, *Targum Onkelos*, and the other Aramaic translations of the Bible contained mystical teachings. His first mystical explanation of a *Targum* was his analysis of a *Fragmented Targum*'s rendering of the Bible's first word.[57] This *Targum* uses *b'chachmah*, "with wisdom," in place of Scripture's *bereishit*, "in the beginning" to teach that God created the world with wisdom. Nachmanides argues anachronistically that this early Bible translation is communicating the later mystical idea of the ten *sefirot*,[58] a concept that did not exist when the *Fragmented Targum* was composed. He argues that the *Targum* is referring to the first of the *sefirot* as the one called *chachmah*. Thus God created the world with the *sefira* of *chachmah*. Nachmanides ignores the facts that *Midrash Genesis Rabbah*, from which the *Targum*'s translator drew material, uses the same word "wisdom" and refers to *Proverbs* 3:19, "The Lord founded the earth with wisdom," and states that "wisdom" signifies the wisdom of the Torah. Since (1) all of the authors of the *Targums* frequently emphasized the importance of Torah study, (2) the translator drew his interpretation that the world was created with wisdom from the *Midrash* that he used consistently and this *Midrash* states that wisdom means Torah, and (3) Nachmanides' mystical notion did not exist when the *Targum* was composed. We will see that this first usage of a *Targum* is emblematic of most of his interpretations of *Targum Onkelos*.

Drazin, "Dating *Targum Onkelos* by means of the Tannaitic Midrashim," *Journal of Jewish Studies*, 50, no. 2 (autumn 1999).

57. There are several different *Fragmented Targums*. The *Fragmented Targums* are Aramaic versions of the Pentateuch that exist in fragments only, and scholars are uncertain whether they were originally written in this fashion on only certain verses, or whether they were translations of the entire Pentateuch and only fragments remain.

58. Y. Leibowitz, *Seven Years of Discourses on the Weekly Torah Reading*, Hebrew (Jerusalem: Keter, 2000), 11, calls the mystical interpretations an insertion of pluralism into Jewish monotheism.

– CHAPTER 5 –

Difficult Nachmanidean Interpretations of the Torah

> Since Nachmanides' Bible interpretations are based on his world views and since his views are different than those held by many modern people, his commentaries are frequently doubtful. A further complicating factor is his idea that a Bible reader can assume that certain events occurred even though the imagined events are not explicit in the passage and are unnatural. A third factor is his practice of forcing an interpretation into a biblical word to prove his notion of what the verse is communicating even though the words do not normally have the meaning he is proposing.

INVENTING A NARRATIVE

As we will see, one aspect of Nachmanides' commentary is his invention of a story out of the Bible's use of a single word or two even though the drama is not even hinted at in Scripture. One example of many is *Numbers* 16:30, which states in the Torah: "But if the Lord *beriah ivrah* [creates a (new) creation], and the ground opens its mouth and swallows them and all that is theirs, and they descend alive to Sheol [meaning, the grave], then you will know that these men caused anger [before] the Lord."

The rabbis differ in interpreting *beriah ivrah*. Rashi understands that the root of the two words is *b-r-h*, and that it means the creation of something from nothing, the same way he understands its usage in the first sentence of the Torah, "In the beginning God created the heaven and the earth." Therefore, relying on the Babylonian Talmud, *Sanhedrin* 110, he says that it was an earthquake that swallowed the rebels, and this special miracle was created during the six days of creation to be executed during the days of Moses. Ibn Ezra, however, points to the fact that since earthquakes had occurred before, it is not an unusual phenomenon, and he defined *beriah* as "cutting"; the rebels were "cut down" by God by being swallowed up in the ground by an earthquake, which was not a new creation.

Nachmanides agrees with Rashi that *beriah* is a new creation of something that did not previously exist, and with ibn Ezra that earthquakes occurred before, but contends that the new event in this case was that the ground opened up to swallow only certain designated people and then immediately closed up. This notion that a miracle occurred, that despite the fact that generally all people standing over an earthquake are swallowed by the fissure, here we have only "designated" people that were killed, is not even hinted at in the Torah.

ANOTHER INVENTED NARRATIVE

Nachmanides tends to invent unreal and frequently unnatural narratives out of his own definition of a single word, or out of thin air with no connection to biblical words, as seen in the next example. In *Numbers* 22:33 he deduces an extended episode from his interpretation of Scripture's *ulai*.

The generally accepted definition of *ulai*, is "unless." In 22:33, the verse would have an angel say to the prophet Balaam who was riding his ass to go curse the Israelites contrary to God's will, "unless she [Balaam's ass] had turned aside from me [when I showed myself to her] I would have surely killed you." Nachmanides argues that *ulai* here means "perhaps," implying a doubt.

Nachmanides states that *ulai* is telling us that the following occurred. The ass felt or saw the angel standing before her with a drawn sword, became frightened, and "because of a doubt [that the angel may have been after her rather than the prophet] she turned aside from before me, although I came to slay you, and I would have saved her life, since it was you who sinned, not the ass." Thus, Nachmanides concludes that the ass saved the prophet's life because she turned aside, and she turned aside because *ulai*, "perhaps," she thought that she might have been the object of the angel's threat.

Needless to say, it is obvious that Nachmanides preferred to define *ulai* as "perhaps" because he felt that he could then use it to support his version of the affair. Secondly, the extended Nachmanidean drama is not implied in this single word even if it is translated as "perhaps."

WHAT IS THE BLESSING OF THE SABBATH?

Nachmanides gives a mystical interpretation to *Genesis* 2:3. Scripture states, "And God blessed the seventh day and sanctified it." Rashi offers a homiletical exegesis. God blessed the Sabbath by distributing a double portion of manna during the days of Moses. Ibn Ezra states that the Sabbath rest affords its observers an additional sense of well-being and a greater ability to function during the following week both physically and mentally.

Nachmanides asserts that the Sabbath "draws its sanctity from the sanctuary on high." This is clearly not even hinted at in the biblical words.

DOES THE TORAH SPEAK ABOUT REWARDS AFTER DEATH?

What does Scripture mean when it says in *Deuteronomy* 4:39 that "He is the God in heaven above and in the earth below, there is no other"? The simple meaning, which fits the context in which this passage occurs, is that there is only a single deity who is everywhere, even "in the heaven above and the earth below," as ibn Ezra states, even in places that humans cannot reach. However, although there is no explicit biblical statement about rewards after death, Nachmanides contends that this verse is teaching that if a person acts properly and observes the divine commandments, the person will be rewarded in heaven after death, and on earth while still alive.

THE DUTY TO HAVE FAITH

The overwhelming majority of Bible commentators maintain that Abram acted properly in *Genesis* 12:11. However, Nachmanides unhesitatingly criticizes the patriarch for committing the great sin of not having faith in God when he lied to save his life, claiming that Sarai was his sister so that the Egyptians would not murder him when they seized her. According to Nachmanides, Abram should have had faith that God would protect him. Nachmanides goes even further. He maintains that as a result of Abram's "sin," his descendants, the Israelites, were enslaved in Egypt for hundreds of years.[1]

---

1. The Babylonian Talmud, *Nedarim* 32a, offers three opinions blaming Abraham for the slavery of his descendants. However, others, such as Abravanel, Sforno, Ran, and Chasdai Crescas state

Nachmanides' notion of the obligation to have faith, contrasts sharply with the worldview of Maimonides. Maimonides contends that the world functions according to the laws of nature that God created and which are good, God does not interfere to help people in trouble, and divine providence means the use of human intelligence; a person is saved from danger if he uses his thought process.[2]

THE NOAHIDE COMMANDMENTS

In his interpretation of *Genesis* 34:13, Nachmanides argues that Maimonides is wrong in how he understands one of the seven Noahide commandments. The commands inform non-Jews what kind of behavior Judaism expects of them. The commands are rabbinic in origin, but the rabbis based their view on their interpretation of biblical verses. The seven are the requirement to establish law courts, and prohibitions of idolatry, blasphemy, bloodshed, incest, robbery, and eating a limb cut from a living creature.

Maimonides explained that the first command requires non-Jews to appoint judges to adjudicate the other six commands. Nachmanides disagreed. He argued that the command to establish law courts included the requirement that the non-Jewish court inform people about all civil laws, even those not included in the remaining six: not to rob, overcharge, seduce women, hurt others, and similar civil laws with which the Israelites were charged.

It is difficult to agree with this understanding because if it is true there would be no need for the six other commandments, since, according to Nachmanides, they are all included in the first. For example, he explicitly lists robbery, one of the seven Noahide commands, in the law court command.

FAMILY RELATIONS

Another difficult Nachmanidean interpretation is *Genesis* 3:16, "[Eve is punished for eating the forbidden fruit] your desire shall be to your husband." Nachmanides quotes Rashi: "This refers to cohabitation. You [women] will not have the

---

that Abraham is blameless. Also, Rashi, Radak, *Avot* 5:2 and *Pirkei de-Rabbi Eliezer* 26 state that this was one of the ten trials that God put upon Abraham and he passed all of them. See Ruth Ben-Meir, "Avraham in Nachmanides' Thought" [Hebrew] in *Avraham Avi ha-Ma'aminim* (The Faith of Abraham in the Light of Interpretation Throughout the Ages), eds. Moshe Halamish, Hannaha Kasher, and Yohanan Silman, (Ramat-Gan, Israel: Bar Ilan University Press, 2002), 155–65.
2. Maimonides, *Guide of the Perplexed* 3:17 and 2:48.

boldness to demand it by word, rather he will rule over you. It will be from him and not from you." Nachmanides criticizes this explanation because "modesty is praiseworthy in a woman." It is unclear why Rashi is being criticized. Rashi states that the woman modestly refrains from requesting cohabitation. Is it possible that Nachmanides did not understand Rashi? Or, perhaps, Nachmanides felt that a woman should have no sexual feelings at all; and this is also perplexing.

NOAH'S FLOOD

Genesis 8:5 recounts the cessation of the flood in the days of Noah. Since the verse says "and God made a wind to pass over the earth," rather than "over the water," Nachmanides imagines an unusual unnatural occurrence. The wind did not come from above the earth, but from "the bowels of the earth." The water entered the emptied space in the earth in the place that the winds evacuated. Leaving scientific questions aside, it is unclear how the words "over the earth" can suggest coming from *below* the earth; and how "earth" suggests the Nachmanidean elaboration when it is used instead of "water."

EVIL INCLINATION

Commenting on *Genesis* 8:21, Nachmanides informs readers that children are born with an evil inclination, which dissipates when the children become older. He concludes that God recognized this human nature and decided that it would no longer be proper to kill human beings because they are so disposed. There is a problem with this idea: God had just finished killing people with the flood. Is Nachmanides saying that although God created humans with this urge, God only realized now that this was done and now decided not to kill people in the future. This would imply that God didn't know the consequences of the past divine act. The Bible states in the first chapter of *Genesis* that God considered what was created and saw it was good. Is God now realizing that creation has a flaw?

THE BIBLICAL USE OF THE SINGULAR

Numbers 19 contains the laws of the red heifer. Verses 1 and 2 contain the words "spoke" and "speak," respectively, in the singular, although both Moses and Aaron are being addressed, and "bring" in verse 2 is in the singular even though the red heifer was to be used by all of the Israelites. Why is the singular used?

Nachmanides supposes that the Torah may have used the singular for "speak" and "spoke" because Moses was more important than Aaron or because God spoke only to Moses, who was required to relay the message to Aaron.

He also supposes that "bring" is singular because God at first wanted Moses to perform the red heifer ceremony alone and then issued it as a command for all the Israelites in verse 10. Nachmanides offers no reason for this behavior.

The issue of the use of the singular can be explained simply. It is the biblical style to use the singular for the plural and vice versa and this occurs very frequently. Indeed, Scripture uses the singular virtually every time that two people are addressed. Apparently C.B. Chavel, who translated Nachmanides' Hebrew commentary into English, had difficulty with Nachmanides' second comment because he deleted it from his English translation.

THE ISRAELITE POPULATION

The biblical Israelite population figures raise more than a dozen questions. One is how it is possible that the Israelite count did not differ by a single person between the enumerations of the first and second year of their stay in the desert. The numbers seem to state that no one died and no one was born during the entire year. It remained at 603,550 males of military age.[3] Many answers were suggested including a midrashic view that indeed a miracle occurred and death was suspended during the year.[4] This solution overlooks the obvious fact that many nineteen-year-olds would have reached the military age of twenty during the seven months between the two countings. Rashi and Nachmanides attempted to explain the count in *Exodus* 30:12. Rashi seems to accept the midrashic miraculous explanation and explains the issue of nineteen-year-olds by saying that birthdays are counted from the month of Tishrei, and the month of Tishrei did not occur during the seven months, so no male increased in age.

Nachmanides could not accept this solution. First, people obviously died during this time frame. Second, as everyone knows, birthdays are calculated from the date of birth, not the first of Tishrei. He suggests, without textual proof, that

---

3. The first census was taken in Tishrei in the exodus' first year and the second, mentioned in *Numbers* 1:2, occurred seven months later on the first of Iyar. The second year began in Nisan, one month earlier.
4. Quoted by Nachmanides.

despite deaths and nineteen-year-olds attaining age twenty, the identical number of 603,550 occurred because the first census included Levites while the second count did not, and the count of nineteen-year-olds that attained the age of twenty was exactly like the count of Levites who were not included in the second census. Again, this solution is not explicit in the text.

MYSTICAL VALUE OF SEVENTY

Nachmanides saw mystical significances in many biblical occurrences, including why God told Moses in *Numbers* 11:16 to select seventy elders to assist him. He states that each of the seventy nations in the word has "a constellation in the heavens [since Nachmanides believed that astrology works, and since he believed that there were seventy nations, each constellation controlled a separate nation] with a prince [meaning an angel] over it." God, he continued, commanded that there should be seventy judges for the Israelites, "because this number includes all opinions [that could be given in a case that they heard] since it [the number] comprises all the powers."

There are several difficulties with Nachmanides' interpretation. First, the seventy elders may have been appointed for administrative and not judicial duties. Second, even if they performed a judicial function, and even if one accepts Nachmanides' notion that there are seventy constellations/angels over seventy nations, it is unreasonable to see a connection between seventy constellations/nations and the number of possible opinions that could be argued in a court case. Every nation must have had many people with different ideas. Third, even if there are only seventy possible arguments, the selection of seventy judges would in no way assure that the seventy chosen judges knew all of them. Fourth, the traditional view of the Sanhedrin, the supreme Jewish court, is that it contained seventy-one, not seventy judges.

THE TORAH IS SPEAKING OF A HEAVENLY SANCTUARY

Numbers 19:13 speaks about a person defiling the *Mishkhan* (Tabernacle) while 19:20 states "for he defiled the *Mikdash* (Sanctuary)." The Bible commentators question why there is a difference in terminology and why there is a need to repeat the admonition. Rashi suggests that the difference in wording teaches the *halakhah* discussed in the Babylonian Talmud, *Shavuot* 16a. Nachmanides states that the simple answer is that the two words are synonymous and there is no repetition since the two verses are speaking of different situations. However, he adds that mystics understand that the *Mikdash* in verse 20 refers to the heavenly Sanctuary.

DOES *PAKAD* MEAN ALL THAT NACHMANIDES READS INTO IT?

In *Numbers* 1:3, Nachmanides notes that Scripture's Hebrew root *pakad*, which *Onkelos* simply translates as "tally," can also mean "remember," as in *Genesis* 21:1, where it refers to God's "remembrance" of Sarah's barrenness. He argues that the Torah used a term that also means "remember" to inform us that the counting of the Israelites by Moses is done through the use of a half shekel and that Moses "should pay attention (*yashgiach*) to the half shekels and thereby know the number of the people." The difficulty here is that *pakad* clearly means "tally" and "pay attention" has nothing to do with "remembrance."

WHY COULDN'T GOD PERFORM A MIRACLE?

Nachmanides asks: why, in *Numbers* 16:21, did God request Moses and Aaron to "separate from this community [of rebels who had joined Korach in a conspiracy against Moses and Aaron]" before punishing the guilty rebels? God certainly had the power to spare them even if people near them perished, just as God saved the Israelites who lived in Egypt from the destruction caused by the ten plagues.

Nachmanides offers two answers, both of which are difficult:

1. The fire and the earthquake that killed the rebels could have killed everyone standing near the rebels "unless a miracle of an unusual nature occurs."

    This answer fails to resolve Nachmanides' question, which was why did God need to have Moses and Aaron move when God could have performed a miracle? Accordingly various attempts have been made to explain Nachmanides' answer, generally rewording it entirely.

2. If Moses and Aaron had not separated from the people then the people would have been saved due to their merit. Many rabbis, including Nachmanides, believed in a concept called *zekhut avot*. Under this concept, when people do a meritorious act, their merit is stored up for them, as if in a bank account, which they can draw upon when they need it to help them. Some rabbis, including Nachmanides, felt that evil non-relatives who are in need can also draw

merit from this account even generations after the death of the meritorious person. This is apparently what Nachmanides was referring to, although it is unclear why they could only draw from Moses and Aaron's account if they were present.

Nachmanides concludes by seemingly reversing himself and saying that both of his answers indicate that Moses and Aaron were instructed to plead for God's mercy and forgiveness for the rebels. If so, and if one believes that their merit alone would save the rebels, why should Moses and Aaron move?

SINGLE AND PLURAL WORDS

When Moses requested that the Edomites allow them to traverse their land during their desert march toward Canaan, *Numbers* 20:18 states, "Edom said to him: 'You shall not pass through my border.'"

Nachmanides supposes that Scripture uses the singular "Edom" because every single Edomite agreed that the Israelites must not be allowed to pass through their border.

There are three problems with his view. First, it is impossible for an entire nation to agree on anything. Second, Scripture very frequently uses the singular when it means the plural; this is especially true when the Bible is describing the general reaction of a country, as in verse 20 where the Bible states that Edom went out to fight against "him," meaning the Israelites. Third, if one wanted to take the singular literally, "Edom" would refer to the king of the country.

ANOTHER EXAMPLE OF SINGULAR AND PLURAL WORDS

God speaks to Moses in *Deuteronomy* 31:19 and instructs that the poem contained in chapter 32 should be written down. The words "write down" are in the plural form in verse 19; however, verse 22 states that "Moses [singular] wrote down this poem." How should this be understood?

Nachmanides states that "the plain meaning of Scripture [is that God] commands both Moses and Joshua to write it because God intended to make Joshua a prophet during Moses' lifetime. Then Moses wrote it (verse 22) while Joshua stood by him, read it, and saw it."

This interpretation is hard to understand. First, as stated frequently,

Nachmanides is inventing a narrative that is not even hinted at in Scripture; Joshua is not mentioned in this part of the story. Second, the command to "write" a poem does not suggest that this was the first time that Joshua prophesied. Third, God, according to Nachmanides, tells Joshua to write; why does he only stand by, read it, and see. Fourth, the term "saw it" is obscure. If it means that Joshua only saw and knew what Moses was writing after he wrote it, this contradicts Nachmanides' interpretation that Joshua was prophesying. If it means Joshua was checking to see that Moses made no error, this can be seen as insulting to Moses. Fifth, why is Joshua distinguished here? We are told earlier in the Torah that Moses transferred the ability to prophesy to seventy people; if Joshua could not prophesy until now, it seems that he was not worthy until this moment.

A simpler explanation, as we indicated previously, is that biblical Hebrew frequently uses the plural when it means the singular and the reverse. Also, ibn Ezra offers the idea that is closer to the plain meaning in that Moses should write it as well as every other capable Israelite, for the poem was composed to alert the Israelites of the consequences of future misbehavior.

WHEN DID THE LEVITES BEGIN WORKING IN THE TABERNACLE?

Numbers 8:24 states, "This pertains to the Levites: They shall participate in performing the service of the Tent of Meeting work from the age of *twenty-five years and up*."

Rashi (based on *Sifrei* and the Babylonian Talmud, *Chullin* 24a) notes that our verse states that the Levites begin their service at age twenty-five, while 4:3 states that the age is thirty. He explains the discrepancy with the suggestion that the Levites came to study the laws of the service at age twenty-five, studied for five years, and began work at the age of thirty. Ibn Ezra and Rashbam suggest that at age twenty-five they could work at carrying the parts of the Tabernacle and at age thirty they could both carry and work in the Tabernacle. Nachmanides felt differently and stated that the Levite service in the Temple began at age twenty-five. Why then was Moses told to count the Levites from age thirty? God had pity on Moses because it would have been too much work for him to identify the Levites who were age twenty-five, since, according to Nachmanides, a person's age is most recognizable at each decade of his life.

WHY WAS A SHOFAR BLOWN IN THE DESERT?

Numbers 10:5 states, "When you sound the alarm [of the shofar], the [Israelite] camps encamped on the east should journey." The Hebrew word translated here as "alarm" is *teruah*.

The Torah does not define *teruah* and does not even hint at whether the word simply means an alarm or is a particular sound or more than one sound; Bible readers can only speculate about it. Rashi relies on *Sifrei* when he suggests that the sound is a threefold blast of a *tekiah*, *teruah*, and *tekiah* (prolonged note, short notes, prolonged note) sounded when the Israelites were called to journey.

Nachmanides agrees that there were three blasts, but he adds a mystical explanation of what occurred. He contends that the *teruah* alludes to God's attribute of justice, while the *tekiah* invokes God's attribute of mercy. He emphasizes that those enlightened in mysticism will comprehend the meaning of his insight.

Since he believed in sympathetic magic, the ability of humans to control nature by their acts, he probably meant that the blasts would magically produce justice against one's enemies and mercy upon oneself.

Ibn Ezra more realistically suggests (on verse 9) that the sound of the *teruah* is a reminder for people to pray to God for protection in time of war. Still more realistically, Maimonides explains the shofar blasts on Rosh Hashanah, and presumably also during Moses's era, as a method of awakening Jews to change their behavior and act properly.

INVENTING HISTORY

The Torah's "Amalek was the first of the nations" in *Numbers* 24:20 is obscure. The *Targums*, Rashi, and ibn Ezra explain that Amalek was the first nation to attack the Israelites. Nachmanides accepts this interpretation as reasonable, but offers another: Amalek was the first among the warriors; that is, the mightiest nation of its time. This understanding fits well with the verse's conclusion: despite its power, Israel was able to defeat it. However, as ibn Ezra points out, Amalek was never the mightiest nation, and Nachmanides developed his interpretation without any historical basis.

ANOTHER INSTANCE OF INVENTING A NARRATIVE

Nachmanides imagines Moses taking a firm restrictive stand against the two tribes,

Reuben and Gad, who petitioned him in *Numbers* 32 to allow them to settle in Transjordan rather than accompanying their fellow Israelites in occupying Canaan. In 32:29, he states that Moses only gave them some of the land they requested – the cities mentioned in verses 3 and 34–38, only enough space for their children and flocks. Moses left the remaining area wasteland, and told Joshua that if these two tribes fulfilled their promise, they should be given the rest of the land of Gilead. However, if they refused to accompany Joshua across the Jordan, he should give them no land in Transjordan, and should take them with him against their will, and after the conquest give them land in Canaan, like the other Israelites.

It is difficult to understand what purpose was accomplished by holding back some parts of Transjordan.

DOES THE TORAH MANDATE LIVING IN ISRAEL?

Numbers 33:53 relates that Moses, who was about to die, gave instructions to the Israelites how to behave when they entered Canaan under the leadership of Joshua. "And you shall drive out the inhabitants of the land, and dwell therein; for unto you have I given the land to possess it."

Nachmanides focuses upon the words "and dwell therein." The plain meaning of this phrase in context is that in the near future, the Israelites will enter Canaan, drive out its inhabitants, and occupy the land. No command is evident in the plain reading and it does not address the distant future.

Nevertheless, Nachmanides insists that the verse is a positive command – one of the 613 biblical commands – that obligates Jews to live in Israel. He disagrees with Maimonides vociferously, in his notes on Maimonides' *Sefer Hamitzvot*, because Maimonides read the verse as a reference to the entry into Canaan and did not include living in Israel as a biblical law.

Maimonides escaped from the persecution of extremist Islam by going to Israel, but left shortly after his arrival when he saw that the Jews inhabiting the land at that time were not the kind of people with whom he wanted to dwell. Nachmanides waited until he was about seventy years old, when he had to escape a threat to kill him for his statements about Christianity, and then fled to Israel, a couple of generations after Maimonides arrived there. He established a synagogue in Israel and remained there until his death.

SHOULD WE EXPLAIN A BIBLICAL EVENT BY STATING IT WAS A MIRACLE?

Numbers 27 and 36 relate a curious event. The Torah clearly wanted each Israelite to settle in Canaan in his/her own tribal land. Moses, understanding this goal, was faced with a challenge. There was a man Zelophehad who died during the forty-year desert wandering and left several daughters, but no sons. The daughters approached Moses and requested that they be given the land as their inheritance because their father would have received it had he been alive. The dilemma was, if they were given the land and later married, the land would descend to their sons; since the tribal identity followed the father, the land would move from their tribe to their husbands' and sons' tribe.

The general consensus among Bible commentators accepts the talmudic view that Zelophehad's daughters could inherit their father's land but they could only marry within their tribe. According to this view this law only applied to the desert generation; no woman was restricted afterwards to marrying only men of her tribe.

Nevertheless, many questions remain. For example, if there were over 600,000 men of military age, there were probably an equal number of women of that age, as well as many older and younger than military age, and among this large number there must have been other females who faced the daughters' predicament; how were their cases adjudicated? Similarly, it was as long as about a decade and a half before Joshua began to divide the land; what law applied to women before the entry into Canaan and what law applied from the time of entry until Joshua began the division? Additionally, what happened to women of the desert generation who were already married to men of a different tribe and would inherit land from their fathers from a different tribe because they had no brothers, and would pass on the land of their father's tribe to their sons who belonged to their husbands' tribes? The Torah offers not even a hint of an answer.

Nachmanides was convinced that God is involved with everything occurring on earth and God performs open and secret miracles daily. He speculates in *Numbers* 36:7: (1) As unlikely as it may appear, there was a miracle that there was no other case among the several million Israelites that was like that of Zelophehad's daughters. (2) A second divine miracle occurred that no case would arise between the moment that Moses addressed the daughters' case until the land was divided. (3) The law of Zelophehad's daughters did not apply after the division of Canaan.

WERE THE EDOMITES CIRCUMCISED?

In his commentary on *Deuteronomy* 2:4, Nachmanides contends, without any biblical support, that the Edomites and Ishmaelites were considered "brethren" because they were circumcised. Two questions arise. First, why should circumcision make a person a brother to the Israelites? Second, there is no historical document that indicates that the Edomites were circumcised, and the Babylonian Talmud, *Sanhedrin* 59b, states that they did not practice circumcision.

READING MORE INTO A WORD THAN IS WARRANTED

The word *mei'itam* "from them," is repeated twice in *Deuteronomy* 2:6, once regarding the Israelite purchase of foods from Edomites and once for the purchase of water. Even though the word does not suggest it, Nachmanides states that "from them" denotes that when you purchase food and drink, you must pay the price that the Edomites set for these two items.

DOES GOD MANIPULATE HUMANS AGAINST THEIR WILL?

Deuteronomy 2:24 and 25 relate that God ordered the Israelites to conquer the land of Sihon in Transjordan: "Begin the dispossession; provoke him to engage in a fight." These passages are followed by 26–28, which describe the Israelites' attempt to make peace with Sihon. The plain meaning of this sequence is that in 24–25, God ordered the Israelites to begin efforts with Sihon, start with peace offers and then, if that does not succeed, wage war. Then 26–28 indicates that the Israelites began the process.

Nachmanides does not read the passage in this way. He understands that 24 and 25 are saying, wage war now. Do not try first to settle the matter peacefully. Thus he contends that the Torah did not place these verses chronologically; the Israelites first attempted peace, then, when the peace attempt failed, God ordered the Israelites to attack. Why, he asks, did the Torah tell the tale backwards? He answers that the Torah wanted to emphasize that "God hardened Sihon's heart," He made Sihon act contrary to his best interest, so that the Israelites would be able to conquer and retain his land.

Contrary to Maimonides' view and the views of others, Nachmanides contends that God is involved with everything occurring on earth, even determining when every leaf and snowflake will fall. He thereby turns humans into puppets and, in this case, turns God into a brutal puppeteer. Nachmanides called his theology "the greatest teaching of the Torah."

DID MOSES AND THE ISRAELITES RECEIVE DIFFERENT VERSIONS OF THE DECALOGUE (THE TEN COMMANDMENTS)?

There are two versions of the Decalogue, one in *Exodus* 20 and a second in *Deuteronomy* 5, with many differences between them. One of the differences is that *Exodus* has the word "remember" in regard to the Sabbath command, while *Deuteronomy* has "observe." Many reasons were offered to explain the differences. Ibn Ezra, for example, states that the *Exodus* version is the true Decalogue, while *Deuteronomy* has Moses' version of it, which includes matters that he wanted to stress.

Nachmanides suggests, however, that Moses heard "remember" and the Israelites heard "observe." His view assumes that God gave two versions of the Decalogue, one version for Moses to observe and another to the Israelites. Nachmanides does not explain why God felt that this was necessary or, more importantly, what did the different words require Moses to do that was not obligatory upon the Israelites.

DID THE ISRAELITES EVER HAVE A DISPENSATION TO EAT NON-KOSHER FOODS?

Deuteronomy 6:10–25 describes how the Israelites should behave when they enter Canaan. Nachmanides interprets this section and the Babylonian Talmud, *Chullin* 17a. The Torah states that when the Israelites come to conquer Canaan and find food in the Canaanite houses and eat it, they should not forget God and worship idols. The Talmud states that since the Torah is speaking of Canaanite foods, it must be allowing the conquering army to eat non-kosher foods, such as pig meat.

Nachmanides contends that this was a special dispensation that allowed the Israelites to consume non-kosher Canaanite foods until all the spoils were eaten, even if the foods were not consumed until after the seven years of conquest. However, despite this food dispensation, Nachmanides continues, the Torah stressed that idolatry was not allowed.

Nachmanides writes that he disagrees with Maimonides who stated in his *Mishneh Torah, Hilkhot Melachim* 8:1 that this permission applies only if the soldiers are starving and cannot find other food to eat. Thus, according to Maimonides, this is not a special dispensation, because people are always able to violate the food laws to save their lives.[5]

DID GOD MIRACULOUSLY KEEP THE ISRAELITES' CLOTHES FROM WEARING OUT FOR FORTY YEARS?

In *Deuteronomy* 8, Moses reminds the Israelites, at the end of their forty year trek though the desert after leaving Egypt, of the many benefits that God gave them during the march. In verse 4, he recalls that during this entire period "your clothes did not wear out." Was Moses stating that this was a miracle?

Ibn Ezra, who preferred to read Scripture as telling natural and not supernatural events, offers several opinions as to what occurred, including: The Israelites brought enough clothes out of Egypt to last them for forty years, or the manna was a food that did not produce perspiration so that the clothes did not wear out.

Nachmanides, who believed that miracles not only occurred in the past, but continue to occur daily today, objects to ibn Ezra's opinions that attempt to remove the miraculous aspects of Israel's existence in the wilderness. He quotes Rashi and a legend from *Midrash Song of Songs Rabbah* and *Pesikta d'Rav Kahana* that the "clouds of glory" that protected Israel in the wilderness also miraculously scrubbed and pressed their clothes, and the clothes that children wore miraculously grew with them as the children became larger.

WHY DID MOSES BREAK THE TWO TABLETS OF THE DECALOGUE?

In *Deuteronomy* 9:17, Nachmanides writes that it is possible that Moses broke the two tablets of the Decalogue for the benefit of the Israelites.

The rabbis likened the Israelites who worshipped the golden calf soon after they received the Decalogue and established a relationship with God to the shamelessness of a bride who acts as a harlot within her own bridal canopy.[6]

---

5. Rashi contends in *Chullin* 17a that the dispensation was granted for only the seven years of conquest. It is possible that he held a view close to that of Maimonides, although this is far from certain.
6. Babylonian Talmud, *Shabbat* 88b, and *Exodus Rabbah*.

Nachmanides took this homily of the sages literally. He wrote that by breaking the tablets, Moses believed that the Israelites, who had not yet received the tablets containing the Decalogue, would be judged more leniently as an unmarried woman, rather than as a married woman who committed adultery under the wedding canopy.

DID GOD WRITE THE SECOND TABLETS?

The Torah describes how Moses shattered the first set of two tablets containing the Decalogue. God then instructed Moses to ascend Mount Sinai and obtain a second set.

In his commentary on *Deuteronomy* 10:1, Nachmanides states that God did not write on the tablets of the second Decalogue as on the first. This is contradicted by the biblical statement in verse 4 that states that God inscribed both sets, "He inscribed on the tablets the same text as on the first."

SUMMARY

Nachmanides often begins his commentary by contrasting it with the explanation of biblical verses by Rashi, Abraham ibn Ezra, and occasionally by Maimonides. These sources take a completely different approach to Torah than Nachmanides.

Nachmanides' approach to *Targum Onkelos* is entirely different. He considered the translation almost if not actually holy. He felt that the targumist who wrote the translation was speaking the truth.

Nachmanides rarely disagrees with the "truthful *Targum*." When he does so, he offers his idea as another idea, as if both are possibly true.

Since *Onkelos* contains the truth, he uses the *Targum*'s language to support his own interpretation. He seems to say: "I am obviously correct because the *Targum* says what I say." This is where he runs into difficulty, as we will see.

PART TWO
Targum Onkelos

– CHAPTER 6 –

The Notion that Targum Onkelos Contains Derash

> People read *Targum Onkelos* today, and search it for *derash, halakhah,* and homiletical teachings. The following will show that the rabbis in the Talmuds and the *Midrashim*, as well as the Bible commentators who used the *Targum* before the thirteenth century, recognized the Aramaic translation as one that only contains the Torah's *peshat* – its plain meaning – and no exegetical material. It will survey how the pre-thirteenth-century rabbis and scholars used *Onkelos*, and how Nachmanides changed the way the *Targum* was understood. It was only after this change, that other interpreters of *Onkelos* read more than the plain meaning into this *Targum*. This chapter also introduces the reader to *Onkelos* and explains why the Talmudic rabbis required that it be read weekly.

THE LAW

The Babylonian Talmud and later Jewish codes mandate that Jews read the Torah portion weekly – twice in the original Hebrew and once in *Targum Onkelos*.[1] Maimonides and Rabbi Joseph Karo, whose law codes are regarded in many circles as binding, felt that it is vital to understand the Bible text through the eyes of its

---

1. Babylonian Talmud, *Berakhot* 8a, b; Maimonides' *Mishneh Torah*, Laws of Prayer 13:25; and Joseph Karo's *Shulchan Arukh, Orach Chayim*, The Laws of Shabbat 285, 1. The requirement does not appear in the Jerusalem Talmud because *Targum Onkelos* did not yet exist when this Talmud was composed. See Drazin, "Dating Targum Onkelos by means of the Tannaitic Midrashim," 246–58, where I date Onkelos to the late fourth century, based on the targumist's consistent use of late fourth-century *Midrashim*.

rabbinically accepted translation – *Targum Onkelos* – and many authorities agree that no other translation will do.[2] This raises some questions.

WHAT IS TARGUM ONKELOS?

The word *Targum* means "translation," thus *Targum Onkelos* means a translation, presumably by someone named Onkelos. *Targum Onkelos* is a translation of the five books of Moses, from the Hebrew into Aramaic. The rabbis placed their imprimatur upon *Targum Onkelos* and considered it the official translation.[3] Although there are other Aramaic translations[4] as well as ancient Greek ones,[5] and later translations into other languages, *Targum Onkelos* is the most literal. Yet despite being extremely literal, it contains over 10,000 differences from the original Hebrew text.[6]

THE SIGNIFICANCE OF *ONKELOS*

Onkelos was extolled by all the Bible commentaries. Rashi makes the statement that the *Onkelos* translation was revealed at Mount Sinai.[7] Tosaphot made a similar statement, and further contends that there are parts of the Torah that we simply could not understand without the *Onkelos* translation.[8]

Some people consider these comments as hyperbolic or metaphoric – that the authors meant that *Onkelos* is so significant that it is as though it were a divine gift, handed to Moses at Sinai. Whether literal or metaphoric, it is clear that these sages

---

2. Although some authorities, such as the *Shulchan Arukh*, discussed below, say that a person can fulfill the rabbinic obligation by reading Rashi.
3. Babylonian Talmud, *Megillah* 3a.
4. The two other complete Jewish Aramaic translations are *Targum Pseudo-Jonathan* and *Targum Neophyti*.
5. The Septuagint, composed about 250 BCE, and the translation by Aquila, composed about 130 CE.
6. There are many reasons for the targumic changes, such as to clarify passages, to protect God's honor, to show respect for Israelite ancestors, etc. These alterations were not made to teach *derash*, as will be shown below. The differences between *peshat* and *derash* is a complex subject. Simply stated, *peshat* is the plain, or simple, or obvious meaning of a text. *Derash* is the reading of a passage with either a conscious or unconscious intent to derive something from it, usually a teaching or ruling applicable to the needs or sensibilities of the later day, something the original writer may have never meant.
7. Babylonian Talmud, *Kiddushin* 49a, s.v. *mecharef*.
8. Babylonian Talmud, *Berakhot* 8a, b, s.v. *shnayim*.

are expressing a reverence for *Onkelos* not accorded to any other book in Jewish history; a reverence approaching the respect they gave to the Torah itself. This veneration is further reflected in the fact that for many centuries, every printed edition of the Pentateuch contained the correlating *Onkelos* text, generally given the preferential placement adjacent to the Torah text.

WHY DID THE RABBIS REQUIRE JEWS TO READ *TARGUM ONKELOS*?

It is significant that the talmudic dictum was written when there were many important exegetical rabbinical collections – both Talmuds, *Genesis Rabbah*, *Mekhilta*, *Sifra*, and *Sifrei*, among others. Remarkably, the rabbis did not require Jews to read these books, filled with interesting *derash*, explanations written by the rabbis themselves. They only mandated the reading of *Onkelos* when reviewing the weekly Torah portion.

Furthermore, by the time the *Shulchan Arukh* was composed in the sixteenth century, and the talmudic law was stated in it, most of the classical medieval biblical commentaries, which included *derash*, were already in circulation. While Rabbi Joseph Karo, its author, suggests that one could study Rashi on a weekly basis in place of the *Targum*, he quickly adds that those who have "reverence for God" will study both Rashi and *Onkelos*. The explanation offered by *Turei Zahav* (a commentary by Rabbi David Ha-Levi Segal on the *Shulchan Arukh*, and commonly abbreviated *Taz*), is that while Rashi enables the student to read the Bible and gain access to talmudic and Oral Law insights, *Onkelos* is still indispensable for understanding the text itself.

Thus, the rabbis, who composed books containing exegetical interpretations, felt that it was so important for Jews to know the plain meaning of the Torah that they mandated that Jews read *Targum Onkelos* every week.[9] When did people stop seeing that *Onkelos* contains the Torah's plain meaning and read *derash* into the wording of the *Targum*?

THE EARLIEST UNDERSTANDING OF *TARGUM ONKELOS*

There was no difficulty understanding the intent of *Targum Onkelos* until the thirteenth century, close to a millennium after it was composed. At that time,

---

9. They may have also been implying that one cannot understand their *derash* unless they first understood the Torah's *peshat*.

Nachmanides was the first commentator to introduce the concept that people should read *Onkelos* to find deeper meaning, meaning that went beyond the plain sense of the text. These included mystical lessons, what Nachmanides referred to as *derekh ha'emet*, the true way.

The conclusion that *Onkelos* contains only the simple meaning of the Torah is supported by an examination of how the ancients, living before the thirteenth century, consistently and without exception, used *Onkelos* only for its *peshat*. Although many of these Bible commentators were interested in, and devoted to, the lessons – *derash* – that could be derived from biblical verses, and although they were constantly using *Onkelos* for the Torah's plain meaning – its *peshat* – they never employed the *Targum* to find *derash* or to support a conclusion that the verse they were discussing contained *derash*. This situation changed when, for the first time, Nachmanides mined the *Targum* to uncover *derash*.[10] Nachmanides used *Onkelos* to support his interpretation of the Torah.

This is significant since many of these rabbinical commentators were far more interested in *derash* than in *peshat*. If they felt that *Onkelos* contained *derash*, they would have used this translation, which they extolled, as Nachmanides later did, to support their midrashic interpretations of the Torah. The following are the ancient sources.

MIDRASH AND TALMUD

The first references to a *Targum* are in the *Midrash* and the Babylonian Talmud. A *Targum* is mentioned seventeen times in the *Midrash*,[11] and eighteen times in the Babylonian Talmud.[12] Each of the thirty-five citations is an attempt to search

---

10. Our view that *Onkelos* was written without *derash* is also supported by the following interpretation of Babylonian Talmud, *Megillah* 3a: The Talmud recalls a tradition that the world shuddered when *Targum Jonathan* to [The books of] the Prophets was written. Why, the Talmud asks, did this not occur when *Targum Onkelos* was composed? Because, it answers, *Onkelos* reveals nothing [that is, it contains no *derash*], whereas *Targum Jonathan* reveals secrets [by means of its *derash* content].

11. See Menacham Mendel Kasher, *Torah Shelemah* 24 (Jerusalem, 1974), 225–38, and Jacob Reifman, *Sedeh Aram* (Berlin, 1875), 12–14. The mention of a *Targum* in the *Midrashim* and Talmuds is not necessarily a reference to *Onkelos*; the wording in these sources frequently differs from that of *Onkelos*.

12. See Kasher, *Torah Shelemah*, 155–61 and Reifman, *Sedeh Aram*, 8–10.

the *Targum* for the meaning of a word. Although these sources were inclined to exegetical explanations, and were scrupulous in naming the source for their teachings, they never tried to draw exegetical interpretations from the *Targum*, and never stated that their exegetical idea is mentioned in *Onkelos*. Thus, the *Midrash* and the Babylonian Talmud understood that the *Targum* is a translation and not a source for *derash*.

DIE MASORAH ZUM TARGUM ONKELOS

A volume of targumic traditions collected in *Die Masorah zum Targum Onkelos* is said to have been composed in the third century, but was most likely written a couple of centuries later,[13] after the Talmuds. It too, makes no suggestion that *Onkelos* contains *derash*. The book attempts to describe the *Targum* completely, but contains only translational traditions about *Onkelos*. If the author(s) believed that *Onkelos* contains *derash*, he/they would have included traditions about it.

SAADIAH GAON

The works of Saadiah Gaon (born in 882 CE) also contain no indication that *Onkelos* contains *derash*. Saadiah Gaon composed a translation of the Bible into Arabic, and used *Targum Onkelos* extensively to discover the plain meaning of words. He never even hinted that his predecessor's work contains *derash*.[14] This is significant since Saadiah Gaon emphasized the Torah's plain meaning, and used *Onkelos* frequently in his Arabic translation.[15] He quotes *Onkelos* on every page

---

13. Abraham Berliner, *Die Masorah zum Targum Onkelos* (Leipzig, 1877). See Drazin, "Dating *Targum Onkelos* by means of the Tannaitic Midrashim," for a summary of the scholarly comments on this volume.
14. See my study of Saadiah Gaon and *Onkelos* in the introduction to Israel Drazin and Stanley Wagner, *Onkelos on the Torah: Leviticus* (Jerusalem: Gefen Publishing House, 2008), xvii–xxii.
15. *Perushei Rabbenu Saadia Gaon al haTorah*, ed. Joseph Kafih (Jerusalem: Mossad HaRav Kook, 1963); "Perushei Rav Saadiah Gaon," in *Torat Chayim*, (Jerusalem: Daf-Chen Press, 1984 and Mossad Harav Kook, 1986). I described Saadiah Gaon's use of *Onkelos* in the 2008 volume on *Leviticus*, in the series *Onkelos on The Torah* (which I co-authored with Dr. Stanley M. Wagner), xvii–xxii. See Erwin I.J. Rosenthal, "The Study of the Bible in Medieval Judaism," *Studia Semitica* (Cambridge: Cambridge University Press, 1971), 244–71, especially 248–49 regarding Saadiah Gaon.
    Saadiah Gaon established Hebrew philology as a prerequisite for the study of the literal sense of the Bible, and he used rabbinic interpretations in his translation only when it com-

without attribution. His reliance upon *Onkelos* as a translation is so extensive, that if readers have difficulty understanding *Onkelos*, they can look to the Saadiah Gaon translation for an illumination of what the targumist is saying.

MENACHEM IBN SARUQ

Menachem ibn Saruq, a tenth century Spanish lexicographer, was explicit on the subject. He called *Onkelos* a *p-t-r*, a translation.[16]

SAMUEL BEN HOFNI GAON

Samuel ben Hofni Gaon headed the Babylonian Academy at Sura in Babylonia during the years 997–1013 and wrote a biblical commentary. He refers to *Targum Onkelos* on several occasions,[17] uses the *Targum* to understand the meaning of words, and always treats it as a literal translation containing no *derash*.

RASHI (RABBI SHLOMO YITZCHAKI)

No biblical commentator relied more often on *Onkelos* than Rabbi Shlomo Yitzchaki, better known as Rashi, born in 1040. He extols *Onkelos*, as stated above, and mentions the targumist hundreds of times – referring to him by the name *Onkelos* or by a variation of the word *Targum*,[18] and incorporates the targumic interpretation without attribution in hundreds of other comments. He has a

---

plied with reason. He stated at the end of his introduction to the Pentateuch that his work is a "simple, explanatory translation of the text of the Torah, written with the knowledge of reason and tradition." He, along with ibn Ezra and *Onkelos*, as we will see, included another meaning only when the literal sense of the biblical text ran counter to reason or tradition. His failure to mention that *Onkelos* contains *derash* does not prove indisputably that he saw no *derash* in the commentary. However, since he copied *Onkelos*'s interpretations so very frequently in his Arabic translation, it is likely that if he saw *derash* in *Onkelos* he would have mentioned it.

16. Menachem ibn Saruq, *Sefer Machberet Menahem* ed. H. Filipowski (London and Edinburgh, 1854), 14a, 16b 17a, 17b, 20a, and others.

17. Samuel ben Hofni Gaon, *Peirush Hatorah L'Rav Shmuel ben Hofni Gaon* (Jerusalem: Mossad Harav Kook, 1978), index on page 111.

18. See the listing in C.B. Chavel, *Perushei Rashi al Hatorah* (Jerusalem: Mossad Harav Kook, 1982), 628–29. For Rashi's struggle against *derash*, see, for example, his commentary to *Genesis* 3:8. While Rashi believed he interpreted Scriptures according to their *peshat*, ibn Ezra criticized him: "He expounded the Torah homiletically believing such to be the literal meaning, whereas his books do not contain it except once in a thousand [times]," G. Lippmann ed. *Safah Berurah* (Furth: Fulda and Zumfdorffer, 1839), 5a. See also S. Kamin, *Rashi's Exegetical Categorization with Respect to the Distinction Between Peshat and Derash*, Doctorial Thesis, (Jerusalem, 1978); M.

non-rigid blend of *peshat* and *derash* in his commentary,[19] and frequently quotes the Talmud and the *Midrash* as the source for his *derash*. He never uses *Onkelos* as a source for his *derash*, nor does he treat the *Targum* as anything other than a translation. It should be obvious that since Rashi relied so extensively on *Onkelos*, which he considered holy, for *peshat*, if he had seen *derash* in the *Targum*, he would have said so.

RASHBAM (RABBI SAMUEL BEN MEIR)

Rashi's grandson Rabbi Samuel ben Meir (also known as Rashbam, about 1085–1174) wrote his Bible commentary, largely, with the goal in mind to liberate people from *derash*, and to show his objection to Rashi's frequent use of *derash*.[20] He seldom mentions his sources, but draws respectfully from *Onkelos*, usually by name. In his commentary to *Genesis*, for example, where Rashi is only named in 37:2, *Onkelos* is quoted in 21:16, 25:28, 26:26, 28:2, 40:11, and 41:45. In his commentary to *Deuteronomy*, to cite another example, *Onkelos* is mentioned in 4:28, 16:2, 16:9, 17:18, and 23:13. While he criticizes his grandfather with and without attribution for his use of *derash*,[21] and occasionally disagrees with *Onkelos*, he never rebukes the targumist for using *derash*.[22] Like his predecessors, he saw no *derash* in *Targum Onkelos*.

Banitt, *Rashi, Interpreter of the Biblical Letter*, (Israel: Tel Aviv University, 1985); and Y. Rachman, *Igeret Rashi*, (Mizrachi, 1991).

19. Rashi said that he was offering *peshat*. He meant that his commentary frequently contains *derash* that seemed to him to reflect the plain meaning of the Torah.

20. M.I. Lockshin, *Rabbi Samuel ben Meir's Commentary on Genesis*, (Jewish Studies, The Edwin Mellen Press, 1989); Samuel ben Meir (Rashbam), *The Commentary of R. Samuel ben Meir on Qohelet*, eds. Sara Japhet and Robert B. Salters, trans. Robert B. Salters (Jerusalem: The Magnes Press, 1985). See especially Rashbam to *Genesis* 37:2 and 49:16 where he criticizes his grandfather using strong language.

21. Lockshin, in *Rabbi Samuel ben Meir's Commentary on Genesis*, 391–99, notes that Rashi's Torah Commentary is the primary focus of Rashbam's own commentary. Of some 650 remarks in the latter's commentary to *Genesis*, only about thirty-three percent concern issues not relevant to Rashi. Of the remaining two-thirds, in only about eighteen percent does Rashbam feel Rashi is correct, and in just over forty-eight percent he is in disagreement with him, consistently criticizing him for substituting *derash* for *peshat* – the very thing Rashi declared he would not do. In view of his sensitivity and opposition to *derash*, it is very telling that he did not sprinkle even one drop of venom on the targumist.

22. See *Genesis* 25:28, for example, where Rashbam issues the accolade: "the plain meaning of scripture is the one offered by the *Targum*." It is significant to note that although Rashbam railed

ABRAHAM IBN EZRA

Abraham ibn Ezra (1089–1164), like Rashbam, was determined to distance himself from *derash* and establish the literal meaning of the biblical text in his Bible commentaries, as he states in his two introductions. He uses *Onkelos* frequently as a translation, and only as a translation, to prove the meaning of words.

Ibn Ezra was the first to note a few isolated instances of *derash* in the *Targum*. This first observation of *derash* in *Onkelos*, I believe, is because *derash* did not exist in the original *Targum* text.[23] Various over-zealous well-meaning scribes embedded it at a later period, probably around the time that ibn Ezra discovered it. Ibn Ezra recognizes that the purpose of *Onkelos* is to offer *peshat* because he states that the targumist is following his (ibn Ezra's) own method, the "straight [or right] way" of *peshat* to interpret the Hebrew according to grammatical rules.[24]

MAIMONIDES

Shortly thereafter, Moses Maimonides, born in 1138, supported part of his rationalistic philosophy by using *Onkelos*. Maimonides recognized that the targumist deviated frequently from a literal rendering of the biblical text to remove

---

against the insertion of *derash* into a biblical commentary, his own commentary was frequently adulterated, as was *Targum Onkelos*, by the improper insertions of *derash* by later hands. See, for example, Deuteronomy 2:20, 3:23, 7:11, and 11:10 in A.I. Bromberg, *Perush HaTorah l'Rashbam* (Israel, Tel Aviv, 1964), 201, note 25; 202, note 111; 206, 7, note 9; and 210, note 3.

23. Chayim Heller and Rabbi Dov Revel were also convinced that the original text of *Onkelos* did not contain *derash*. However, neither of them recognized Nachmanides as the first commentator to argue the opposite. The first is in Chayim Heller, *A Critical Essay on the Palestinian Targum to the Pentateuch*, (New York, 1921), 32–57. The second is in Dov Revel, *Targum Yonatan al Hatorah* (New York, 1924–5), 5. See also Bernard Grossfeld in "Targum Onkelos, Halakhah and the Halakhic Midrashim," in *The Aramaic Bible*, eds. D.R.G. Beattie and M. McNamara (Sheffield: Sheffield Academic Press, 1994), 228–46.

24. In an epigram prefacing one of the editions of his commentary on the Pentateuch, ibn Ezra writes that he intends to mention by name only those authors "whose opinion I consider correct." He names *Onkelos* frequently. In his commentary to *Numbers*, for example, the *Targum* is cited in 11:5 where he gives another interpretation, but respectfully adds, "he too is correct," and in 11:22 he comments, "it means exactly what the Aramaic targumist states." See also 12:1; 21:14; 22:24; 23:3; 23:10; 24:23 and 25:4. Asher Weiser, *Ibn Ezra, Perushei Hatorah* (Jerusalem: Mossad Harav Kook, 1977).

While he treats *Onkelos* respectfully, ibn Ezra uses the strongly derogatory terms "deceivers" or "liars," for the *derash*-filled *Targum Pseudo-Jonathan to Deuteronomy* 24:6. See Revel, *Targum Yonatan al Hatorah*, 1–2.

anthropomorphism and anthropopathisms – to avoid portraying God in a human fashion – for this is "a fundamental element in our faith, the comprehension of which is not easy for the common people."[25] Maimonides never uses *Onkelos* for *derash*.

JOSEPH BECHOR SHOR

Rabbi Joseph Bechor Shor (born around 1140) adopted the literal methodology of Rashbam.[26] However, he is not as consistent as Rashbam; he inserts homiletical comments along with those that are literal. Bechor Shor mentions Rashbam only twice by name, but quotes *Onkelos* dozens of times to support his own definition of a word when his interpretation is literal. Although he used *Onkelos* and *derash*, he never states or even suggests that *Onkelos* contains *derash*,[27] and never uses *Onkelos* to support his homiletical remarks.

RADAK (RABBI DAVID KIMCHI)

Rabbi David Kimchi (known as Radak, c. 1160–1235) wrote biblical commentaries using the text's plain sense in contrast to the homiletical elaborations that

---

25. The "fundamental element" that *Onkelos* addresses is the avoidance of a literal translation of most anthropomorphic and anthropopathic phrases. See the listing in Moshe ben Maimon (Maimonides), *The Guide of the Perplexed*, translation and introduction by Shlomo Pines (Chicago: University of Chicago Press, 1963), vol. 2, 656, and 658, and 1:28 for the quote.

Maimonides based his interpretation of negative commandments 128 and 163 in part upon our *Targum*. Charles B. Chavel, trans. *Maimonides, The Book of Divine Commandments* (Soncino Press, 1967), 116–17 and 155–56. This was not because *Onkelos* deviated from the plain meaning to teach *halakhah*. Commandment 128 forbids an apostate Israelite to eat the Passover offering. *Onkelos* translates the biblical "no alien may eat thereof" as "no apostate Israelite" (*Exodus* 12:43). The targumist may have thought this was the necessary meaning because *Exodus* 12:45 and 48 state that a sojourner and an uncircumcised Israelite could not eat this sacrifice; thus the earlier verse must be referring to someone else. Commandment 163 prohibits a priest from entering the Sanctuary with disheveled, untrimmed hair. Maimonides notes that *Onkelos* translates *Leviticus* 10:6's "Let not the hair of your heads go loose" as "grow long." Again, the targumist may have thought that this was the verse's simple sense because it is the language used by the Torah itself in *Numbers* 6:5, and because when one loosens one's hair, it becomes longer. Indeed, Rashi states explicitly that the *peshat* of "loose" in this instance is "long."

26. He is believed to have been a student of Rashbam's brother Rabbenu Tam. See the source in the next note.

27. Jehoshapat Nebo, *Perushei Rabbi Josef Bechor Shor al Hatorah* (Jerusalem: Mossad Harav Kook, 1994), 11. Bechor Shor went beyond *Targum Onkelos* in his concern about biblical anthropomorphisms and his attempts to exonerate the patriarchs.

were prevalent during his lifetime. He followed the methodology of ibn Ezra and stressed philological analysis. He refers to *Onkelos* frequently and always treats the *Targum* as a translation. He, like ibn Ezra, occasionally inserted homiletical interpretations into his commentary from exegetical legends to add zest and to delight readers, but he never used *Onkelos* for this purpose.

CONCLUSIONS FROM READING THE ANCIENT COMMENTATORS

The consistent history of *all* of the commentators using *Onkelos* only for the plain meaning of the Torah, and never mentioning seeing *derash* in the *Targum,* is quite persuasive that no *derash* was contained in the original *Onkelos* text. If any of the commentators who lived before the mid-thirteenth century believed that *Targum Onkelos* contained *derash* – especially those who delighted in, or who were concerned with *derash* – they would have said so. None but ibn Ezra did, and he called attention to only a very small number of, probably, recently unauthorized insertions.

Where, then, did the *derash* that many people today think they see in *Targum Onkelos,* come from? First of all, I am convinced that most of the instances in *Onkelos* that readers recognize as *derash* were really intended by the targumist as *peshat* – the text's simple meaning; people differ in what they see. Second, C. Heller has shown us many examples where most, if not all, of the presently found *derash* did not exist in the original *Targum* text.[28] His findings are supported by the previously mentioned history showing that ibn Ezra was the first to observe any *derash* at all in our *Targum*.

NACHMANIDES WAS THE FIRST BIBLE COMMENTATOR TO READ *DERASH* INTO *ONKELOS*

Nachmanides was influenced by *Kabbalah,* Jewish mysticism. He equated *Kabbalah* with truth[29] and felt that, since Torah is truth, it must contain *Kabbalah*.[30] He held that no one can attain knowledge of the Torah, or truth, by his own reasoning. A person must listen to a kabbalist who received the truth from another

---

28. See note 23.
29. *Genesis* 6:13, 18; 31:42; 33:20; 35:13; and others.
30. This could be seen as a kind of syllogism. Torah is truth. *Kabbalah* is truth. Thus, Torah "must" contain *Kabbalah*.

kabbalist, generation after generation, back to Moses, who heard the kabbalistic teaching directly from God.[31] He decided to disseminate this truth, or at least hint of its existence, and was the first to introduce mystic teachings of the Torah into a biblical commentary.[32]

Nachmanides extended his exegetical methodology into his interpretations of our *Targum*.[33] He felt that this was appropriate. *Onkelos*, he erroneously believed, "lived in the age of the philosophers immediately after Aristotle," and like the philosopher was so interested in esoteric teachings that, though born a prominent Roman non-Jew, he converted to Judaism to learn Torah, and to later teach its secret lessons through his biblical translation.[34]

We will see how Nachmanides dealt with *Onkelos* in part three of this book but first we need to understand how *Onkelos* changes the wording of the biblical text and why it does so.

---

31. Chavel, *Ramban, Writings and Discourses*, 174.
32. Chavel, *Ramban, Commentary on the Torah, Genesis*, xii. Chavel points out that the extensive kabalistic influences on future generations can be traced to Nachmanides.
33. This is my original idea. It is based on several facts. First, we know that he was the first to read *Kabbalah* in the Torah words and phrases. Second, we know that he had enormous respect for *Onkelos*; he referred to *Onkelos* 230 times in his Bible commentary and, although he criticized others, he treated *Onkelos* with great respect, even reverence. He considered *Onkelos* to be generally expressing the truth. Thus it is reasonable to assume that he applied the same syllogism to *Onkelos* that he applied to the Torah. Finally, we know of no one before him who read mysticism into the targumist's words.
34. Chavel, *Ramban, Writings and Discourses*, 75–76. Nachmanides' error in dating *Targum Onkelos* "immediately after Aristotle" was not his only historical mistake. He believed that the Talmud's implied dating of Jesus at about 100 years before the Common Era was correct. See Hyam Maccoby, trans. and ed., *Judaism on Trial* (Littman Library of Jewish Civilization in association with Liverpool University Press, 1993), 28–29.

– CHAPTER 7 –

Differences between Onkelos and the Hebrew Bible

> Nachmanides' problematical interpretations of the readings in *Targum Onkelos* are based in part upon his failure to understand the methodology that the targumist used in creating his translation. The author of *Onkelos* inserted over ten thousand deviations from the Hebrew Bible text.[1] He made these differences purposely for a number of reasons. We will categorize them and give some examples.

CLARITY

The *Onkelos* translator, called the targumist, made over half of his changes from the original biblical text in order to clarify the meaning of the Hebrew text for the general population. Thus, he explained many metaphors, which the average Bible reader might find to be obscure, by substituting a clear statement. For example "flowing with milk and honey" (*Exodus* 13:5) is replaced by "producing milk and honey"; "with heaviness" (14:25) becomes "with difficulty"; "arm" (15:16) is "strength"; and "give ear" (15:26) is "obey." Similarly, *elohim* in 7:1 is explained as "teacher" and the noun "people [of his house]" is inserted in 1:1 to make it clear that the Israelites brought people to Egypt and not buildings.

He added, in about a quarter of his changes, the letter *daled*, "of," "that," "which," "who," or "in order to," when this preposition is missing from or only implied in the biblical text, or where the Hebrew has the construct state and the *daled* was customarily used in the Aramaic language. It is inserted in *Exodus* 1:1, for example,

---

1. The Palestinian *Targums Neophyti, Pseudo-Jonathan,* and the various *Fragmented Targums* deviate more frequently from the original biblical Hebrew and they contain a wealth of fanciful midrashic material.

in place of the *hay* in *habaim*, "who came," and added in 1:5 to *haya*, "was in Egypt," transforming it to "who was [already] in Egypt."

These alterations that total about three-quarters of the differences between the original Hebrew and the Aramaic translation made the text more easily understandable and less confusing, and they minimized ambiguities and obscurities for the *Targum*'s readers. Sometimes the targumist made these clarifications by changing one or more words or by adding a word or words. In some instances, he replaced the number or tense of a word for the sake of consistency, such as a participle to perfect, and infinitive to imperfect, imperative to imperfect, singular to plural. In other verses, he exchanged a rhetorical question, which could easily be mistaken for a positive proposition, with an affirmative statement. There are also several dozen cases in which he updated the names of biblical nations and historical sites to the names used during his own age.

He also altered the text to avoid biblical exaggerations; used direct, forceful, and vivid language in place of the indirect and passive and retained Hebrew words when the Hebrew term was known or understood better by his audience. Sometimes two interpretations are inserted into the translation, although one of them was probably a later placement by an overzealous and over helpful scribe. Occasionally he presents a rendering contrary to what is explicit in the Hebrew original, reads letters differently, and changes the order of words or omits them.

He made these and other changes to clarify the text subtly, usually by the addition or substitution of only one or two words. Yet, despite the large number of alterations, he did not explain every verse, for to do so he would have had to transform his work from a translation into a commentary.

RESPECTFUL CONCEPT OF GOD

The second largest category of differences made by the targumist between the Hebrew and Aramaic, after those made to clarify the text, are alterations made to present the readers with a respectful concept of God. There are 1,650 of these modifications, about sixteen percent of the total changes. Our targumist shuns anthropomorphisms and anthropopathisms, statements that depict God with human attributes and emotions, because these descriptions might give the populace an unseemly conception of the incorporeal God. These occur 396 times throughout the Pentateuch. Thus, for example, God does not "hear" in *Exodus*

2:24, "see" in 2:25, "know" in 2:25, or "appear" in 3:2, because these are anthropomorphisms, portrayals of God in human terms. Similarly, the targumist supplants "mountain of God" in 3:1, which could convey the idea that the deity is restricted to a single location or give the mountain an intrinsic holiness, by using "mountain upon which the glory of the Lord was revealed." Yet he does not remove every anthropomorphism: "the Lord remembered" is retained in 2:24 (even though it seems to suppose that God can forget as humans do) and also the Lord's "anger" in 32:11 (a portrayal of God with a human emotion).

Since the Bible spoke in language that humans could understand, it abounds in anthropomorphic descriptions and metaphors. The targumist changed only several hundred of these phrases, because to do more would have so altered his translation to the extent that it would be seen as a commentary rather than a translation of Scripture.

Maimonides mentions *Onkelos*'s avoidance of anthropomorphisms in a number of places in his *Guide of the Perplexed*. For example: "Consider this well, and you will observe with wonder how *Onkelos* keeps free from the idea of the corporeality of God, and from everything that leads thereto, even in the remotest degree."[2]

Maimonides purposely overstates his point to highlight his conviction that God is incorporeal, a view he codified as the second of his list of the 613 biblical commands, following the command to know God.[3] He discusses this subject in about half of the first three volumes of his *Guide* so frequently because this was a view that was vigorously rejected by many, if not most of his contemporaries, including Nachmanides, as I will discuss.

How did the targumist change the text to avoid the corporeal depictions of God? One of his methods is to remove some anthropomorphisms and anthropopathisms by substituting a select group of words. Thus, for example, there are 188 places in the Pentateuch where he adds the term *memra* to avoid an anthropomorphism or anthropopathisms that he felt diminished the concept of the divine.[4]

What is a *memra*? It is an Aramaic equivalent of the Greek term *logos*. It denotes God's "wisdom," "word," "command," "will," "teaching," "inspiration," "power,"

---

2. Maimonides, *Guide of the Perplexed*, 1:28, trans. M. Friedlander, 37.
3. Chayim Heller, *Maimonides, Sefer Hamitzvot L'harambam* (Jerusalem: Mossad Harav Kook, 1995).
4. It is also added in a few instances out of respect for humans.

"protection," and the like, as the verse's context may require. It suggests that God is not carrying out the act corporeally, as a literal reading of the biblical text may suggest, but, rather, the act is being performed by or through God's "word" or "wisdom." Thus, in *Deuteronomy*, for example, it is not God corporeally "fighting" (1:30, 3:22, 20:4), or "moving" (31:6), "demanding" (18:19), "charging" (11:1), "taking" (4:37), "helping" (2:7, 20:1, 23:15, 31:8, 31:23), or even making the world (33:27), but it is His *memra* that is doing so.

The notion that "wisdom," rather than God, is acting is found in the book *Wisdom of Solomon*, composed in the first or second century BCE, some 500 years before the composition of *Onkelos*.

> Wisdom delivered a holy people and blameless race from a nation of oppressors. She entered the soul of a servant of the Lord, and withstood dread kings with wonders and signs. She gave to holy people the reward of their labors; she guided them along a marvelous way, and became a shelter to them by day and a starry flame through the night.[5]

The author is visualizing the miracles of the exodus in a rational instead of a supernatural manner, and rationalizes the divine appearance to Moses, the threats to Pharaoh, and the pillar of clouds that guided the Israelites in the desert. Kugel writes: "It is not hard to see how the whole idea of wisdom in this book functions between two domains that are otherwise completely separate, the spiritual and the material. God's spirit may fill this world, but he Himself remains aloof, somewhere in heaven. Indeed, the things that happen in the material world may take place because of Wisdom's inspiration or underlying presence."

The targumist uses other similar Aramaic terms to preclude the appearance of God from performing acts as if he were a human being. These include *yekara*, "glory," *Shekhinah*, "divine presence," *qadam*, "before," and *dachal*, "fear."

He inserts *yekara*, "glory," into twenty-one texts in the Pentateuch so as not to depict a seeming corporeal divine appearance. Instead of God appearing, the Israelites experience a *feeling* of the presence of divine "glory."

He places *Shekhinah*, "divine presence," into his translation for the same

---

5. David Winston, "The Wisdom of Solomon," *Anchor Bible* (New York: Doubleday, 1979). Also, J.L. Kugel, *The God of Old* (The Free Press, 2003), 22.

purpose forty-nine times when the Bible asserts that God is "dwelling." Significantly, his translation is radically different than that of *Pseudo-Jonathan* and *Neophyti*, more midrashic Aramaic translations of the Pentateuch, who portray the *Shekhinah* performing all kinds of activities, as if the *Shekhinah* is a physical being. Contrary to the other targumists and contrary to Nachmanides,[6] *Shekhinah* is not God and not a separate entity created by God; it is a human *feeling* of God's presence on earth (a feeling of the imminence of God) or in heaven (His transcendence).

Our targumist also inserts *qadam*, "before," in front of "God," 659 times as a sign of respect and to soften an anthropomorphic portrayal. Thus, for example, the words of the Israelites were not heard *by* God in *Deuteronomy* 1:34, which may suggest that a corporeal being with ears listened to the Israelites, but the words are heard "before the Lord."

The Aramaic translation, adds *dachal*, "fear" or "service," in forty-five places to avoid picturing unacceptable behavior, such as the Israelites forgetting or approaching God.[7] They only forgot his "service," or to "fear" Him, or they approached His "service," but did not physically come near Him.

Similarly, our translator spells the Hebrew *Elohim*, which is in the respectful majestic plural in Scripture, by replacing *Elohim* with the Tetragrammaton, the Hebrew four-letter noun for God, because he was concerned that the plural could lead uneducated readers to be confused and believe that the Torah is hinting at the existence of many gods. He evades this problem 204 times.

The nouns *El*, the singular form for God, and *Elohim*, the plural form, occasionally refer to idols or important human officials. Accordingly, in eighty-eight passages, *Onkelos* explains these terms as "idol" or "fear" (a disparaging adjective for idol).

All of these alterations, the 1,650 targumic deviations from the biblical text purposely made by the targumist to depict God in a respectful manner, are significant not only in grasping the methodology of the *Targum*, but in understanding Nachmanides. I will discuss Nachmanides' opinion on this subject when we examine *Genesis* 46:1. In a word, we will see that despite the 1,650 deviations, Nachmanides

---

6. As we will see in our discussion of *Genesis* 46:1.
7. Or as a substitute for "idol."

remarkably insists that *Onkelos* does not change the biblical text in the Aramaic translation to avoid anthropomorphisms.

HONORING ISRAEL'S ANCESTORS

The targumist also deviates from rendering the biblical text literally to preserve the honor of Israel's ancestors. This occurs in 194 verses. He deletes, changes or at least softens many statements of a derogatory nature. He depicts the attitudes and reactions of Israel's ancestors with great delicacy, and sometimes even erases the remotest suggestion of any wrongdoing on their part. Thus, for example in *Exodus* 1:8, thinking that Joseph would be belittled if a new Pharaoh was ignorant of his life works and enormous achievements in Egypt, our targumist substitutes "who did not fulfill Joseph's decrees" for Scripture's "who did not know Joseph." He adds, "that was heavy upon them" in 2:23 to remove the detestable notion that the Israelites attempted to shirk all kinds of work, even the simplest labors.[8] He does not allow the Egyptians to rudely drive out the Israelites from Egypt, for the Israelite ancestors were *certainly* treated with respect, but they "cause(d) them to descend" (6:1; 14:5 is similar). He steers clear of the portrayal of the Israelites passively and emotionally "groaning" over their bondage in Egypt by softening it slightly to the more dignified, active, and intellectual "complaining" (6:5).

Strictly speaking, the activity "prayer" is not found in the Pentateuch. Nevertheless, our translator introduces it by exchanging quite a few biblical words to "prayer." These include verbs such as "cry" and "groaning." The change elevates and ennobles the Israelites' activities and removes the negative emotional and unmanly connotations.

The targumist also trades the Hebrew word "to" for "with" when God speaks with humans. "With" suggests a more friendly conversation rather than "to," which may be seen as a dictatorial discourse.[9]

ALTERNATIVE TRANSLATIONS

In addition to the targumic deviations that we described above, the *Targum* has hundreds of words that are not departures from a literal rendering of the text, but

---

8. Sources are from Drazin and Wagner, *Onkelos on the Torah* (*Exodus*).
9. In *Numbers*, for example, this occurs seventy-six times.

rather a preferred way, out of several possibilities, of translating a word. Thus, for example, *vayeit* in *Genesis* 38:1 could be translated as "camped" or "turned." Similarly, in 38:2, *canaani* could mean "Canaanite" or "merchant." One of the many values of the *Targum* is to see how the "rabbinically authorized translation" has treated a word.

ONKELOS AND HALAKHAH

Many readers of classical bible commentaries suppose that since rabbis have accepted a commentary as a valuable and worthy document it must contain the understanding of the scriptural text that conforms to rabbinic *halakhah*. This, however, is not true. Virtually every Bible commentator will occasionally introduce non-halakhic interpretations into his commentary.

We can understand how this misconception crept into the interpretation of *Onkelos*. Since *Onkelos* was called *Targum didan*, "our translation," or "the authorized *Targum*," by the rabbis in the Talmud,[10] some people assumed that no non-halakhic elements could have entered the translation.[11] Actually, the targumist's goal was to present the simple meaning of the biblical text, focusing on the precise meaning of each word as it should be understood in the context of the entire passage. As a result, there are many instances in which our translator renders words and verses contrary to the interpretation given by the rabbis to support a *halakhah*, for the *halakhah* was often based on an oral tradition and not on the literal meaning of the verse.

There are many times when our targumist renders the biblical words literally and does not incorporate the halakhic wording.[12] There are also instances when he changes the literal wording of the text and interprets a word or phrase to reflect the passage's plain meaning when the *halakhah* uses the literal wording to denote halakhic behavior.[13] There are other verses where he adds a word or words, which are implied in the simple understanding of the sentence, or which may be nothing

---

10. Babylonian Talmud, *Megillah* 3a.
11. See, for example, Nathan Adler, *Netina La'ger* (Vilna, 1886).
12. For example, in sources from Drazin and Wagner, *Onkelos on the Torah* (*Exodus*) (Jerusalem: Gefen Publishing House, 2008). *Exodus* 23:19, 34:26; *Numbers* 19:17; *Deuteronomy* 14:21, 19:21, 25:6, 25:12.
13. For example, in *Numbers* 5:13 and *Deuteronomy* 21:14, 21:18.

more than a characteristic targumic addition, but the insertion gives the text a meaning not intended by the *halakhah*.[14]

SUMMARY

Virtually all *Targum* scholars know that the *Onkelos* targumist generally translated the Pentateuch literally, but deviated from a literal translation in about ten thousand instances for the purposes that we outlined above. Nachmanides is an exception. As we saw in the prior chapters, Nachmanides was the first to read mystical interpretations into the Bible. He also wanted to do so with *Targum Onkelos*, which he respected. It was as if he said to himself, "The Torah is holy, therefore it must contain mysticism, which is holy. Similarly, the *Targum* is holy and must also contain mysticism." This drive to find the mystical elements led him, as we will see, to give problematical interpretations of the *Targum*.

---

14. For example, *Numbers* 5:19–20, 5:29, 6:14, 15:8, 29:39; *Deuteronomy* 17:5. A more detailed discussion of the subject, with many examples is contained in Rabbi Dr. Israel Drazin, *Targum Onkelos to Deuteronomy* (New York: Ktav, 1982), 10–14, 16–17, 51–57, as well as I. Drazin's other *Targum* books.

PART THREE
Nachmanides Misunderstands *Onkelos*

– CHAPTER 8 –

Reasonable Interpretations in Genesis

> Nachmanides mentions *Targum Onkelos* in his *Commentary to the Pentateuch* while analyzing 230 verses. Most of his attempts to see the targumist as teaching homiletic lessons and mysticism seem forced. He reads more into the Aramaic than the words themselves state.

SOME STATISTICS

There are 129 puzzling interpretations of *Onkelos* in these 230 verses. This represents about 56 percent of the total 230. However, fifty-five of the 230 Nachmanidean comments are merely references to the *Targum* without any analysis. When these fifty-five comments are subtracted from the total 230, we are left with 175 instances in which Nachmanides analyzes the *Targum*. The 129 challenging interpretations represent about seventy-five percent of the 175 times that the sage discusses *Onkelos* and uses it to support his interpretation of the biblical verse.

Nachmanides mentions *Targum Onkelos* in his *Bible Commentary to Genesis* eighty-two times. Forty-one, exactly half of these instances are difficult. He refers to the *Targum* in eighteen verses without any analysis. There are twenty-three passages where he explains *Onkelos* in what appears to be a reasonable manner.

His interpretations are troubling in *Genesis* in forty-one instances because he read more into an Aramaic word than its literal meaning warrants, felt the *Targum* was teaching mysticism, explained *Onkelos* based on his rather unique notion that the targumist does not deviate from the biblical text to avoid anthropomorphisms, and did not recognize that the targumist was simply using a characteristic targumic technique such as where *Onkelos* changed the text to preserve the honor of Israelite ancestors.

The puzzling aspect of the Nachmanidean interpretations apparently bothered the Bible commentator Bachya ben Asher. Although he was an enthusiastic follower of Nachmanides; shared his penchant for interpreting the Bible in a mystical manner; mentions Nachmanides very frequently in his commentary, and on other occasions borrows from him without attribution; paid close attention to the *Targum Onkelos* renderings and sometimes mentions them; and despite the fact that he generally agrees with the Nachmanidean explanations, Bachya rarely mentions Nachmanides' readings of *Onkelos*. In his commentary to *Genesis*, Bachya quotes and agrees with the Nachmanidean interpretation only twice.

I will show the apparent difficulties in the 129 interpretations in the upcoming chapters. However, before doing so, I will show the reasonable interpretations that are in *Genesis* so that readers will be better able to understand the Nachmanidean methodology.

THE FOLLOWING ARE NACHMANIDEAN INTERPRETATIONS THAT SEEM REASONABLE

1. In a brief statement, Nachmanides observes in *Genesis* 4:22 that *Onkelos* connects this verse with verses 20 and 21 that have the word *avi*, which is *ribhon* (master) in *Onkelos*. The targumist adds *ribhon* in verse 22 to show that Tubal-cain, mentioned in verse 22, was also a master craftsman like Jabal in 20 and Jubal in 21.
2. In his commentary to *Genesis* 4:23, Nachmanides states that biblical commentators depended on *Onkelos*'s rendering of 4:15 to understand the passage. The obscure text of 4:24 reads, "whosoever slays Cain sevenfold vengeance shall be taken on him." In 4:15, *Onkelos* explains that God is consoling Cain that he will not be punished for a long time, only "after seven generations will punishment be exacted of him.[1]
3. Nachmanides explains that the shameful act of *Genesis* 9:18 that Ham committed against his father Noah, during the latter's drunken sleep, was that he saw his father's nakedness and should have covered the nakedness and told no one what he saw. Instead, Ham mentioned it to his brothers and many people "outside" (the word used by scripture) and disgraced him. Nachmanides

---

1. *Pseudo-Jonathan* is like our *Targum*. See also *Onkelos* and *Pseudo-Jonathan* to 4:24 and *Genesis Rabbah* 23:4.

correctly states that *Onkelos* emphasized this heinous misdeed by replacing "outside" with "in the street" in verse 22. The targumist typically uses the phrase "in the street" to indicate public notice. In this case, Ham ridiculed his father openly, where everyone could hear about his drunken conduct.[2]

4. Nachmanides mentions in *Genesis* 12:8 that *Onkelos* explains the biblical "[Abram] called [upon God]" as "prayed." This is correct. The targumist usually renders ambiguous biblical statements more concretely, and the concept of prayer is introduced twenty-three times in *Genesis*. This is the first time that Nachmanides' student Rashba's student Bachya ben Asher mentions in his Bible commentary what Nachmanides states about *Onkelos*. However, although he says the same thing as Nachmanides, and although he mentions the Nachmanidean commentary frequently, he does not ascribe this idea to Nachmanides. Bachya includes another targumic interpretation in his commentary to this verse. He notes correctly that the *Targum* treats *hahara* as *l'tura*; both mean "to the mountain."

5. Nachmanides notes correctly that our *Targum* sometimes renders place names literally as nouns and sometimes conveys the sense of the expression. Thus, "Eil Paran" in *Genesis* 14:6 is altered to "plain of Paran" by our targumist.[3]

6. *Genesis* 14:22 describes Abram saying to the king of Sodom: "I lift up my hand" to God. Nachmanides quotes Rashi that the words signify an oath.[4] He also correctly states that *Onkelos* understood that the act was one of "prayer." Without criticizing the targumist he explains that in his view, lifting one's hand denotes devoting an object to God.[5] Abram gave a tenth of the items he acquired during the battle to the priest.[6]

7. "And He [God] said unto him [Abram]: 'Take Me a heifer *meshuleshet* (*Genesis* 15:9).'" *Onkelos*: *telata*.

   The ancient biblical commentators differed in how to interpret *meshuleshet*.

---

2. For a similar reason, *Onkelos* replaces "outside" by "street" also translated "market-place" in *Genesis* 39:12, 13, 15, and 18. Joseph not only flees the sexual advances of Potiphar's wife "outside" her house, he runs to the safety of the more public "street."
3. This translational technique occurs twenty-three times in the *Targum* to *Genesis*.
4. This understanding is also in *Sifrei*, Va'etchanan 33, and in *Daniel* 12:7.
5. See *Exodus* 35:22, 24 and *Leviticus* 27:28.
6. *Onkelos* adds the concept of "prayer" frequently in the Aramaic translation. It occurs twenty-three times in *Genesis*.

Did Abram offer as sacrifices "three" heifers, she-goats and rams or "a three-year old"? In other words, does *meshuleshet* signify the number or the ages of the sacrifices? *Genesis Rabbah* 44:14, *Onkelos*, Rashi, and Radak take it to mean "three." *Pseudo-Jonathan*, ibn Ezra, etc., chose the latter definition. Nachmanides agrees with *Onkelos*, which he mentions briefly, that it means "three."

8. In *Genesis* 17:18, Nachmanides mentions *Onkelos*'s rendering of 17:1 without any analysis of the *Targum*. The verse describes God being revealed to Abram and telling him to "walk before Me." The targumist avoids a possible anthropomorphic misunderstanding that a human was accompanying God on a stroll by substituting "serve [or worship] before Me." Bachya mentions this interpretation as being correct without mentioning Nachmanides or *Onkelos*.

9. Nachmanides quotes Rashi who had an erroneous literal rendering of *Onkelos* to *Genesis* 18:19. Both the Hebrew and Rashi's Aramaic state that God spoke about Abraham and said, "I have known him." (*Onkelos*, in a proper version, reads "it is revealed before Me," a change that *Onkelos* made to soften the possible anthropomorphic sense of knowing.) Rashi states that both the Hebrew and Aramaic "know" is an expression of affection.

Nachmanides rejects Rashi's interpretation, mentions the *Targum* and states that the biblical "known" here means that God watches over righteous people like Abraham to make certain that no harm befalls them. He does not claim that this theological notion is contained in the *Targum*'s literal rendering.[7]

10. *Onkelos* exchanges *Genesis*'s 19:31 "firstborn" (Lot's eldest daughter) to "the older." Nachmanides correctly explains that the biblical "firstborn" does not necessarily denote that the elder of Lot's daughters who accompanied him in the escape from the destruction of Sodom was the first out of his wife's womb. The term is used metaphorically and simply means the elder of the two daughters who left Sodom with him. Thus Lot's married daughters, mentioned in verse 14 that failed to escape, could have been older, and as was customary, married before their younger siblings.[8]

11. Nachmanides correctly explains *Onkelos*'s rendering of *Genesis* 20:17. The next

---

7. Bachya mentions Nachmanides here but not *Onkelos*.
8. See *Genesis* 29:26.

verse states that God punished Abimelech's household: He "closed up all the wombs of the house of Abimelech" because the king kidnapped Abraham's wife Sarah. When he released Sarah, verse 17 states that God "healed Abimelech and his wife, and his maidservants, and they bore children." However, Abimelech, as a male, had no womb that needed to be healed. The verse probably means that Abimelech, his wife and staff were healed of the illness, the women's wombs were closed and he was impotent, and the women were now able to bear children. However, our targumist, as usual, did want to present a lengthy explanation. So he resolved the problem of Abimelech bearing children by changing the wording and having everyone "relieved."

12. The literal reading of *Genesis* 25:31 describes Jacob requesting Esau to sell him his birthright *kayom*, "like this day" (instead of *hayom*, "today"). *Onkelos* retains *kayom* but adds *dilhein*, "that": "Sell me your birthright as on that day." Rashi explains the *Targum*: "Just as this day is certain, so make a certain [binding] sale."

    Nachmanides, somewhat more plausibly, points out that since the birthright only has significance after the father's death, our targumist understands *kayom dilhein*, as Jacob saying, "Sell me the birthright in a sale that will become effective on the day that it will come into your possession."[9] While Nachmanides' interpretation of our *Targum* is possible, it must be recognized that it is far from certain. First, the addition of the single word "that" does not in itself imply what Nachmanides reads into it. Another interpretation of the targumic wording is possible. Thus, he may be reading more into the added Aramaic word than is warranted.[10]

13. In *Genesis* 26:1, Nachmanides refers to verse 28, where Isaac and Abimelech are making a covenant, where *Onkelos* clarifies Scripture's recollection of the words of Abimelech's servants, "let there now be an oath between our two parties" as "let there now be an oath that existed between our fathers." Thus, Nachmanides correctly states, the targumist understood that the Abimelech

---

9. This is also the interpretation of *Targum Pseudo-Jonathan*.
10. A later *Midrash* interprets Scripture as suggesting that Esau sold Jacob his share in the world-to-come while the two were in the womb, M. Friedmann, ed. *Nispahim l'Seder Eliyahu Zuta* (Jerusalem, 1960), 2nd edition, chapter 19, beginning page 26.

with whom Isaac dealt was different than the one that was involved with his father Abraham, and that Abimelech was a title, like Pharaoh.

14. In *Genesis* 29:27, Nachmanides notes that *Onkelos* adds "my work" in verse 27, which reads, "my days are finished": Jacob claims Rachel as his wife because "my days of my work are completed" to explain what "days" were meant.

15. Similarly, Nachmanides states that *Onkelos* identifies the *dudaim* that Reuben brought to his mother Leah in *Genesis* 30:14 as "mandrakes."

16. Nachmanides reports that *Onkelos* rendered *zeved* in *Genesis* 30:20 literally as "portion."

17. Again, in *Genesis* 30:23, Nachmanides simply states that *Onkelos* translates *osaph* literally as "gathered."

18. So, too, in *Genesis* 30:32, he only reports that our targumist rendered *chum* literally as "reddish."

19. Still again, he points out that the targumist translates *hamekusharot* and *u've-ha'ateef* in *Genesis* 30:41 and 42 literally as "the early-breeding sheep" and "the late-breeding sheep."

20. Nachmanides notes that Jacob's statement to his father-in-law Laban, "and the fear [Hebrew: *u'fachad*, Aramaic: *u'd'dachil*] of Isaac had been on my side" in *Genesis* 31:42 is subject to various interpretations. "Fear" could refer to the God of Isaac, as Rashi maintains, or the frightful day of Isaac's binding as stated by ibn Ezra,[11] or the kabbalistic attribute of justice as Nachmanides believes. *Onkelos*, he correctly states, takes the first position when it writes "He whom Isaac fears." Bachya ben Asher mentions *Onkelos*, but not Nachmanides, and gives the same interpretation of the *Targum*.[12]

21. Jacob returns to Canaan after some twenty years and sends a message to his brother Esau. In it, he refers to God. In *Genesis* 32:11, he states, "I am not worthy of all the mercies and all the truths that you [God] have shown to your servant." Nachmanides explains that *Onkelos* clarifies the idiomatic abstract Hebrew expression "truths" as "benefits" because Jacob wasn't thanking God for "all the truths" but for "all the goods" that the deity had bestowed upon

---

11. See *Genesis* 22.
12. This is the seventh time that both Nachmanides and Bachya mention *Onkelos*.

him. Bachya mentions *Onkelos*, but not Nachmanides, and agrees with Nachmanides' understanding of the *Targum*.[13]

22. Nachmanides observes that Rashi translates *akhaprah* in *Genesis* 32:21 as "appease" as *Onkelos* does, while he defines it as "ransom."
23. *Genesis* 36:6 is difficult. According to the Bible, Esau took his family and property acquired in the land of Canaan "and went to a land from before his brother Jacob." *Onkelos* explains the scriptural phrase as "and went to another land away [from] his brother Jacob." Nachmanides notes that targumic clarification, and without commenting upon it, offers an alternative view.
24. Nachmanides states that Rashi and *Onkelos* understand *Genesis* 37:26 similarly. Judah asked his brothers what profit they would gain by killing Joseph, and "conceal his blood." Rashi explains the last phrase as "and hide the fact of his death." Rashi drew the explanation, as he frequently does, from *Onkelos*, which reads "and conceal concerning [*al*] his blood." *Onkelos* and Rashi addressed the relevancy of the covering of the blood and explained that the brothers were concealing the murder. Without criticizing the targumic view, Nachmanides contends that the correct interpretation of the passage is the literal one: murderers kill in secret, bury the victim, and conceal any shed blood by covering it with earth.[14]
25. *Onkelos* translates *hatabachim*, "slaughterers," a word used in Hebrew for killing animals, in *Genesis* 37:36, as "executioners," a term for human executions. Nachmanides explains that the Bible's statement in 40:3 that Joseph was placed in a prison and it is reasonable to assume that the head of the prison was responsible for human executions rather than that Potiphar was the administrator of the prison, influenced the targumist's rendering: since Potiphar administered the prison, it is reasonable to assume that he was responsible for human executions rather than animal slaughtering. Additionally, *t'vichah* is used elsewhere in Scripture as a metaphoric way of describing human killings.[15]
26. In *Onkelos* to *Genesis* 38:2, Judah married the daughter of a "merchant," rather than a "Canaanite,"[16] precluding the idea that Judah transgressed the prohibition

---

13. This is the eighth parallel mention of *Onkelos*.
14. As in *Exodus* 2:12.
15. *Isaiah* 14:21, *Lamentations* 2:21, and *Daniel* 2:14.
16. See also *Genesis* 28:1, 24:3, Babylonian Talmud, *Pesachim* 50a, and *Targum* to *1 Chronicles* 2:3.

of intermarriage with Canaanites.[17] This is one of the 104 instances where our targumist changed the translation to protect the honor of Israel's ancestors in *Genesis*.[18] Nachmanides does not acknowledge the deviation methodology but mentions that the targumist wanted to say that Jacob's sons kept Abraham's command not to marry Canaanites.[19] Bachya interprets *Onkelos* in the same way.[20]

27. Nachmanides reports without any analysis of the *Targum* that while he believes that Pharaoh imprisoned "eunuchs" with Joseph – because he translates the biblical *saris* as "eunuch" – *Onkelos* to *Genesis* 40:2 (and 39:1 and 37:36) and *Targum Jonathan* to *II Kings* 20:1 translate the term as "officers" or "chiefs."

28. *Genesis* 40:16 tells how Joseph interpreted the dream of his fellow prisoner the chief baker after the baker saw that Joseph interpreted the chief cup-bearer's dream *tov*. This idiomatic Hebrew usage of *tov* literally means "good," but could also mean "properly" and is so rendered in *Targum Onkelos*.[21] Nachmanides writes that our targumist is stating that the chief baker was persuaded to ask Joseph to interpret his dream when he saw that Joseph explained his friend's dream properly.

29. Rashi to *Genesis* 41:1 states that the Hebrew *ye'or* only refers to the Nile. Nachmanides differs and states that both *ye'or* and *nahor* denote "river." He notes that *Onkelos* renders *ye'or* as *nahar*, thus showing that both denote "river," contrary to what Rashi maintains.[22] Bachya ben Asher makes the same statement as Nachmanides about *Onkelos*.[23]

30. The Hebrew *tzenumot* in *Genesis* 41:23 – the seven ears of grain in Pharaoh's dream were *tzenumot* – is obscure. Rashi translates it as "hard as a rock," but

---

Canaanite is also understood as "merchant" in *Isaiah* 23:8, *Zechariah* 14:21, *Proverbs* 31:24 and *Job* 40:30.

17. The Berliner edition of *Onkelos* lacks this rendering, but it is in the Sperber version.
18. See Drazin, *Targumic Studies to Genesis*, 35, 39–40, 42–43, 48, 52–55, 59, 63, 74–75.
19. *Genesis* 28:1 and 24:3.
20. This is the tenth parallel passage of Nachmanides and Bachya.
21. Saadiah, has "[for good] results." Rashbam and Radak refer to the Babylonian Talmud, *Sotah* 9b, and *Berakhot* 55b, and state "he recognized that it was true" because the two officials saw the interpretation of the other's dream during their own dreams. Chazkuni writes simply that he believed Joseph.
22. *Onkelos* does this consistently except in *Exodus* 7:19 where the targumist needed to retain *ye'or* since he had already used *nahar* to translate another word. According to Nachmanides, *ye'or* denotes both "river" and "canal," while *nahor* is only a natural "river."
23. This is the eleventh parallel statement.

reports that *Onkelos* has the opposite *natzan lakyan*, which Rashi explains means "withered" or "shriveled" or "beaten."[24] Rashbam notes that the word is found only here in Scripture and it must be interpreted according to the context; it probably denotes, as in the Talmud,[25] "hard as rock." Ibn Ezra also notes its uniqueness but defines it as "beaten," as does Radak.[26] Nachmanides understands the word in the same way as *Onkelos*, whom he cites.

31. In his commentary to *Genesis* 41:45, Nachmanides states that Pharaoh's daughter knew at least some Hebrew and gave Moses the Hebrew name Moses, but Egyptians called him Munyos because they changed the original name into a language they understood. Nachmanides claims this is like the pattern of *Onkelos* who occasionally changes biblical names into the current name understood by the targumic audience. This is a rare instance where Nachmanides recognizes a targumic methodology.[27]

32. Nachmanides explains that *Onkelos* paraphrases Scripture's *l'hitgoleil*, which literally means "to roll over us," in *Genesis* 43:18, as "'to lord it over us,' that he [Joseph] elevates himself over us [his brothers] as a sea raises its waves." He is correct. However, he would have been more correct had he stated, "This is a common targumic style to explain biblical metaphors that the translator thought his readers would have difficulty understanding."[28] Bachya ben Asher mentions *Onkelos*, but not Nachmanides, and agrees with the *Targum*.[29]

33. In *Genesis* 45:1, Nachmanides mentions the interpretations of Rashi, ibn Ezra, and *Onkelos* of *l'hithapeik* and then agrees with the definition given by *Onkelos*.

34. In *Genesis* 45:12, Nachmanides relates that Rashi, ibn Ezra, Radak, and *Onkelos* explain Joseph's statement to his brothers that the brothers can see that he is indeed Joseph because "it is my mouth that speaks to you." They explain that Joseph is saying you can identify me because I am able to "speak to you in your language."

Nachmanides rejects this view arguing that Hebrew was the common

---

24. Although not noted by Rashi, *Onkelos* uses the same Aramaic word in this sense in verse 27.
25. Babylonian Talmud, *Bava Batra* 18a.
26. Referring to the Babylonian Talmud, *Berakhot* 39a.
27. There are twenty-three cases where the names of biblical nations or historic sites are changed for those in use during the talmudic age. See Drazin, *Targumic Studies*, 13 and 14.
28. See other *Genesis* examples in Drazin, *Targumic Studies*, 7 and 8.
29. This is the twelfth parallel.

language of the Canaanites and was known in nearby countries such as Egypt by many of its inhabitants. He prefers to accept the figure of speech "my mouth speaks to you" literally: I am the ruler of Egypt; if I tell you something it is certainly true. Bachya ben Asher agrees with Nachmanides, but does not relate this meaning to the *Targum*.

35. Commenting on *Genesis* 45:26, Nachmanides states that *Onkelos* renders "the spirit of Jacob their father revived [when he heard the news that Joseph was alive]" as "the spirit of prophecy rested upon their father Jacob."[30] He explains that the targumist is expounding upon the word "spirit."

36. Nachmanides differs with Rashi in interpreting *Genesis* 48:6. Rashi states that Joshua divided Canaan among the conquering Israelites by population; i.e., each person received an equal share. Nachmanides declared that the land was divided by tribes, with each tribe receiving the same amount of land, no matter their population. The only exception was Ephraim and Menasheh, the sons of Joseph, who were given a full share each. This represented the double portion of the first-born granted to Joseph by his father Jacob.[31]

Nachmanides presents several proofs for his position. He includes as proof the words of *Onkelos* to *Genesis* 49:22 "they shall receive *chulka v'achsanta* [a portion and inheritance]" and claims that *chulka* denotes the extra share of the firstborn and *v'achsanta* the ordinary inheritance. A dispassionate reader, with a dictionary in hand, would not see this meaning in these words. This is especially so when one recognizes that Nachmanides apparently overlooked the fact that the two Aramaic words are an exact Aramaic equivalent of the frequently repeated biblical *chelek v'nachalah*, which is a phrase that denotes a single portion.[32] Bachya mentions Nachmanides' interpretation of *Onkelos* and agrees with it. This is the second and last time, of fifteen parallel interpretations in *Genesis*, that Bachya agrees with Nachmanides.

---

30. Our text reads "holy spirit," the wording in the *Midrash Tanchuma A. Vayeshev* 2. The wording "spirit of prophecy" was taken from *Targum Pseudo-Jonathan*. It is possible that both versions were not in the original *Onkelos* version, but were later additions. See also the *Midrashim Pirkei d'Rabbi Eliezer*, chapter 38 and *Socher Tov* 24, 3, 102b.
31. See the Babylonian Talmud, *Horayoth* 6b and *Bava Batra* 121b, 123a.
32. For example, *Genesis* 31:14, *Deuteronomy* 10:9, 12:12, 14:27, 14:29, 18:1, etc.

37. *Onkelos* inserts "to go" into *Genesis* 49:6, "I was not present in their secret when they [Simeon and Levi] assembled *to go*…," supplying what the Hebrew text does not say explicitly, but clearly implies. Jacob was not furious with his sons because they assembled to discuss the rape of their sister Dinah. He was angry that they decided to go and exact revenge. Nachmanides notes this and agrees.

38. The Hebrew *m'cheiroteihem* in *Genesis* 49:5 is obscure. Rashbam associates it with its use in Ezekiel 16:3 and interprets it as "sojourning." So too does *Genesis Rabbah* 49:7, Rashi, ibn Ezra, Radak; *Onkelos*, and others. Nachmanides notes this and agrees.[33]

39. Jacob says that his sons Simeon and Levi disabled an ox (*shor*) in *Genesis* 49:6. *Genesis* Rabbah 99:6, *Onkelos, Pseudo-Jonathan, Neophyti*, Vulgate, *Peshitta*, Aquilas, Symmachus, Saadiah, Chazkuni, ibn Ezra, and others, treat *shor* as if it were pronounced *shur*, "a wall." Thus, Jacob is not portrayed as saying that his sons inhumanly disabled cattle, but the "wall of the enemy."[34] This is not the only interpretation of *shor*. Rashi and Radak understand "ox" as a metaphor for Hamor and Shechem.[35] Nachmanides understood *Onkelos*'s interpretation, but rejected it, stating he preferred a literal reading, that Jacob's sons killed all the men of Shechem's city and plundered the cattle and the other items in the city.

40. Nachmanides cites our *Targum*'s paraphrase of *Genesis* 49:12 and agrees with it:[36] *Onkelos* reads: "His [the tribe of Judah] mountains will be red with his vineyards, his wine-presses will overflow with wine." He uses the targumic paraphrase to prove that Judah's land had an abundance of wine and milk. Bachya mentions *Onkelos*'s interpretation and agrees with it, without mentioning Nachmanides.

41. Although *Genesis*'s 49:16 Hebrew original uses the word "judge,"[37] *Onkelos* reads, a man will arise [Samson] who will deliver the Israelite tribes.

---

33. There are other interpretations of the obscure word, as noted by ibn Ezra.
34. "Enemy" was also added by *Onkelos* to clarify whose wall was demolished.
35. The Babylonian Talmud, *Megillah* 9a, states that this verse is one of the fifteen that the Septuagint translators did not translate literally to protect the honor of Israelite ancestors. Jacob's sons did not kill a man and maim an ox, as indicated in the original Hebrew, but "killed an ox and… uprooted the manger."
36. The Bible has, "His eyes are darker than wine; his teeth are whiter than milk."
37. "Dan will judge his people, as one of the tribes of Israel."

Nachmanides explains that "judge" is understood in the sense of "avenge," as in *Deuteronomy* 32:36 and *Psalms* 43:1.

42. Nachmanides mentions our targumist's rendering of *Genesis*'s 49:22 *bein Porath* as one of two possible correct interpretations.[38] *Onkelos* reads "Joseph is my son who will be numerous."

---

38. "Joseph is a *bein porat*, a *bein porat* by the spring." *Onkelos* understands *bein* as "son," and *porat* as an expression of fruitfulness.

– CHAPTER 9 –

Genesis Problematical interpretations

> As noted in chapter 7, Nachmanides mentions *Targum Onkelos* in his *Commentary to Genesis* in eighty verses. Thirty-eight, or close to half of these instances are problematical. He refers to the *Targum* in eighteen verses without any analysis. There are twenty-four passages where he explains *Onkelos* in what appears to be a reasonable manner. His interpretations are problematical in *Genesis* in twenty-three instances because he reads more into an Aramaic word than its literal meaning warrants, including once where he felt that the *Targum* was teaching mysticism. In four instances, he explained *Onkelos* based on his rather unique notion that the targumist does not deviate from the biblical text to avoid anthropomorphisms. In eleven places he did not recognize that the targumist was simply using a characteristic targumic technique, including three verses where *Onkelos* changed the text to preserve the honor of Israelite ancestors.

BACHYA IS TROUBLED BY NACHMANIDEAN INTERPRETATIONS

The problematical aspect of the Nachmanidean interpretations apparently bothered the Bible commentator Bachya ben Asher. Although he was an enthusiastic follower of Nachmanides and shared his penchant for interpreting the Bible in a mystical manner, and although he mentions Nachmanides very frequently in his commentary and on other occasions borrows from him without attribution, and although Bachya paid close attention to the *Targum Onkelos* renderings and sometimes mentions them, and despite the fact that he generally agrees with the Nachmanidean explanations, Bachya rarely mentions Nachmanides' readings of *Onkelos*. In his commentary to *Genesis*, Bachya quotes and agrees with the Nachmanidean interpretation only twice.

THE PROBLEMATICAL INTERPRETATIONS FOUND IN
NACHMANIDES' *COMMENTARY TO GENESIS*

1. "And God said: 'Let the waters swarm (*yishretzu*) with swarms (*sheretz*) of living creatures…" (*Genesis* 1:20). *Onkelos*: *yirchashun…rechesh*.

    Nachmanides mentions *Onkelos* for the first time in his commentary to *Genesis* 1:20 where he states that he differs with Rashi's definition of the biblical *sheretz*. Rashi writes "every living thing that is not high from the ground is called a *sheretz*." Nachmanides seems to understand that Rashi is stating that the root of the term *sheretz* denotes "something that is close to the ground."[1] Nachmanides points out that the root of the word is *ratz*, "run," and the animal is named *sheretz* because *shehu ratz*, "[it is] that which runs." Nachmanides supports his definition by referring to *Onkelos*: "*Onkelos's* opinion is [like mine] that *shritzah* (swarming) implies movement, for he says [in *Leviticus* 11:44] of both *sheretz* and *remes*; *ruchasha d'rachish* (moving things, things that move)." Actually, Rashi understood that *sheretz* means "movement" and explicitly says so in his commentary to *Leviticus* 11:10 and 44. Rashi was not defining the word here, but simply informing us which animals are called *sheretz*. Furthermore, *Onkelos* was not taking a position on the matter, but simply rendering the Hebrew literally into its Aramaic equivalent. Thus Nachmanides appears to have misread Rashi and used *Onkelos* to support his view when the *Targum* was only giving a literal rendering.[2]

2. *Genesis* 1:31 states: "And God saw everything that He made, and, behold, it was very good (Torah: *tov meod* – Onkelos: *takin lachada*)."

    This verse describes the results of the sixth day of creation as "very good." The *Onkelos* translator, who prefers to clarify ambiguous biblical phrases with more specificity (good in which way), renders it "well established," implying that the world was established firmly. He may have been calling to mind *Psalms* 93:1, "the world also is established that it cannot be moved" and *Psalms* 96:10, "the world also shall be established that it shall not be moved."

    Nachmanides reads into the *Onkelos* words "well established" that the

---

1. The commentary is rather obscure.
2. M. Jastrow, *A Dictionary of the Targumim, the Talmud Babli and Yerushalmi and the Midrashic Literature*, 2 vols. (Philadelphia, 1886–1902), vol. 2, 1470.

targumist is teaching that creation contains evil, "the order [of the world] was very properly arranged that evil is needed to preserve what is good."[3] This interpretation is a good homily, but is not the plain meaning of the *Onkelos* words. It is problematical because "well established" neither suggests "containing evil" nor implies that evil is necessary to preserve what is good.

3. After creating man, God, according to *Genesis* 2:7, "breathed into his nostrils the breath of life, and man became a living being." The bible uses *nefesh* for "breath" and "being." In later Hebrew, *nefesh* came to mean "soul," a meaning it did not convey in the Pentateuch. Since the Hebrew "breath of life" does not indicate how humans supersede other creations, *Onkelos* alters the text and clarifies that "man acquired the power of speech," *ruach memalela* (literally, "speaking breath"). Thus, humans transcend animals by their intelligence in general, and their ability to speak, communicate, and reason, in particular. This is the Aristotelian concept, accepted by Maimonides, i.e. that the essence of a human is intelligence, and people are duty bound to develop that intelligence.[4]

Nachmanides, the mystic, disagreed with Maimonides, the rationalist, and anachronistically interpreted the biblical *nefesh* as "soul." The Hebrew verse, he declares, alludes to the superiority of the soul that is composed of three forces: growth, movement, and rationality.[5] *Onkelos*, he maintains, is reflecting this

---

3. The *Midrash Genesis Rabbah* 9:5, which is the source of this teaching, mentions "death" and 9:9 "the evil inclination in man" as examples of seemingly bad things, which are good from a non-personal world-wide perspective. R. Bachya ben Asher, the student of Nachmanides' student Rashba, who was also a mystic, mentions 9:9, but not the *Targum*. He did not see this idea in *Onkelos*.

4. Maimonides, *Guide of the Perplexed* 1:1. The Greek term *psyche* had a similar etiological history as the Hebrew *nefesh*. T. Cahill, *Sailing the Wine-Dark Sea* (Doubleday, 2003), 231:

> *Psyche* was, to begin with, a Greek word for "life," in the sense of individual human life, and occurs in Homer in such phrases as "to risk one's life" and "to save one's life." Homer also uses it of the ghosts of the underworld – the weak, almost-not-there shades of those who once were men. In the works of the early scientist-philosophers, *psyche* can refer to the ultimate substance, the source of life and consciousness, the spirit of the universe. By the fifth century BCE, *psyche* had come to mean the "conscious self," the "personality," even the "emotional self," and thence it quickly takes on, especially in Plato, the meaning of "immortal self" – the soul, in contrast to the body.

5. R. Bachya ben Asher also mentions the parts of the soul, but not the *Targum*, again not seeing Nachmanides' idea in *Onkelos*.

concept of the tripartite soul, and that the rational soul that God breathed into man's nostrils became a speaking soul. How the two Aramaic words, literally meaning "speaking breath," suggest this elaborate tripartite theology, is problematical. Again, Nachmanides seemingly desired to have *Onkelos*, which he admired, reflect and support his own idea even though what he reads into the *Targum* is not its plain meaning.

4. *Genesis* 4:1 states that when Eve gave birth to Cain, she exclaimed, "I have acquired a man with the Lord." Since this statement has an anthropomorphic sound, suggesting physical help from God, our *Targum* adds *qadam*, "before [the Lord]," thereby supplanting, or at least ameliorating, this implication of physical aid, in that it distances God from the birth.

   The word *qadam* was inserted in *Onkelos* in verse 4, as well as in seventy other instances in *Genesis*, for the same reason – to ameliorate an anthropomorphic depiction, this is in addition to the 585 instances in *Targum Onkelos* in the other volumes of the Pentateuch.[6] Nachmanides ignores the targumist's frequent use of *qadam* to avoid anthropomorphism and its plain meaning.[7] He states that the correct interpretation of the biblical Hebrew is that Eve said: "This son will be an acquisition from God for me, for when we die he will exist in our place to worship his creator." Nachmanides assures us that this was *Onkelos*'s opinion, as proven by the addition of the word *qadam*. Thus, Nachmanides drew a conclusion from the *Targum*'s use of a single word, a word that is used over five hundred times for an entirely different purpose, and which cannot, by itself, connote and support his interpretation. Furthermore, *qadam* does not have this meaning in the hundreds of other instances where it appears.

5. "And the Lord God planted a garden in Eden (*mikedem*)...." (*Genesis* 2:8). *Onkelos: milekadmin.*

   Nachmanides uses *Onkelos*'s Aramaic rendering as evidential support for his view against that of Rashi in *Genesis* 2:8. Rashi explains that "God planted a garden *mikedem* in Eden" means "east" of Eden. *Onkelos* translates *mikedem* as *mileqadmin*, which Nachmanides translates as "in ancient times" and states

---

6. See the five books by I. Drazin on *Targum Onkelos* published by Ktav Publishing House. Each contains a listing of the deviations by the targumist from the Hebrew original.

7. In my discussion of *Genesis* 46:1, I show that Nachmanides was convinced that *Onkelos* never deviates to avoid anthropomorphisms.

that the targumist is reflecting the midrashic idea that the garden of Eden existed before the world was created.[8] "And this is the correct explanation."

It is true that *mileqadmin* could mean "in ancient times,"[9] as he states, but it also means "in the east,"[10] as Rashi contends, in *Genesis* 3:24. Thus, the Aramaic word is as ambiguous as the Hebrew it is translating and cannot be used to support Nachmanides' position.

6. *Genesis* 2:9 states that the tree of life and the tree of knowledge of good and evil were "in the midst" (*betokh hagan*) of the garden of Eden. *Onkelos: bimtzi'ut ginta*.

Nachmanides explains that the "simple meaning" of the biblical word that is translated into English as "in the midst of" indicates that the trees were set in "a known place." (He does not identify who knew the place.)[11] He says that this is the reason why *Onkelos* translated the word as "in the middle [of the garden]." He concludes that this being so, "we must say that in the middle of the garden there was the likeness of an enclosed garden-bed made which contained these two trees."[12] How Nachmanides derived the non-sequitor is unclear: neither "in the midst" nor "in the middle" implies "a known place" and, even if they did, "a known place" does not require one to deduce that the garden contained "the likeness of an enclosed garden."

7. In his commentary to *Genesis* 12:15, Nachmanides uses an incorrect *Onkelos* text. The Bible states "and they [the Egyptians] praised her [Abram's wife Sarai] to Pharaoh." Nachmanides states that the Egyptians saw that Sarai was so beautiful that she was only fit for Pharaoh. He supports his interpretation by quoting *Onkelos's levat*, which he defines as "for," and understands that the

---

8. *Genesis Rabbah* 15:4, the Babylonian Talmud, *Pessachim* 54a and *Nedarim* 39b, and *Targum Pseudo-Jonathan*. *Onkelos's mileqadmin* has the same root as the word used to translate "In the beginning" in *Genesis* 1:1. Bachya states that the "kabbalistic approach to our verse understands... *mekedem* as since primeval times... to an era preceding that described in the Torah in chapter 1." However, he does not ascribe this notion to our targumist.

9. Gustaf Dalman, *Grammatik des Jüdisch-Palästinischen Aramaisch* (Leipzig, 1905), 214.

10. Ibid., 217.

11. Bachya ben Asher argues that since Scripture states that both trees were in the midst of the garden and since two things cannot exist in the same place, "we must assume that they had a single trunk." He does not mention the *Targum* to this verse.

12. Chavel, *Ramban, Commentary on the Torah*, Genesis, 71.

Egyptians were speaking among themselves and said to one another, "she is only fit *for* Pharaoh." Actually the correct targumic text has a *lamed*, which means "to," just as the Hebrew. There is no targumic change. Also, *levat* does not mean "for," but "to."[13]

8. "And they turned and came to En-mishpat" (*Genesis* 14:7).

   When *Onkelos* renders the place name "En-mishpat" as *"pilug dina,"* for the above-stated reason, Nachmanides tells us that he does "not know what this means." He supposes that *pilug* suggests a "stream" or "fountain" as in Isaiah 30:25, and concludes that *Onkelos* is stating "a fountain of judgment" will flow on this plain. The *Targum*, he remarks, is telling us that this is a fitting site for kings to occupy when they judge their citizens. His final remark about the *Targum* is correct, even though his steps to his conclusion are not. The term *pilug* means "decision" and the phrase *pilug dina* is an idiom (as defined by Jastrow, *Dictionary*, page 1163) for "judgment." Thus *Onkelos* should not be translated "[the plain of] a fountain of judgment," but as "[the plain of] Judgment."[14]

9. *Genesis* 14:19 states that God is the *konei* of heaven and earth. In biblical Hebrew *konei* means "creator," while in later talmudic Hebrew it had the exclusive meaning of "acquirer," as in *Genesis Rabbah* 43:7 and the Babylonian Talmud, *Kiddushin* 16a; see also the *Dictionary* of Abraham Even-Shoshan.

   Onkelos changes the word to "whose possessions are" to avoid the anthropomorphic image and theological problem of God receiving the heaven and earth from somebody or something else. A "possession" does not have to be "acquired" from another person or thing. Nachmanides, who was convinced that *Onkelos* does not change the scriptural wording to remove anthropomorphisms,[15] apparently felt forced to claim that *konei* does not mean "acquire," but "possessor," and that the *Targum* is literal.[16]

---

13. Jastrow, *Dictionary*, 701. Michael Sokoloff, *A Dictionary of Jewish and Palestinian Aramaic of the Byzantine Period* (Ramat Gan, 1990), 279.
14. The root *p-l-g* denotes a division and not a stream of water (M. Sokoloff, *Dictionary*, 433). *Targum Pseudo-Jonathan* and Rashi understand that this statement predicts the future site where Moses and Aaron would be judged and sentenced to die in the wilderness. See *Numbers* 20:12–13. *Numbers Rabbah* 19:14 and *Tanchuma*, Lekh Lecha 8–end.
15. See our discussion of 46:1.
16. Bachya ben Asher also argues that the true meaning of *konei* is "one who has a rightful claim," but does not mention Nachmanides or the *Targum*.

10. In *Genesis* 17:17, *Onkelos* changes a significant detail in the Aramaic translation. Abraham does not "laugh" (Hebrew, *vayitzchak*) when he hears he will have a child in his old age, but "rejoices" (Aramaic, *vachadi*). This alteration is not made in 18:12, where Sarah "laughed" when she heard the same news. Rashi explains that the couple reacted differently. Abraham trusted God and rejoiced at the good news, while Sarah lacked trust and sneered, and therefore God chastised her in 18:13.

    Nachmanides asserts that the *Onkelos* rendering in 17:17 is correct because the word *tzachak* also means rejoice, and Abraham and Sarah's reactions, he contends, were the same – proper "rejoicing."

    Actually, as defined by the Even-Shoshan dictionary and others, *tzachak* is an outward expression, a "laugh," and not an inner feeling of contentment. R. Bachya ben Asher mentions the Aramaic rendering, but he does not mention Nachmanides. He recognizes, contrary to Nachmanides, that *tzachak* does not mean rejoice, but rather laugh. He states that the targumist made the change to "rejoices" because in the context in which the word appears here it should be understood as an expression of joy. This example, while not expressing a theology, as in the first three instances, also shows Nachmanides insisting by use of a forced interpretation that the targumist understands the Torah in the same way he does.

11. *Onkelos* replaces the Torah's "Is anything too wondrous for the Lord," in *Genesis* 18:14, with "Is anything hidden from before the Lord." The Hebrew "wondrous" is somewhat vague, and is seemingly not exactly on point within the tale of Sarah's laughter. The Aramaic explains the text and relates that Sarah's laughter, mentioned in the prior verse, although it was not done openly, was not "hidden" from God. This is also the interpretation of Saadiah Gaon, Rashi, Chazkuni, ibn Ezra, Radak, etc. Thus, in short, all that the targumist is doing is clarifying the text, a task he performs over a thousand times in his translation.

    However, Nachmanides states that *Onkelos* uses "hidden" in the translation to teach a mystical lesson. Nachmanides, as is his habit, does not explain the lesson, but the explanation is in Bachya ben Asher and Recanati. Bachya writes that God added the letter *heh* to Abram's name, transforming it into Abraham, and "the letter *heh* alludes to God's transcendental powers"; thus, God gave Abraham the power to have a son. Abraham, he continues, exemplified the divine attribute of mercy, and Isaac the divine attribute of justice, and now both attributes would exist on earth. It is difficult if not impossible to read this Nachmanidean mystical interpretation of *Onkelos* into the word "hidden."[17]

12. *Genesis* 21:7 quotes Sarah's excited exclamation of joy,[18] "Who [meaning what person] would have said to Abraham [that I would give birth at the advanced age of ninety]." The *Targum* renders her statement as a thankful praise of God, "Faithful is he who said to Abraham," and avoids the risk of the general population reading the translation and misunderstanding Sarah's reaction as one of surprise; for she should not have been surprised. God had assured Abraham a year earlier that he would have a son.[19] Thus, by making the change, the *Targum* shows that she not only is not surprised, but also is thankful that God fulfilled the earlier promise.

Nachmanides interprets the Torah's "Who would have said to Abraham" to mean that everyone will join Abraham and Sarah in rejoicing over the birth of Isaac because it is such a "surprise"; the possibility of such a birth would never have occurred to anyone. He writes that the *Onkelos* rendition is "close" to his interpretation of a community celebration. Actually, as we stated, *Onkelos*'s "Faithful is he who said to Abraham" is quite the opposite. Rather than focusing on the people and their reaction to the unexpected event, the targumist deviated from the Hebrew text to avoid depicting Sarah as having been surprised. His Aramaic version concentrates on God, not the community, and on how the divine promise was fulfilled.

13. *Onkelos* frequently renders the biblical "call," which is somewhat vague, with the more concrete "prayed." Thus, in *Genesis*'s 21:33 "and he [Abraham] called there in the name of the Eternal God" is elevated to "and he prayed."

Nachmanides notes this, and uses it to attempt to disprove a statement of Maimonides.[20] "The Rabbi said in the *Guide* that this ['the Eternal'] alludes to [the principle of] the preexistence of God [before the creation of time] because he [Abraham] informed people of his [God's] existence before [the

---

17. Bachya mentions neither Nachmanides nor *Onkelos*, again not seeing the Nachmanidean interpretation in the *Targum*.
18. The "joy" is mentioned in the *Targum* to verse 6.
19. *Genesis* 17:19.
20. Maimonides, *Guide of the Perplexed*, 2:13 and 3:29.

creation of] time [when he 'called' there]. But *Onkelos* states that 'he called' refers to 'prayer' [and not to a discourse with people]." The fact that *Onkelos* rendered "call" as "prayer" is irrelevant to Maimonides' statement, since (1) Maimonides' view that God preexisted time is based on the word "Eternal" meaning existing forever, and not on "called," and (2) Maimonides statement that Abraham informed people about this fact is not based on the *Targum*, but on the Torah reading.

In his commentary, Bachya ben Asher also understands the verse as Nachmanides, but does not mention him. He does mention *Onkelos* – this being the third time that he parallels Nachmanides – but he specifically states that this teaching about the existence of God has nothing to do with the *Targum*.

14. *Genesis* 22:2 recounts God commanding Abraham to take his son Isaac to "the land of Moriah," and to offer him there as a sacrifice. Mount Moriah was traditionally understood to be the later place of the Jerusalem Temple,[21] and the targumist therefore renders "Mount Moriah" as "the land of worship," to help his readers in identifying the location. This is a typical targumic methodology. The *Targum* changes the names of places mentioned in the Bible, and gives their later known names.[22]

Nachmanides contends that *Onkelos* is referring to an exegetical teaching that was recorded, years after the targumist's death, in *Pirkei d'R. Eliezer*:[23] God pointed to the site and told Abraham that this is the place where Adam, Cain, Abel, and Noah had sacrificed, and the site was named Moriah because Moriah is derived from the word *mora*, fear, for the people feared God there and worshipped Him.

There are several problems with Nachmanides' analysis. First, as we already pointed out, our targumist would frequently update the name of a site to

---

21. See *II Chronicles* 3:1.
22. Rashi offers an additional explanation why "Mount Moriah" is rendered "the land of worship." He connected "Moriah" to "myrrh," which was an ingredient of the sacrificial incense, and an important part of the Temple worship. Rashi states that this is the targumic interpretation. Rashi may be explaining why the site was called Moriah, which would not be *derash*, but rather the plain sense of the word. Nachmanides' interpretation goes far beyond a simple definition. See *Genesis Rabbah* 55:7, *Exodus* 30:23ff, and Babylonian Talmud, *Keritut* 6a.
23. Chapter 31.

help his readers identify its location,[24] and this is a reasonable and consistent explanation of the targumic rendering. Second, the targumic words "land of worship" do not suggest the elaborate exegetical story that was not recorded until long after the death of the targumist. Third, the story is a legend; there is nothing in any text to indicate that God had such a conversation with Abraham, or that the ancestors sacrificed in this area. Furthermore, it is contrary to the targumist's style to incorporate legends into his translation.

15. *Onkelos* renders Abraham's request to his neighbor Ephron to sell him a burial plot for his deceased wife Sarah in *Genesis* 23:13, "if only you would hear me," as "if you would do me a favor." Nachmanides states that the biblical Hebrew should be read as though "if" is stated twice, "if you, if you will hear me"; and states that the Bible frequently uses redundancy to emphasizes the matter; and adds that Abraham is emphasizing his arguments here. He concludes: "Perhaps this is the view of *Onkelos* who writes, "if you would do me a favor," meaning, "if you will do my will as you have said."

Actually, the targumist is explaining the figure of speech "hear," as he does many times elsewhere when he renders "hear" as "accept" when it is used as a figure of speech.[25] He does not substitute "accept" in this passage, even though it is a figure of speech, because Abraham's point was not that Ephron should pay attention, because "accept" would be an ambiguous. Therefore, he explains what "hear" and "accept" imply, "do me a favor."[26] Furthermore, the Aramaic alternative words "if you would do me a favor" do not at all imply "as you have said."

16. Ephron replies to Abraham in *Genesis* 23:15 that he has "land of 400 *selah* of silver." *Onkelos* clarifies the passage by adding "worth" after "land."

Nachmanides states that the Aramaic change was made to inform its readers that the land had a fixed price and was actually "worth" 400 *selah*. He wonders why the translator took this position since the rabbis understood that Ephron was demanding an exorbitant arbitrary price.[27] He does not see that *Onkelos*

---

24. This occurs twenty-three times in *Genesis* alone.
25. For example, verses 6 and 15 in this chapter.
26. *Targum Onkelos*'s rendering also raises the question as to how the targumist understood *lu*. The Septuagint, Samaritan Bible, and *Pseudo-Jonathan* read it as *li*, with a final *yud* instead of a *vav*.
27. *Genesis Rabbah* 58:9.

GENESIS PROBLEMATICAL INTERPRETATIONS · 99

is only translating what is in Scripture, but with slightly greater clarity. This passage was part of Ephron's reply, his attempt at negotiation; he was claiming that it was worth 400 *selah* when it may have been worth considerably less. The additional "worth" does not in and of itself imply that there was price fixing in that land. Bachya ben Asher mentions *Onkelos*'s interpretation – the fifth time that he mentions *Onkelos* when Nachmanides does so – but ignores Nachmanides' understanding of it.

17. *Genesis* 24:62 states that when Abraham's servant returned from his mission to find a wife for Isaac and brought Rebecca for his wife, Isaac happened to meet them just before they reached their destination: "Now Isaac had just come." The Hebrew *ba mibo* can be translated (1) as we stated "just come," or (2) *ba* could mean "come," and *mibo* could be a noun, and the verse would be stating, "Now Isaac had come from *mibo*," or (3) *mibo* could be taken as the infinitive construct, "Now Isaac had come (back) from coming," meaning that he was returning from wherever he went. *Onkelos* opts for the third treatment.

    Nachmanides maintains that the targumist is stating that Isaac was returning from the place where he constantly went for prayer, the well of *lachai-roi*. There are several problems. The *Onkelos* wording only states that Isaac returned from an undisclosed trip. Proof that the destination of this trip is obscure is that a *Midrash* gives another interpretation of Isaac's prior destination: Isaac went to bring Hagar home to Abraham.[28] Additionally, there is no indication in the Aramaic that this was a habitual journey, as Nachmanides maintains. Furthermore, many rabbinic sources understand the passage to say that Isaac did not come from prayer, but went to this field to pray.[29] Bachya ben Asher does not mention Nachmanides or *Onkelos* and suggests that the passage is stating that Isaac had just returned from a three-year period of solitude at Mount Moriah.

18. In *Genesis* 24:64 Rebecca reacts when she saw her future husband Isaac for the first time: "she fell from the camel." The verb "fell" is certainly not meant to be taken literally; it is a typical biblical dramatic hyperbole for "she alighted from

---

28. *Genesis Rabbah* 60:14 and *Tanchuma B*, Chayei Sarah 9, page 123.
29. Jerusalem Talmud, *Berakhot* 4, 1, 7a; Babylonian Talmud, *Berakhot* 26b and *Avodah Zarah* 7b; *Genesis Rabbah* 60:14; Jacob Z. Lauterbach, trans. *Mekhilta d'Rabbi Ishmael* (Philadelphia: Jewish Publication Society, 1933), vol. 2, 206.

the camel," and probably means that she hurried to alight. *Onkelos* renders it this way either because the targumist understood "fell" as a figure of speech, as we said, or, if he took it literally, he changed it to protect the honor of the Israelite ancestor whom he did not want to portray in an unfavorable light.[30] Rashi is similar to the *Targum*: "she let herself slide towards the ground."

However, Nachmanides maintains that Rebecca did not get off the camel. He states that the *Targum*'s "she alighted from the camel" means that Rebecca bent herself toward one side in order to humbly turn her face from him. Nachmanides recognizes that the targumist states "from the camel," but argues that although he used the *mem* in *mei'al*, "from on," he did not want it to be translated: "it is a redundant letter."[31] This is unlikely. There is no other instance where *Onkelos* says one thing and means another. Bachya ben Asher rejects Nachmanides' interpretation of the *Targum* for the sixth time. However, he states that the *Targum* means, "she inclined her head as one does prior to falling off an animal," but he does not explain why she did it.[32]

19. Genesis 24:67 lacks "of." It literally states, "And Isaac brought her [Rebecca] into the tent, Sarah his mother." Radak explains that in those days wives had separate tents, and when a man wanted to join his wife, he went to her tent. *Onkelos* could have rendered the text simply by adding an Aramaic letter *d*, "of [Sarah his mother]." However, our *Targum* text adds, instead, five Aramaic words.[33] "And he saw, and behold her deeds were as proper as the deeds of [Sarah his mother]."[34] Nachmanides did not have this unusual midrashic insertion in his *Onkelos* text but, instead, another erroneous rendering: "and Isaac brought her into the tent which was the tent of his mother Sarah." While the cryptic targumic language Nachmanides had could refer to many different

---

30. There are 103 other instances in *Genesis* where our targumist deviates to preserve the honor of Israelite ancestors. See Drazin, *Targumic Studies*, 3.
31. As in the biblical texts of *Isaiah* 65:20 and *Psalms* 148:4.
32. Ibn Ezra understands that she purposely fell off of the camel so that she could prostrate herself before Isaac.
33. This uncharacteristic, unnecessary, and fanciful midrashic supplement is probably a late scribal insertion.
34. The insertion parallels *Genesis Rabbah* 60:15. "Before Sarah died, there was a blessing of miraculous increase in the dough," which stopped when she died and reappeared when Rebecca entered her tent.

things, such as the plain meaning Radak gave to the verse, or to Rebecca's looks, height, or fondness for him, he opted to read the above-stated *Midrash* into this cryptic targumic language, that her deeds were as proper as Sarah's deeds, even though the *Targum* generally avoids midrashic interpretations.

20. *Onkelos* frequently translates biblical ethnic and place names as if they were not names. There are fifteen instances of this in the *Genesis* translation,[35] including three in 25:3, "Asshurim, Letushim and Leummim." These three clans or clan chieftains are replaced by "camps, settlements and islands."[36] Nachmanides states that our targumist had to translate as he did because the Bible uses the word *hayu*, "and the children of Dedan *hayu* [were] Asshurim, Letushim, and Leummim." He argues that if the three words were names of children Scripture should have said "begot." Actually, a form of *hayu* is also used in *Genesis* 36:11 and 22, to cite just two examples, to denote births, and *Onkelos* retains the proper names.

21. In his commentary to *Genesis* 25:17, concerning the death of Abraham's son Ishmael, Nachmanides states that the biblical word *gviyah* denotes a wakening of the body prior to death,[37] and that *Onkelos*'s rendering *ve'itnegid*, which he understands as "fainting," reflects this view. Actually when *gviyah*, which means "expire," is mentioned in respect to the righteous Israelite patriarchs, our targumist softens it euphemistically to *ve'itnagid*, which also means "he was withdrawn [from those who are living]."[38] When the term is used for other people, the more explicit *mait*, "died," is used.[39]

22. The Hebrew of *Genesis* 27:42 is difficult. It states that Rebecca warned her younger son Jacob that his elder brother Esau "consoles himself against you to kill you." If Esau was consoled, why did he seek revenge? *Onkelos* exchanges the verb and renders "[Esau] is plotting against you." This is what the context implies.

Nachmanides recognizes this, but unnecessarily adds that the targumist

---

35. See Drazin, *Targumic Studies*, pages 14–15.
36. *Genesis Rabbah* 61:4 translates them as "merchants, flaming ones, and heads of people."
37. This is the interpretation of *Genesis Rabbah* 62:2.
38. As in *Genesis* 25:8, 25:17 35:29, and 49:33 regarding Abraham's son Ishmael whom the rabbis maintain repented before his death. Sokoloff, *Dictionary*, defines *nagid* as "pull away" and "flow."
39. As in Drazin and Wagner, *Onkelos on the Torah*, *Genesis* 6:17 and 7:21.

understood Esau did two things: he acted as if he were consoled (a word that is not in the *Targum*) while he still plotted revenge.

23. Before entering Canaan after his some twenty year absence and crossing the Wadi Jabbok, Jacob encountered a man (who some commentators contend was an angel) *vayei'aveik* with him (*Genesis* 32:25). The verb is usually translated as "wrestled;" however, *Onkelos* has *ve'ishtadeil*. Nathan Adler states that the Aramaic denotes a verbal struggle: *Onkelos* wanted to avoid portraying an anthropomorphic physical wrestling match between a human and an angel.[40]

   Maimonides maintains that the episode was a prophetic dream because, as noted by Adler, it is impossible for a human to wrestle with an incorporeal being.[41] The targumist avoids the impossible portrayal because most readers would not recognize that this episode was a dream.

   Nachmanides, as we will see when we discuss 46:1, was convinced that the *Onkelos* translator did not alter his translation to avoid anthropomorphic portrayals. He understands the Aramaic as cunning.[42] He states that *Onkelos* was not intentionally deviating; he was unable to find a more proper word for "wrestling," and used "cunning" because all struggles including wrestling, require cunning. Nachmanides' idea has two problems. First, *Onkelos* does change the translation to avoid anthropomorphisms. Second, in 25:22, *Onkelos* uses *v'dachakin*, "pushed," for scripture *vayitrotzetzu*, "struggled," and could have used the word here; "pushed" is certainly closer to "wrestled" than "cunning."

24. The *Onkelos* targumist avoids identifying an altar with God in *Genesis* 33:20 by rendering Scripture's "and he [Jacob] called it [*lo*, meaning the altar] 'God, the God of Israel'" in Aramaic as "he worshipped on it [*bo*] before God, the God of Israel." He generally dislikes endowing a place with God's name, considering such a thing degrading, or fearing that naming an object might lead his unsophisticated readers to believe that a corporeal God could be isolated to a single area.

   Nachmanides, as we saw previously and will see again, was convinced that the *Onkelos* translator did not change the biblical wording in his translation to

---

40. M. Lowenstein, *Nefesh Hager*, Pietrokov, 1906, 112. *Genesis Rabbah* 67:2 and *Canticles Rabbah* 3:5 also describe it as a verbal strife. *Onkelos* changes the translation of 30:8 for the same reason.
41. Maimonides, *Guide of the Perplexed* 2:42.
42. As in *Exodus* 22:15.

avoid anthropomorphisms.[43] He states that *Onkelos* must be understanding *lo*, "it," as *bo*, "on it," and changed the meaning of the passage solely for this reason. It is more reasonable to suppose that our targumist was not led to his translation by his understanding of *lo*, but by the anthropomorphism. Once he decided to address the problem of the anthropomorphism, he did so by treating *lo* as *bo*.

25. Nachmanides maintains that *Onkelos* inserts *khashar*, "proper," into *Genesis* 34:7, "it is not proper to be done," to emphasize that the act performed by Jacob's sons was forbidden. Actually, our targumist is not making this point; the original Hebrew itself, "it is not to be done," already clearly states that the act is forbidden. *Onkelos* adds "proper" frequently. It is an explanatory Aramaic supplemental adjective that is customarily used in Aramaic and unnecessary in idiomatic Hebrew.[44] Additionally, contrary to Nachmanides' assertion, and as we saw when we examined the reasons for the targumic changes,[45] our targumist changes the text to protect the honor of Israelite ancestors in 104 instances in *Genesis* and does not make any alteration to denigrate them.

26. Esau's descendant Anah in *Genesis* 36:24 found *yeimim* in the wilderness. This noun is obscure and has been the subject of various explanations, such as "mules."[46] Our targumist connects *yeimim* with *eimim*, "fearsome ones,"[47] and reads "valiant men."

    Nachmanides records the targumic rendering but then reads an adventure story into the translation of the single word and states that this is *Onkelos*'s intent. Anah was attacked by a nation called Yeimim. They robbed him of his father's asses. Without any help, he fooled the robbers, conquered them, saved the asses, and became known as a powerful hero. Needless to say, the single word does not suggest the elaborate tale. What we see here and several of the next discussions are paradigmatic example of the Nachmanidean proclivity to

---

43. See our commentary to *Genesis* 46:1.
44. It is also, for example, in *Onkelos on the Torah – Genesis* 24:23, 25, 31 and *Numbers* 32:1.
45. In chapter 4.
46. *Pseudo-Jonathan*; Jerusalem Talmud, *Berakhot* 8, 6, 12b; Babylonian Talmud, *Berakhot* 54a; *Genesis Rabbah* 82:14.
47. This is the view of Babylonian Talmud, *Chullin* 7b, although the Talmud identifies the fearsome ones with wild mules. See also Drazin and Wagner, *Onkelos to Deuteronomy* 2:10, 11 where the *eimim* are warriors.

read his elaborate interpretations into single characteristic targumic changes that do not suggest what Nachmanides attributes to it. This is the first of the nine instances until now that Bachya ben Asher quotes both Nachmanides and *Onkelos* and accepts Nachmanides' interpretation of the *Targum*.

27. *Onkelos* explains *Genesis* 37:2 description of Joseph *v'hu ma'ar*, "he was a youth [together with the sons of Bilhah and Zilpah]," as "he grew up [with them]." This is nothing more than a clarification of what the Bible itself states.

    However, Nachmanides insists that *Onkelos* is suggesting a drama in a single word, *merabei*, "grew up." The sons of Bilhah and Zilpah, according to this non-biblical elaboration, raised Joseph and treated him well. He repaid them by maliciously bringing false reports about their behavior to their father Jacob. Understandably, this began the strife between the brothers. Whether this story is true or not is irrelevant. What is significant is that it is not hinted in *Onkelos*'s "he grew up." Bachya ben Asher interprets the biblical verse like Nachmanides, but does not read the interpretation into the *Targum*.

28. Our *Targum* makes a change in *Genesis* 37:3 "for he [Joseph] was the son of his [Jacob's] old age" to "for he was a wise son to him" to defend Jacob against a possible charge of unjustified favoritism to Joseph and to explain why Benjamin, Jacob's youngest child, was not called "the son of his old age." Thus, Joseph deserved to be favored since he was a wise son. The targumic alteration of the Hebrew original is one of 104 instances in *Genesis* alone where our targumist preserves the honor of Israel's ancestors.[48]

    Nachmanides shows no knowledge of this characteristic frequent targumic technique. Instead, as we noted previously, he reads a lengthy tale in the one Aramaic word, "wise." It was an ancient custom that elders selected one of their younger sons to attend them. This child was called *ben z'kunav*, the child who attended to him in his old age. Jacob chose Joseph for this function. When our targumist called Joseph "a wise son," says Nachmanides, he was referring to this practice and telling us why Jacob elected Joseph to perform the task of serving him instead of another child.

---

48. See Drazin, *Targumic Studies*, "Concern for Israel's Honor in *Onkelos* and the other *Targums*," 35–76.

29. Nachmanides states that Rashi and *Onkelos* understand *Genesis* 37:26 similarly. Judah asked his brothers what profit would they gain by killing Joseph and if they "conceal his blood." Rashi explains the last phrase as "and hide the fact of his death." Rashi drew the explanation, as he frequently does, from *Onkelos*, which reads "and conceal concerning [*al*] his blood." *Onkelos* and Rashi addressed the relevancy of the covering of the blood and explained that the brothers were concealing the murder. Without criticizing the targumic view, Nachmanides contends that the correct interpretation of the passage is the literal one: murderers kill in secret, bury the victim, and conceal any shed blood by covering it with earth.[49]

30. *Genesis* 38:15 is another instance where the targumist altered his translation to protect the honor of Israelite ancestors, but Nachmanides reads the targumic change as a disparaging statement. The Bible states that Tamar was sitting at a cross road, and that when Judah saw her, he supposed that she was a "harlot." The *Targum* softens the description of this ancestress of King David somewhat by saying "one who goes outside."

    Nachmanides states that when Tamar dressed as a harlot to deceive her father-in-law Judah, she did not cover her face entirely. Harlots sat at the cross roads wrapped in a veil with part of their face, throat, neck, and hair uncovered to entice the passersby. He attempts to prove that his description is correct by referring to a *Mishnah* and our *Targum*.[50] The *Mishnah* states that a head net of a *yotza'at chutz*, literally "she who goes outside," a euphemism for "harlot," is not susceptible to corpse uncleanness since it is not a garment that one lies on, nor is it a full head covering. It is a small garment that covers only part of a face. He argues that since *Onkelos* uses the Aramaic equivalent of *yotza'at chutz*, namely *nafkat bara*, the targumist must be referring to the type of head covering mentioned in the *Mishnah*.

    There is a problem with this reasoning. *Onkelos* uses *nafkat bara* only here and in *Genesis* 34:31 concerning Dinah. The targumist does not utilize the term in other verses where "harlot" is mentioned. Thus it appears that these two are instances where the targumist used the euphemism so as not to disparage

---

49. As in *Exodus* 2:12.
50. *Keilim* 24:16.

Israelite ancestors. Dinah and Tamar were by no means common harlots. Both "went outside," the literal meaning of *nafkat bara*.[51]

31. In *Genesis* 38:18, Tamar requests that Judah give her three objects: Judah's seal, *p'tilekha*, and staff. The middle item has been variously interpreted. For example, Saadiah, Chazkuni, Sforno, and Rashbam have "belt"; Rashi, stating that he is taking his interpretation from *Onkelos's shoshipakh*, "cloak"; and Radak has two ideas, either *Onkelos's shoshipakh* (which he defines as "cloak" in his *Sefer Hashorashim, p-t-l*) or "hat."

Nachmanides states that Rashi is wrong. He insists that *shoshipakh* cannot mean "cloak" since (1) Judah would not leave and wander the streets naked, (2) the Hebrew in verse 25 is in the plural form (would Judah wear two "cloaks"?), (3) how could Judah leave without his cloak which "obviously" had *tzitzit*? He would certainly obey the mitzvah of *tzitzit* of *Numbers* 15:38, and not disparage the *tzitzit* by giving it to a harlot. Therefore, Nachmanides maintains that *Onkelos's shoshipakh* must be a "hat" or a piece of cloth containing an imprint of his seal that he carried with him.

There are two problems with this reasoning. First, the three apparent problems do not make the new interpretation necessary. (1) Judah could have worn an overgarment, such as a coat, above his regular clothes, and he gave Tamar this cloak. (2) The plural form in verse 25 is a larger problem than what Nachmanides recognized. How could Judah give a single garment in verse 18 that turns into more than one in verse 25? *Onkelos* resolves the difficulty by rendering verse 25 in the singular. Thus there is no tense inconsistency in the *Targum*. (3) In regard to Nachmanides' question about the observance of the command of *tzitzit*, Judah either did not anachronistically observe the later Mosaic law of *tzitzit* or he wore a cloak that did not have four square corners, and therefore, was not required to have *tzitzit* on the garment.

Second, and even more importantly, *shoshipakh* means "cloak" as recognized not only by Rashi, but also Radak. Furthermore, it is used in this sense in *Targum Onkelos to Deuteronomy* 22:17 and *Targum Jonathan to Isaiah* 3:22.[52]

---

51. Dinah went out in *Genesis* 34:1.
52. Nachmanides notes these verses but attempts to explain that they refer to small scarves. Jastrow, *Dictionary*, 1543, also defines *shoshipakh* as a cloak that was also used as a bed-sheet. He

Bachya ben Asher mentions Nachmanides' interpretation, but does not ascribe it to the *Targum*.

32. *Genesis* 40:10 narrates the disturbing dream that the cup-bearer told Joseph. He saw a vine with three branches and "and when it budded, it brought forth sprouts, its clusters ripened into grapes." *Onkelos* adds "sprouting flowers" just after "brought forth sprouts," to clarify the phrase.[53] The vine began to sprout, the sprouts blossomed into flowers, and then ripened into grapes.[54]

Nachmanides, however, states that the targumic addition, in his view, was added to explain that this was not a gradual growth, but that as soon as the vine budded, it immediately brought forth large sprouts, its blossoms shot up, and its clusters ripened into grapes. The problem with this interpretation is that the targumic supplement "sprouting flowers" does not imply speed, as Nachmanides suggests. This was apparently recognized by Bachya ben Asher who interprets the passage like Nachmanides, but does not ascribe this view to the *Targum*.

33. *Genesis* 41:47 states, "The earth produced [grain] during the seven years of plenty *likmatzim*." *Onkelos* recasts the entire verse and renders it, "The inhabitants of the land gathered grain for the granaries [of Egypt] during the seven years of plenty [so that food would be available in the future predicted seven years of famine]."

Rashi and all other biblical commentators define *likmatzim* as "handfuls," while, as we indicated, in the *Onkelos* paraphrase *likmatzim* became "granaries."

Nachmanides supposes that the biblical *likmatzim* is not Hebrew, but Aramaic, and means "pits" and assumes that the pits were used as granaries. He states that this meaning of *likmatzim* prompted the targumic paraphrase.[55] It

---

does not agree with Nachmanides that it was a small garment. Sokoloff, *Dictionary*, 543, also defines it as a cloak.

53. This is a virtual quote from the Hebrew and Aramaic of *Numbers* 17:23, and the *Targum* is simply quoting *Numbers*, which explains the occurrence more explicitly.

54. As stated in *Numbers* 17:23. However, it is also possible that this is a conflation of two targumic interpretations of the Hebrew *altah*.

55. *Targum Jonathan* to *II Samuel* 17:9; 18:17; *Isaiah* 24:17, 18; *Jeremiah* 48:43, 44. The Babylonian Talmud, *Berakhot* 3b, also relates *kumtza* to pit. The *Targums Neophyti* and *Pseudo-Jonathan* to 41:47 also render "granaries."

is more likely that the targumist understood *likmatzim* in its Hebrew sense of "handfuls," as defined by most commentators, and saw it as a figure of speech for the "plenty" (that is, the grain) that Joseph stored in the granaries. Bachya ben Asher understands the passage like Nachmanides, but does not attribute this view to the *Targum*.

34. In his commentary to *Genesis* 41:48, Nachmanides distinguishes *ochel*, "food," from *bar*, "grain," in 41:35 and other verses,[56] and observes that *Onkelos* translates both words the same.

If Nachmanides is simply stating that *Onkelos* renders both words alike, he is of course correct. He is also correct, that *bar* means "grain" or "seed," as ibn Ezra also points out. However, it would be incorrect to state that our targumist saw no difference between the meanings of the two terms. *Onkelos* is characteristically clarifying the text by rendering a general biblical term (in this case "food") by what it specifically intends in the context of the narrative ("the stored grain"). Additionally, Nachmanides misses that *Onkelos* also renders *shever*, "food for sale," as "grain" for the same reason.[57] Thus this may be another instance where Nachmanides fails to recognize a targumic technique.

35. Rashi defines the biblical *amtachato* in *Genesis* 42:27 as "his sack," while *Onkelos* has *toanei*, which could mean "his sack," "bag," "load" or "the object into which the load is placed."[58] The targumist did not use the Aramaic *sackei*, "his sack," because it is his characteristic methodology not to repeat words,[59] and *sackei* is already used in the verse to translate the Hebrew *sako*.

Nachmanides fails to notice this customary technique where the targumist is simply using a synonym for "sack" and is rendering the biblical verse literally. Nachmanides reads more into the targumic rendering than is warranted: "It seems from his [*Onkelos*'s] opinion that each [of Jacob's sons] had a large sack and smaller ones to equalize their loads, and the total load was called *amtachat*."

---

56. This occurs three times in verse 35, once in 36, three times in 48, and once in 49.
57. See 42:7 and 43:2 where *Onkelos* renders *shever* as "grain."
58. The Bible uses a form of *amtachat* fifteen times in this episode and nowhere else in Scripture. The Hebrew word is related to the Assyrian *matachu*, "to bear," to carry," or to lift up."
59. When the Bible repeats words, *Onkelos* will generally find a synonym for the second one.

36. The Hebrew word *bi*, in *Genesis* 43:20 and other verses such as 44:18, is probably an expression of entreaty and supplication as stated by Rashi. However, Nachmanides defines it as "by myself." Rather than allowing *Onkelos*'s "please" to contradict him, he maintains, without any support that the targumist is not defining *bi* but is merely rendering it in accordance with its context.
37. Nachmanides cites Maimonides' view that *Onkelos* generally avoids portraying God anthropomorphically,[60] that is having corporeal aspects.[61] He notes that Maimonides recognizes that the *Targum* fails to deviate in *Genesis* 46:1 and renders Scripture's "I [God] will go down with you [Jacob] into Egypt, and I will surely bring you up again" literally.[62] He also notes that Maimonides explains that while the targumist generally avoids anthropomorphic depictions of God, there was no need for a deviation in chapter 46 since verse 2 states explicitly that this was a dream, and the masses, reading the literal Aramaic, would recognize that a person could have all kinds of impossible notions expressed in their dreams, and would not be misled to think that God is corporeal.

    Nachmanides disagreed and insisted that *Onkelos* does not evade anthropomorphisms. He cites nineteen verses where the *Targum* appears to change the biblical text to avoid anthropomorphisms, but states that actually there are other reasons that prompted the targumist to paraphrase the scriptural words. He insists that *Onkelos* does not make even a single alteration of the biblical wording in the translation to avoid portraying God in a corporeal manner. For if so, why are changes absent when God is "saying," "speaking," or "calling." These expressions certainly signify corporeality; a person cannot "speak" without a mouth. He cites fifteen examples where the *Targum* does not change anthropomorphic texts. He also mentions seven examples where *memra*, "word" or "wisdom," is added by the targumist when, in his opinion, there is no fear or apprehension of corporeality in a biblical wording, such

---

60. Maimonides, *Guide of the Perplexed*, 1:21, 27, 28, 48, 64, 65, 66, etc.
61. *Targums Pseudo-Jonathan* and *Neophyti* deviate even more frequently than *Onkelos* to avoid portraying God corporeally.
62. *Targum Pseudo-Jonathan* resolves the anthropomorphic problem somewhat by having the *memra*, "word" or "wisdom," perform the first activity, "go down," while *Neophyti* uses *memra* for the second, "bring you up."

as "between me and you" being rendered as "between my *memra* and you."[63] He states that these seven instances and many like them were added by the targumist to teach a mystical lesson "and their secret meaning is known to the learned students [of the mystic lore of the Torah]."[64]

"It is not only *memra*," he continues, but "all these subjects,[65] [some of which are rendered literally and some of which are paraphrased, are not influenced by a fear of using terms denoting corporeality but rather by secrets] of the *Kabbalah* known to *Onkelos* and Jonathan ben Uziel,[66] and the secrets thereof are revealed to those who know the mystic lore of the Torah."[67]

Nachmanides concludes by giving us his reason why *Onkelos* did not change the text of 46:1. It teaches the rabbinic lesson contained in *Mekhilta Shira* 3 and the Babylonian Talmud, *Megillah* 29a that God's *Shekhinah*, "presence," will accompany the Israelites into exile.

There are about a half dozen problems with Nachmanides' analysis.

First, Nachmanides cites only nineteen times where our *Targum* changes the biblical wording to show a more respectful concept of God and not portray the divine in a corporeal manner. By using this small number, he minimizes the phenomenon. He does not seem to know that there are actually 1,650 such instances in the *Onkelos* translation of the Pentateuch. Surely even he would recognize that all 1,650 passages were not changed in the Aramaic translation to teach *Kabbalah*.

Second, the targumist obviously felt that he could not change every expression signifying corporeality, such as "saying," "speaking," "seeing," and "calling." Nachmanides claims that if the targumist had an agenda to remove anthropomorphisms, he should have removed all of them. Actually, had the translator removed every anthropomorphic statement, the above-stated number would be more than quadrupled and the translation would no longer be recognized as the Bible. The translator treated anthropomorphisms as he treated

---

63. *Genesis* 9:12.
64. Chavel, *Ramban, Commentary on the Torah, Genesis*, 549.
65. I.e., all the deviations which Maimonides and others state are for the honor of God and to avoid anthropomorphisms.
66. The translator to the Prophets.
67. Chavel, *Ramban, Commentary on the Torah, Genesis*, 551 and 552.

metaphors that he changed to assure that his readers would understand the text. He explains hundreds of metaphors, but not all of them. A line had to be drawn to maintain the integrity of the document. The drawing of this line is subjective and there were others who felt that the targumist acted improperly by not changing the text. Indeed, *Pseudo-Jonathan* and *Neophyti* have many more such deviations than *Onkelos*. In any event, this failure to remove every anthropomorphic statement does not in itself prove that he did not remove 1,650 of them.

Third, *memra*, meaning "word" or "wisdom," was not inserted into any of the *Targums* to teach mystical lessons. It was added, as Maimonides and others stated, to preclude a depiction of the deity acting like a human and an inappropriately close connection between humans and God. Thus it is God's "wisdom" that accomplishes a certain act, and not God Himself. If *memra* taught a mystical lesson, each of the 188 times that *Onkelos* introduced it, why did the *Fragmented Targums*, *Pseudo-Jonathan*, and *Neophyti* use the term more frequently than *Onkelos*? Did they have a deeper and more perceptive understanding of *Kabbalah* than the *Onkelos* targumist? Nachmanides, who believed *Onkelos* was holy and true, would never accept this disparagement of this *Targum*.

Fourth, his naked statement that the 1,650 targumic changes of the biblical text were not influenced by a desire to avoid depicting God in a corporeal manner and that they teach the secrets of mystic lore, does not, in and of itself, prove anything. He does not overcome the consistency of when and how the changes are made and does not reveal the supposed secrets of *Kabbalah*.[68]

Fifth, Nachmanides claims that *Onkelos* does not have deviations to avoid anthropomorphisms. Therefore, he should have answered Maimonides: "there is no deviation here because there is no need for one. *Onkelos* does not replace anthropomorphisms." Curiously, by seeking a better answer than the one given by Maimonides, Nachmanides seems to forget his own position that there is no need for a change in the translation of *Genesis* 46:1.

Finally, and most significantly, the reason he gives is problematical. It does not appear logical to state that *Onkelos* renders 46:1 literally to teach that the

---

68. The consistency can be seen clearly in the author's various *Onkelos* commentaries.

Shekhinah accompanied the Israelites into exile. The contrary is true. If the targumist wanted to inform his readers that the *Shekhinah* accompanied the Israelites, he should have added the noun *Shekhinah* in the translation: "My *Shekhinah* will go down with you."[69] The fact that the *Targum* is literal, that it left out the noun *Shekhinah*, seems to say just the opposite of what Nachmanides proposes to read into the sentence. By learning out "*Shekhinah*" from the Aramaic rendering, it certainly seems that the *Onkelos* translator did not intend to let the readers think that the *Shekhinah* accompanied Jacob into Egypt.

Nachmanides' argument – his refusal to acknowledge that the respected Aramaic translation of *Onkelos* avoids anthropomorphisms – only makes sense if we understand that he was convinced that God is corporeal and that the *Shekhinah* is a part of God. Thus, he was arguing that *Onkelos* did not deviate in 46:1 because the translator wanted to tell us that the *Shekhinah* physically traveled to Egypt with Jacob.[70]

Nachmanides wanted the *Targum*, which he felt was sacred, to support his view. The twelfth-century talmudist Rabad of Posquieres, Nachmanides' contemporary, at the beginning of his critique of Maimonides' *Sefer Hamitzvot*, wrote that there are many wise Jews who believe in a corporeal deity. Thus if Nachmanides were one of them, he would not be unique.

There are quite a few Nachmanidean statements that appear to suggest that he believed in a corporeal God who appeared to and was seen by humans.

Nachmanides, like Rabad, disagreed with many ideas presented by Maimonides in his *Sefer Hamitzvot*. Commenting upon Maimonides' first positive command, he writes that we know about the biblical commands because "the *Shekhinah* was revealed to our eyes."[71]

What is the *Shekhinah* that "was revealed to our eyes" as Nachmanides stated?

The term *Shekhinah* was introduced around the beginning of the Common Era about 2000 years ago. It literally means "dwelling." *Onkelos* uses the noun in a very restrictive manner to paraphrase some biblical Hebrew words with

---

69. *Shekhinah* is added forty-nine times by *Targum Onkelos* in the pentateuchal translation.
70. Thus when the verse says that God went with Jacob to Egypt, the verse should be understood literally that either God himself or his *Shekhinah* accompanied Jacob.
71. Chavel, *Sefer Hamitzvot La'Rambam im Hasagot haRamban*, 152.

anthropomorphic implications, but only to describe the feeling of the divine presence either on earth or in heaven. The *Onkelos* targumist, unlike the other later Aramaic translators, was thus careful to depict the *Shekhinah* "as a mental state,"[72] a human feeling or thought process, and not a separate physical entity performing tasks such as traveling with the Israelites.

The Talmuds and *Midrashim* extended the description and activities of the *Shekhinah* to indicate a divine presence at a particular place or upon a certain individual or group, even though God existed at the same time throughout the world.

Some Jewish philosophers were more careful. They evaded the possible anthropomorphic and polytheistic implications of the concept by stating that it was an independent entity, created by and separate from God.[73] Others suggested that it was a prophetic mental experience,[74] a human feeling of "divine glory," "divine influence or inspiration,"[75] or simply a metaphor.[76]

However, kabbalistic literature, in the 12th and 13th centuries, saw the *Shekhinah* as the tenth, the lowest level of the *sefirot*, the feminine aspect of God.[77] Unlike the philosophers, these mystics did not oppose anthropomorphisms, strict monotheism, and the concept of an unseeable God.[78]

Nachmanides, as we will see, fell into the latter group: "the essence of God as manifested in a distinct form."[79]

In *Genesis* 46:1, he states that the term *Shekhinah* is not a human feeling or intuition that God is present, but that the term "is identical with God." Thus, he wrote that when *Mekhilta Shira* 3 and the Babylonian Talmud *Megillah* 29a state, "when [the Israelites] were exiled in Egypt, the *Shekhinah* went with

---

72. Maimonides, *Guide of the Perplexed*, 1:21.
73. Saadiah ben Joseph al-Fayyumi, (Saadiah Gaon), *Book of Beliefs and Opinions*, ed. D. Sluzki. Leipzig, 1864. Trans. S. Rosenblatt. (New Haven: Yale University Press, 1948), 2:10
74. Maimonides, *Guide of the Perplexed*.
75. Judah Halevi, *Kuzari* 2:20
76. Hermann Cohen, *Religion der Vernunft aus den Quellen des Judentums* (Weisbaden: Fourier 1978), 53.
77. Martin Buber, *On Judaism* (New York: Schocken Books, 1967), 6 and 27.
78. Babylonian Talmud, *Hagigah* 5b.
79. Siegmund Maybaum, *Die Anthropomorphism und Anthropopathien bei Onkelos und spateren Targumim* (Breslau 1870), 51–54.

them," he is suggesting that God literally traveled to Egypt. He claimed as we saw that *Onkelos* had to render this verse literally, "I [meaning, God] will go down with you to Egypt," because God literally accompanied Jacob and his family to Egypt.

In *Exodus* 19:19, and 20, to cite another example, Nachmanides contends that God "came down upon Mount Sinai and He was there in fire." Moses did not go up to heaven to communicate with God, but up to Mount Sinai where God had descended.

In *Exodus* 24:10, Nachmanides understands Scripture's, "They saw the God of Israel" literally. He contends that *Onkelos* shared his view. "He translated and they saw the glory of the God of Israel, but did not render it, 'and the glory of God revealed itself to them,' as is his way of translating in other places." Nachmanides is suggesting that the targumist is stating that they saw God.[80]

In *Exodus* 30:13, he informs us that God's language is Hebrew: *hu halashon shehakadosh barukh hu yitbarakh shemo medaber bo*, "this is the language that [God] speaks." He does not state that God communicates in Hebrew by creating a voice that people hear, but contends that God speaks Hebrew. This, as he admitted, is an anthropomorphism.[81]

Most remarkable is his commentary on *Genesis* 3:8. Nachmanides rejects the view in *Genesis Rabbah,* ibn Ezra and Maimonides (*Guide of the Perplexed* 1:24) that it is the voice of God that is figuratively "walking" in Gan Eden. He states that it is *gilui Shekhinah b'makam hahu oh histalkuto min hamakom sheniglah bo*, "the appearance of the *Shekhinah* in that place [not a revelation] or the departure to from the place where it had appeared." He also states that generally the appearance of the *Shekhinah* is accompanied with "a great and strong wind." However, in this instance God revealed his *Shekhinah*, which Nachmanides stated in 46:1, "is identical with God, in conditions like the wind of ordinary days, so they [Adam and Eve] would not be frightened [by the divine appearance]."

In his commentary to the Torah on this verse, Bachya ben Asher admits

---

80. Actually, contrary to Nachmanides' understanding, the targumist deviated to avoid this anthropomorphic notion; they saw only the "glory," i.e., they had a vision or a sense or feeling of God's presence, but did not see the deity.
81. See his argument against Maimonides at the start of this section.

that the plain meaning of "I will go down to Egypt with you" is "an assurance by God that He will be with Jacob during his descent into Egypt." Like Nachmanides, he argues that the "kabbalistic approach" to the verse is that the *Shekhinah* will accompany Jacob when he goes to Egypt. He states that *Onkelos* "hints at this" by not using "I will be revealed" and retains the physical anthropomorphism. He concludes, *"This is especially remarkable considering the care that Onkelos takes to avoid using anthropomorphic terms for God and His activities"* (emphasis added). Thus, we see two significant things: (1) Like Nachmanides, Bachya felt that the *Shekhinah* is a physical being since he said that this is why *Onkelos* retained the physical description to hint at the *Shekhinah*. (2) Bachya disagreed with Nachmanides' basic argument in this commentary that *Onkelos* does not avoid anthropomorphisms. Further proofs that Bachya understood the *Shekhinah* to be a physical being is his comment on *Genesis* 18:2 where he states, "when [the Bible says that] Abraham saw the three angels [approaching him] he ran to them, [it means that] he was actually running after the *Shekhinah* to welcome it [to his dwelling]." Also, in his commentary to *Genesis* 19:24, he states that the reason why Lot's family were told not to turn around and look at the destruction of the city of Sodom was because if they turned they would see the *Shekhinah* and "this would be fatal.... Lot's wife felt compassion for her married daughters who remained [in Sodom] and this is what caused her to turn around. She wanted to see if her daughters were following them. She saw the *Shekhinah* instead and turned into a pillar of salt."

38. Nachmanides differs with Rashi in interpreting *Genesis* 48:6. Rashi states that Joshua divided Canaan among the conquering Israelites by population; i.e., each person received an equal share. Nachmanides declared that the land was divided by tribes, with each tribe receiving the same amount of land, no matter their population. The only exception was Ephraim and Menasheh, the sons of Joseph, who were given a full share each. This represented the double portion of the first-born granted to Joseph by his father Jacob.[82]

Nachmanides presents several proofs for his position. He includes as proof the words of *Onkelos* to *Genesis* 49:22, "they shall receive *chulka v'achsanta* [a portion and inheritance]" and claims that *chulka* denotes the extra share of

---

82. See the Babylonian Talmud, *Horayoth* 6b and *Bava Batra* 121b, 123a.

the first-born and *v'achsanta* the ordinary inheritance. A dispassionate reader, with a dictionary in hand, would not see this meaning in these words. This is especially so when one recognizes that Nachmanides apparently overlooked the fact that the two Aramaic words are an exact Aramaic equivalent of the frequently repeated biblical *chelek v'nachalah*, which is a phrase that denotes a single portion.[83] Bachya mentions Nachmanides' interpretation of *Onkelos* and agrees with it. This is the second and last time, of fifteen parallel interpretations in *Genesis*, that Bachya agrees with Nachmanides.

39. In *Genesis* 48:15, Nachmanides attempts to prove from *Onkelos* to 48:6 that although Scripture is silent on the subject, Joseph had sons after he received Jacob's death-bed blessing. The Bible has Jacob say, "and the children that were born to you," in the past tense, while the *Targum* changes the words to "that will be born to you," in the future.

Actually, the tense change does not prove Nachmanides' point because the *Targum* is only explaining the obvious scriptural intent. Jacob is clearly saying, *if* you have additional sons in the future they will receive part of Menasheh and Ephraim's share, but not an additional portion. Secondly, the future is the only logical interpretation of the passage, because If Joseph had children beside Menasheh and Ephraim, why is there nothing in the Bible to indicate why these two sons of Joseph merited more than any of their brothers. Thirdly, there is nothing surprising in the fact that the past tense is used; the Bible frequently uses the past tense when the future tense is meant and virtually all the ancient biblical commentators understand this verse as just another example of this fact of biblical grammar.[84] Finally, *Onkelos* usually makes such changes for the sake of clarifying passages, and for no other reason. Thus, the change in the *Targum* cannot be used to prove whether Joseph had additional sons.[85]

40. The patriarch Jacob blessed the tribe of Gad on his death bed in *Genesis* 49:19 with the words *gad gadud y'gudenu*. Biblical commentators disagree whether

---

83. For example, *Genesis* 31:14, *Deuteronomy* 10:9, 12:12, 14:27, 14:29, 18:1, etc.
84. For example, Saadiah, Rashi, Rashbam, ibn Ezra, Chazkuni, Radak, etc.
85. For example, in *Numbers* alone, there are 296 instances where *Onkelos* changes the number or tense, such as singular to plural, plural to singular, active to passive, present to future, future to present, verb to noun, etc. See Rabbi Dr. Israel Drazin, *Targum Onkelos to Numbers* (New York: Ktav, 1998), 37–39.

he was saying, "Raiders will raid Gad" or "Gad will raid." Is the tribe being raided or are they the ones who are raiding.[86]

Onkelos gives Gad the active favorable role: "From the house of Gad armed hosts will cross the Jordan before their brethren to do battle," referring to the role played by the tribes of Gad, Reuben and half the tribe of Menasheh in proceeding the remaining tribes in the Israelite conquest of Canaan.[87]

Nachmanides disagrees with *Onkelos* and states that the correct interpretation, found in the Jerusalem Talmud,[88] is that foreign bands will assail the tribe of Gad, but the tribe will ultimately defeat them.[89] It is possible that the targumist read the biblical text as Nachmanides but decided to paraphrase the text to predict a better future for the tribe. The verse as written in Scripture suggests a long period of border warfare and insecurity only relieved by a late victory. *Onkelos* frequently deviates from the biblical wording to change or elevate seemingly disparaging comments about Israelite ancestors.[90] Thus Nachmanides apparently failed to understand the targumic style.

---

86. Radak, ibn Ezra and others take the first passive position, while Rashi, Rashbam, Chazkuni, *Pseudo-Jonathan*, *Neophyti* and others prefer the second active role.
87. *Numbers* 32:16–32, *Deuteronomy* 3:18ff, *Joshua* 1:12ff; 4:12f.
88. Jerusalem Talmud, *Sotah* 8:10.
89. The second half of the verse states: "but he will troop upon (their) heel."
90. For example, there are thirty-three such instances in the book of *Numbers*. See Drazin, *Targum Onkelos to Numbers*, 56–58. See Drazin, *Targumic Studies*, 35–76, for a listing of such changes in *Genesis*.

– CHAPTER 10 –

Exodus

> Nachmanides refers to *Onkelos* sixty times in his commentary to *Exodus*. Thirty-four, about fifty-eight percent of these comments are problematical. Of the remaining twenty-six, he simply mentions the *Targum* fifteen times without comment, and he explains *Onkelos* in a reasonable manner in eleven instances. In seventeen of the thirty-four comments that are problematical, Nachmanides appears to read more into an Aramaic word than its definition.

NACHMANIDES DISCOVERS MYSTICISM IN ONKELOS

Nachmanides finds a mystical teaching six times in the *Targum* that the words themselves do not indicate. He does not seem to notice that the targumist is following his usual translation methodology and seeks interpretations that do not seem to be supportable by the plain meaning of the Aramaic words in fourteen verses, including three times that the targumist is avoiding anthropomorphisms.

As stated previously, Bachya ben Asher apparently disagreed with the problematical interpretations of *Targum Onkelos*. In *Exodus*, he quotes such an Nachmanidean reading five times out of the thirty-four that are problematical, or under fifteen percent.

THE THIRTY-FOUR PROBLEMATICAL NACHMANIDES INTERPRETATIONS IN EXODUS

1. Nachmanides had an *Onkelos* text that translates *Exodus*'s 3:14 *Eheyeh Asher Eheyeh* as God's statement to Moses, "I will be with him that I will be *Eheyeh*."

    Nachmanides understands that the targumist is stating that God's name is *Eheyeh*. There are two problems with this understanding. First, the wording is a scribal error and no conclusion should have been drawn from the mistake.

The generally accepted *Targum* texts retain the Hebrew for all three words in the Aramaic translation,[1] most likely because the targumist considered all three words as God's name or because the three words were a well-known and widely discussed Hebrew phrase that did not require translation.[2]

Second, and more significantly, even If Nachmanides' *Targum* text is correct, the words "I will be" in "I will be with him that I will be *Eheyeh*" does not clearly mean: "Moses, my name is *Eheyeh*."[3]

2. Nachmanides cites *Onkelos*'s reading of *Exodus*'s 5:4 figure of speech *taphri'u* – Pharaoh asks Moses and Aaron "do you [want to] cause the people to *taphri'u* from their work" – as "rest," as proof that Rashi's definition "separate" is incorrect.[4]

    Actually, Rashi is defining the word, while the targumist is paraphrasing it. *Siftei Chachamin* explains that the *Targum* chose not to use the literal "separate" (the true meaning of *taphri'u*, as Rashi correctly defines it) because "separate" is inappropriate; Moses and Aaron had not yet been instructed by God to "separate" the Israelites away from their work, and they did not do so. Thus, the *Onkelos* translator chose to use another word in his translation and no one should attempt to prove the definition of *taphri'u* from his paraphrase.[5]

3. *Exodus* 12:6 relates God's command that the Israelites should take a sheep and "kill it *bein ha'arbayim*."

    Nachmanides explains *bein ha'arbayim*, literally "between the evenings" – a two word expression denoting the single idea of "eventide" or "dusk" – as the time between the two afternoons.[6] He also attempts to read the rabbinic *halakhah* into the two biblical words and contends that the Hebrew plural

---

1. Berliner and Sperber.
2. See the Babylonian Talmud *Berakhot* 9b. *Neophyti*, *Peshitta*, and the *Samaritan Targum*s also retain the Hebrew. *Pseudo-Jonathan* paraphrases: "the one who spoke and the world came into being, spoke and all was."
3. Bachya ben Asher mentions Nachmanides several times in his interpretation of this verse, but does not mention anything about Nachmanides' view of *Onkelos*.
4. By relying on *Onkelos* for the correct definition, Nachmanides shows again his respect for the correctness of the translation.
5. The *Targum* also uses the word in verses 5, 8, 9, 17 and 32:25.
6. *Bein ha'arbayim* appears in *Exodus* 12:6; 16:12; 29:39, 41; 30:8; *Leviticus* 23:5; *Numbers* 9:3, 5, 11; 28:4, 8.

form (the ending *im*) refers to the greater and smaller afternoons.⁷ One is "the time from six-and-a-half hours after the beginning of the day" and the other "from nine-and-a-half hours after the start of the day until sunset."⁸ He understands the Torah's *bein*, "between," as "within (the three hours between six and a half and nine and a half)."⁹ He argues that *Onkelos's bein shimshaya*, literally "between the suns" – which is also an expression in the plural denoting "eventide" or "dusk" – reflects his interpretation. The time, he writes, is between "when the sun is in the east and [when] the sun is in the west."

The problem with his interpretation is that *Onkelos's* plural form is simply a literal rendering of the biblical plural and is, therefore, clearly not written to denote a law, *halakhah*. Second, at six-and-a-half hours after the beginning of the day, the sun is not in the east, as Nachmanides contends; it has already begun its descent in the west. Third, the *Targum's* "between the suns" is not the same as "between the afternoons," as Nachmanides states, and "suns" does not even suggest "afternoons." Finally, the targumic words are nothing more than an Aramaic expression denoting "dusk" and are understood as such in *Midrashim* and Talmuds.¹⁰ In fact, both the Hebrew and Aramaic expressions are common folk language for the short period prior to the night, several hours after the time mentioned by Nachmanides. It is therefore quite clear that *Onkelos* was translating the Hebrew literally and did not intend to reflect the *halakhah*.¹¹

4. *Onkelos*, as stated frequently, generally translates the biblical Hebrew literally into its Aramaic equivalent. This occurs in *Exodus* 14:10 when the frightened Israelites saw their Egyptian pursuers and "cried out" to God.

Nachmanides cites this literal *Onkelos* rendering but reads more into the

---

7. Maimonides, *Mishneh Torah, Hilkhot Temedim Umusaphim* 1:3. The issue is when is the pascal lamb sacrificed.
8. Chavel, *Ramban*, 124.
9. Amos Chacham, *Sefer Shemot* (Jerusalem: Mossad Harav Kook, 1991), 183, 184.
10. In the Babylonian Talmud, *Pessachim* 58a, for example, it states "*bein ha'arbayim* starts when the sun begins to set."
11. See Chacham, *Sefer Shemot*, 184, note 10, for various opinions regarding the origin of the presently obscure "between the evenings" and "between the suns." Chacham explains that the short biblical time frame of several minutes was extended to accommodate the large number of Israelites who desired to bring the pascal sacrifice when the tribes settled in the land of Israel. Thus, *bein haarbayim* probably means between two evenings, sunset and dark and *bein shimshaya*, an Aramaic synonym, probably means between the two suns, the sun of the day and the moon of the night.

Aramaic word than is warranted. He uses it to prove his position: the Israelites did not pray to God,[12] but complained loudly. Since *Onkelos* is not interpreting Scripture, it is unreasonable to say that he is doing so.

5. *"Israel saw the great hand, that which God did to Egypt" Exodus 14:31. Onkelos:* "Israel saw the strength of the great hand...."

Nachmanides again attempts to use the *Onkelos* rendering to prove that Rashi is wrong.[13] Rashi explains that the biblical metaphor God's "great hand" signifies that God handled the Egyptians with "great power." "But," Nachmanides objects, "*Onkelos* did not interpret 'great hand' as 'power.'"

Actually the opposite is true. The targumist inserts this very word: "Israel saw the power of the great hand," and thereby softened the apparent anthropomorphism: the Israelites saw the "power" of the hand, but not a divine appendage.[14]

6. Occasionally, commentators of *Targum Onkelos* or scribes copying the text inserted their own words into the original translation, sometimes replacing the targumist's words, and at other times, adding the interpretation that titillated their fancy.[15] This sometimes produced doublets, as in *Exodus* 15:1. The Torah's *ki gaoh gaah*, "for he is highly exalted," is rendered in *Onkelos* as both "He has been exalted above the boastful [Egyptians]" and "Pride is his." The second version is an uncharacteristic targumic rendering because it portrays God as unsuitably prideful, a coarse human trait that our translator generally avoids applying to God.

Nachmanides failed to notice that our *Targum* text is faulty and contains an inappropriate doublet. He thought of God, as we noted,[16] in anthropomorphic and anthropopathic terms and cited the incorrect doublet to prove still again

---

12. As maintained by *Mekhilta d'R. Ishmael* and Rashi to this verse. However, Bachya ben Asher understands "cry" as "prayer."
13. The Babylonian Talmud, *Berakhot* 58a and Saadiah translates like *Onkelos* and Rashi. The metaphor "great hand" is also in *Exodus* 3:20, 6:1, and 7:4.
14. Nachmanides preferred to read a mystical interpretation into the biblical passage, that "hand" refers to the attribute of justice, and, as stated in the discussion of *Genesis* 46:1, he apparently believed in a corporeal deity and did not accept the idea that *Onkelos* avoided anthropomorphic metaphors. Bachya ben Asher agrees with Nachmanides on his interpretation of *Onkelos* on this verse, the first time he does so in *Exodus*.
15. This scribal adulteration occurred to many ancient documents.
16. In the discussion on *Genesis* 46:1.

that Rashi was wrong. Rashi, like the correct targumic language, interpreted *ki gaoh gaah* as: God is lofty and above human praise.

7. Nachmanides wonders why *Onkelos* to *Exodus* 15:18 changed the biblical future tense, "The Lord will reign forever and ever," and paraphrased it and added the present, "The Lord, his kingdom endures in this time and forever." He interprets the biblical verse as an Israelite prayer that God will reign in the future and wonders why the targumist needed to speak about the present time when there was no need for a prayer.

    Nachmanides' difficulty disappears when it is realized that the targumist did not interpret these words as a prayer. The Israelites were viewing God's assistance at the Sea of Reeds and extolled him; they recognized that he is all-powerful and that his earthly rule exists at present and will continue to exist in the future.[17]

8. Nachmanides states that the wonder inherent in the miracle of the manna with which God fed the Israelites in the dessert was extremely great. In fact *Avot* 5:6 states that this was one of the miracles that God prepared during the six days of creation. He supports his view by saying that *Onkelos* rendered *Exodus*'s 16:7, "And in the morning you will *see* the Glory of God" literally.

    One should not attempt to derive an interpretation from a literal rendering. Additionally and more significantly, *Onkelos* usually adds "glory" to the text to avoid anthropomorphisms:[18] the Israelites did not see a corporeal God; they only saw the impact of divine aid: the delivery of the manna showed the "glory of God." Our translator understood "glory" in this way. He did not have to add "glory" in this verse to avoid the anthropomorphism since the Bible has the word. In short, "glory" refers to God, and not the delivery of the manna as Nachmanides contends.[19]

---

17. This interpretation is in Chazkuni. *Onkelos*, as well as the original Hebrew, can also be an acceptance by the Israelites of the yoke of God's worship, Chacham, *Sefer Shemot*, 279. Bachya ben Asher does not mention Nachmanides here, perhaps because he disagrees with him, and offers two other interpretations of *Onkelos*'s present tense, both of which are mystical.
18. For example, "glory" is added ten times in the Aramaic translation of *Exodus*.
19. Bachya ben Asher does not mention Nachmanides to this verse. He recognizes that "glory" refers to God and not the manna, as Nachmanides contends. In accordance with his mystical bend, he interprets "glory" as God's "attribute of justice."

9. Targumic scholars differ as to whether the *Onkelos* translator included doublets – that is, two different alternative translations – or whether one of the doublets is a later addition.[20] Occasionally, there are instances where commentators differ as to whether a particular targumic rendering is a doublet at all. Frequently, the first question can be resolved when one recognizes that one of the two renderings does not fit in with the targumic methodology.

    In his Commentary to *Exodus* 16:14, Nachmanides states that *Onkelos* translates many biblical texts in two different ways. See item 6 above.

10. Nachmanides turned to *Onkelos* to prove the correctness of his interpretation in his commentary to *Exodus* 16:23. Rashi states that the Torah's "bake that which you will bake" means "what you want to bake in the oven bake today, [bake] all for two days."[21] Moses is advising the Israelites on Friday to bake for Friday and the Sabbath. Rashi's view of the verse is in contrast to Abraham ibn Ezra who states that Moses only told the Israelites to bake Friday's meal. They ate manna on the Sabbath raw.

    Nachmanides argues that when *Onkelos* added the single word *athidin*, "intending,"[22] he was reflecting his and Rashi's view. *Onkelos* has "bake what you are intending to bake."

    Actually, this single word supports neither side. *Onkelos* adds "intending," which is implied, to help enhance the clarity of the sentence. However, the word does not illuminate the ambiguity involved in the Rashi–ibn Ezra positions. It could even support ibn Ezra: "bake what you are intending to bake, meaning the Friday food that you are accustomed to prepare, but not the extra measure for the Sabbath since you are not accustomed to prepare the manna for the following day."

11. Jethro advises Moses to appoint judges to relieve him of judicial duties that are interfering with his other tasks. Among other things, Jethro suggests in *Exodus* 18:21 that the candidates should hate *vetza*. The Hebrew word denotes "profit" or "money." *Onkelos* defines it as money, rather than profit, because of

---

20. There are about a half dozen doublets in *Exodus*.
21. Unnoticed by Nachmanides, this is also the interpretation of Saadiah and others.
22. The word means "preparing" in *Esther* 3:14.

the context of the verse "[hate] to receive money," using the exact words in *Mekhilta d'R. Ishmael* 183:63.

Nachmanides reads more into this literal Aramaic translation than is warranted. He argues that *vetza* does not mean a money bribe, but a gift or loan of money to prompt a favorable decision. Needless to say, the Aramaic, like the Hebrew, is ambiguous. "Money" does not preclude a bribe and does not necessitate the interpretation of a gift or loan.[23]

12. Our targumist, as we said frequently, generally recoils from ascribing human attributes to God, such as God clenching the Israelites and bringing them into the divine presence as stated in *Exodus* 19:4, "I [God] brought you in to me." He alters the text and has them only "brought near," not to God but "to my service."

Nachmanides believed that our targumist did not change his translation to remove anthropomorphisms.[24] Thus he apparently felt he had to insist that the Aramaic changed wording is simply "an expression of respect" to God. But, he does not explain how the Aramaic words show greater respect than the Hebrew and why bringing the Israelites to the divine service rather than to God enhances respect for the deity.

13. The *Onkelos* targumist translates *Exodus* 20:3 literally: "You shall have no other god [before My face]." Adler explains that the targumist could not substitute *elohim*, "god," with "idol," as he usually does, because the reader might think that idols exist and God is comparable to them.[25]

Although there is no hint of it in the *Targum*'s literal rendering, Nachmanides maintains that *Onkelos* is teaching a prohibition against worshipping angels or any heavenly entities that are also called *elohim*, "gods." Bachya ben Asher mentions Nachmanides in his commentary and agrees with him in how he defines *elohim*, but does not ascribe this view to *Onkelos*.

14. *Onkelos* characteristically changes the end of *Exodus* 20:3 "before My face" to "besides Me" to avoid the anthropomorphic portrayal of God having a face.

Nachmanides, as pointed out frequently, maintains that *Onkelos* does not

---

23. Nachmanides' interpretation may be the result of his thinking that the rule against taking a bribe is already explicitly forbidden by the Torah in *Exodus* 23:8. However, he does not state how Jethro knew this later biblical command.
24. See our commentary to *Onkelos on the Torah – Genesis*, 46:1.
25. Adler, *Netina La'ger*.

avoid anthropomorphisms. Accordingly, he explains the targumic change by referring to his Commentary of *Exodus* 19:20. He asserts that "besides me" is reflecting a teaching of the *Kabbalah*: "Do not worship *elohim acheirim* [other gods], since they were all created, excepting God, who is eternal and has not been created by any being."[26] Needless to say, this is not apparent in *Onkelos*'s characteristic rendering. Again, Bachya ben Asher mentions Nachmanides, agrees with him, but does not read the interpretation in *Onkelos*.

15. *Onkelos* paraphrases the anthropomorphic Israelites' fear of God in *Exodus* 20:16, "but let not God speak with us [lest we die]" with "do not let it be spoken with us from before the Lord [lest we die]." The targumic change removes the unacceptable notion that God has human organs that he can use to speak and that God would appear to the Israelites and talk to them. The alteration, being passive, suggests that some voice unconnected to the deity is speaking.

Nachmanides, as usual, accepts the anthropomorphic depiction literally and even elaborates it. He imagines that God descended from heaven to Mount Sinai and dwelt there for a period of time to speak to Moses. When the people expressed their dread of hearing God speak with them as with Moses, "but let not God speak with us," they were clearly stating, according to Nachmanides, that they were able to hear and understand the divine commands at the same level as Moses, but were afraid to do so. Accordingly, says Nachmanides, to protect Moses from this depiction of the Israelites outrageously claiming they were as wise and pious as Moses, our targumist separated the people from God in his translation by using the passive form.[27]

Actually, the targumist does not state or suggest that God descended and resided on Mount Sinai, as Nachmanides contends, and the targumic change was made to avoid the anthropomorphic depiction that he enlarged.

16. Scholars differ as to what *Onkelos*'s rendering of *Exodus*'s 21:18 *b'egrof*, "fist," as *bekhurmeiza* means. Rashbam, Nachmanides and others interpret *Onkelos* as "clod of earth," but Jastrow, *Mini Targuma* and others state it is a literal rendering

---

26. Chavel, *Ramban*, 291, N. 299. Compare Nachmanides' comment on 22:19.
27. Nachmanides mentions and criticizes Maimonides' interpretation of *Onkelos*'s rendering of this verse. However, Nachmanides' version of Maimonides is incorrect. See, for example, Chavel's note to this verse in his Hebrew edition. Bachya ben Asher interprets that the Israelites were miraculously elevated to the level of prophecy attained by Moses, but nevertheless Moses could approach closer to God. He does not mention Nachmanides or *Onkelos*.

"fist." The latter are probably correct since *Onkelos* generally translates the Hebrew literally, the word is used in this sense in the *Targum* to *Isaiah* 58:4 and *Midrash Psalms* 22:6, the *Targums Neophyti* and *Pseudo-Jonathan* have "fist," and the *Midrash Mekhilta*,[28] from whom *Onkelos* frequently borrows its translation, also has "fist."[29]

17. *Exodus* 21:22 rules that if a man strikes a pregnant woman and kills her child but not the woman, the assailant must pay "as much as the woman's husband determines." Nachmanides notes that rabbinical law understands that the adjudication is made by judges, not the woman's husband, and he wonders why *Onkelos* translates literally contrary to rabbinical law.

    Nachmanides fails to notice that all three of the Aramaic *Targumim* render the phrase literally because of how they understand the next statement about *pelilim*, which they interpret as "judges." They render it: "He should pay it by verdict of the judges." As we pointed out, our targumist derived his interpretations from the tannaitic *Midrashim*. In this instance, *Mekhilta d'R. Ishmael* 66:52 states: "I might think this [phrase] to mean, whatever he [the husband] pleases; Scripture therefore says, 'and he shall pay as the *pelilim* decide,' and *pelilim* always means 'judges.'"

18. *Exodus* 21:29 states that the owner of an ox that habitually gores and kills a human, should be stoned and its owner shall die. *Onkelos* changes "shall die" to "killed."

    Nachmanides states that the *Onkelos* rendering is contrary to the *halakhah* that the owner is punished by God, but not killed by the court.[30]

    The commentary Mizrachi justifies *Onkelos* by stating that the Aramaic *qatal* is used sometimes to refer to a heavenly death.[31] Mizrachi's observation is supported by *Pseudo-Jonathan* who uses *qatal* and indicates that the death is from heaven.

    More importantly, there is no problem of a conflict with *halakhah* once

---

28. In its commentary on this verse.
29. Although *Mekhilta* exists for only twelve *Exodus* chapters, *Onkelos* deviates one-hundred-and-fifty-eight times reflecting interpretations found in this *Midrash*, including ninety-five instances where the targumist uses *Mekhilta's* word. See Drazin, *Targum Onkelos to Exodus*, 32–33.
30. *Mekhilta*, and the Babylonian Talmud, *Sanhedrin* 15b.
31. As in the *Mishnah Avot* 1:13.

one recognizes that *Onkelos* is a translation designed to capture the *peshat*, the simple overt meaning of the text and the targumist does not attempt to even hint at the *halakhah*.[32]

19. *Exodus* 22:2 legislates that if a thief breaks into another's house and is killed by the homeowner, the latter is innocent. However, if "the sun be upon him [the thief]," the homeowner is liable for murder. *Onkelos* renders the biblical "sun" metaphor with an obscure statement: "if the eye of witnesses fell on him."

    Nachmanides and the others understand *Onkelos*'s "witnesses" in a halakhic sense, which raises all kinds of difficulties. For example, what were the witnesses doing during the encounter? Did they warn the thief that he was acting improperly and could be punished or killed, as required by rabbinic law?

    The problem vanishes entirely when we remember that our targumist does not teach *halakhah*; and is using "witnesses" in a non-technical sense as an observer. *Onkelos*, as usual, is deriving its interpretation from the *Midrash Mekhilta d'R. Ishmael*: "if the owner of the house had someone to protect him from the attack by a burglar and the owner nevertheless kills him, he is guilty." What is necessary here as elsewhere, is not to attempt to read and interpret a specific text in isolation, but to try to understand it in light of the general targumic methodology.

20. *Exodus* 22:15 decrees that if a man *yefateh* a virgin, he is subjected to certain penalties. *Onkelos* renders the act *yeshadeil*, which Rashi explains as speaking to her heart until she consents; that is "seduction" or "enticing."

    Nachmanides argues that Rashi is incorrect. He contends that *Onkelos* uses the Aramaic word either as a specific expression of cunning in order to have the other act as he pleases (as is done here), or, more generally, as an effort involving skill with which a person attempts to achieve something. This seems to be a distinction without a difference. Nachmanides is interpreting the *Targum* as Rashi even though he insists that he is not doing so.

21. Nachmanides attempts again to prove that Rashi is incorrect when Rashi interprets *mohar* in *Exodus* 22:15 as "dowry." He says it means "gift" and supports his view with *Onkelos*'s rendering of *Genesis* 34:12's *mohar u'matan* by

---

32. In *Targum Onkelos to Exodus*, 34–35, we give eleven examples where Onkelos to Exodus is contrary to the halakhah.

pluralizing both words *moharim u'matman*, and states that the plural could not refer to many dowries.[33]

There are two problems with his argument. First, since *matan* in *Genesis* clearly means "gift," *mohar* must be something else, not "gifts and gifts" as he contends. Second, the targumist is using the plural in *Genesis* to portray Shechem as wanting Dinah so much that he is willing to give more than the usual bridal dowry and gift, "Ask of me many dowries and gifts and I will pay it, whatever you tell me, just give me the girl as a wife."[34]

22. Nachmanides insists that *Onkelos* is hinting at a kabbalistic lesson with its insertion of "name" into *Exodus* 22:19, sacrifices may only be offered "to the name of the Lord alone," but not to angels.

This interpretation is unlikely for five reasons. First, our targumist only incorporates the *peshat* into his translation, the simple overt meaning of the text. Second, the prohibition about sacrificing to angels is not explicit in the *Targum*. Third, *Pseudo-Jonathan*, which includes "to the name" and is more prolix than *Onkelos* and adds midrashic interpretations, uses it for a different purpose: "therefore you should not worship [anything] but the name of the Lord alone."[35] Fourth, it is possible that our targumist used "to the name," instead of *qadam*, "before," because it is found in *Mekhilta d'R. Ishmael* 136:95.[36] Fifth, Bachya ben Asher, who believed in mysticism like Nachmanides and who composed his own commentary using that of Nachmanides and who frequently mentions him, does not include Nachmanides' notion and explains *Onkelos* as "sacrifices must be addressed to God's essence, to His name."

23. "My angel shall go before you [in front of the Israelites]" *Exodus* 23:20.

Nachmanides maintains that the mystic teachings of *Kabbalah* reveal that this passage is promising that the angel Metatron will come and lead the Israelites to Canaan. He feels that *Onkelos* was, like him, also mystically minded

---

33. He is presumably arguing that a husband only gives his future wife one dowry.
34. *Mohar* is mentioned elsewhere solely in *Exodus* 22:16 and *1 Samuel* 18:25. *Onkelos* renders 22:15 as "he must surely commit himself to her" because the word is used there as a verb. The *Targum* is literal in the other instances where it is a noun.
35. It is possible that the addition of "name" was copied by a scribe into *Onkelos* from *Pseudo-Jonathan*, a not altogether infrequent occurrence.
36. Compare Nachmanides' comment on 20:3.

and purposely hints this kabbalistic revelation when it renders verse 21, "My name is in him [in the angel]" as "he speaks in my name." Literally, "in my name is his *memra* [*memra* means 'word' or 'wisdom']."

There is nothing in the targumic words to suggest who the angel is or that he will do more than the Hebrew implies: act as an agent for God. The targumist is simply explaining the Hebrew.[37]

24. The rationalist Abraham ibn Ezra states that Moses, Aaron, Nadab, Abihu, and the seventy Israelite elders did not actually see God, as *Exodus* 24:10 ("They saw the God of Israel") seems to imply. Instead, they had a prophetic vision of the deity.

    Nachmanides, who appears to have believed in a corporeal deity,[38] contends that *Kabbalah* teaches that the seventy elders saw more than the rest of the people who only "saw God through a partition cloud and thick darkness." He states again that *Onkelos* reflects this *Kabbalah*. The *Targum* changes the verse to read "They saw the glory of the God of Israel," adding "glory," to avoid the impossible notion that people saw a physical God. *Onkelos* adds "glory" frequently to describe the impact of God's presence, in this case, upon the assemblage of Israelites.

    There are several problems with Nachmanides' proof. First, there is nothing in the Aramaic rendering that even hints at a comparison between what was seen by the elders and the masses and that the elders had a greater theophany. Second, the targumic style is to keep as close to the original Hebrew as possible. Therefore, *Onkelos* only added "glory" and "of" in this phrase. The first avoids the thought that the deity was seen, they only saw (or experienced) the divine "glory." The second "of" is required by Aramaic grammar. Third, the word "revealed" is only inserted by our targumist when the verse requires it. Thus, in *Numbers* 16:19, *Onkelos* substitutes the passive "was revealed" for

---

37. We have seen elsewhere that Nachmanides reads unwarranted mystic lessons into *memra* – which means nothing more than "word" or "wisdom" and which the targumist inserted into his translation to avoid an anthropomorphism as explained in chapter 4. He ignores the fact that even if he feels he can argue in his comment to some passages that it be interpreted mystically, it is clearly impossible to do so in all twenty-eight instances where *memra* is introduced.
38. See discussion of *Genesis* 46:1.

Scripture's anthropomorphic active "appeared," as in *Numbers* 14:10, *Exodus* 16:10, *Leviticus* 9:23, *Deuteronomy* 31:15, and other passages.

25. *Exodus* 25 recalls the donations that the Israelites made to the ancient sanctuary. Rashi translates verse 7's *v'avnei milu'im* as "stones for setting." Nachmanides disagrees and defines the words as "whole stones"; the stones must not be hewn, chipped or cut, but must remain in their natural state. He supports his definition by referring to *Onkelos's ashlamuta*, which he understands as "whole" or "complete."[39]

    Nachmanides is apparently incorrect. Jastrow defines *ashlamuta* as "set" or "insert,"[40] as Rashi states.

    Bachya mentions Nachmanides' interpretation of *Onkelos* and agrees with him, making this the second time he concurred.

26. The noun *umenakiyotav* (one of the items used in the sanctuary) in *Exodus* 25:29 is obscure and has been translated variously. The Babylonian Talmud, *Menahot* 97a, understands it as "attachments." *Onkelos* has *v'm'chibteh*, which Rashi understands as "supports."

    Nachmanides defines the Aramaic noun as "measures," the meaning the word has elsewhere.[41] However, he declines to use this definition here because *Onkelos* would then differ from the *Mishnah*[42] that states that there were only two dry measures in the sanctuary – the tenth and half-tenth of an *ephah* – while our targumist would be introducing a third – a two-tenth measure. To avoid having the Aramaic contrary to the authoritative *Mishnah*, Nachmanides suggests that the Aramaic word in this passage means a form-mold made to shape the dough, even though he has no linguistic support for this translation.

    His belief that our targumist does not translate the Bible contrary to the *halakhah* is unfounded. Once we recall this, we readily realize that Nachmanides' forced interpretation is unnecessary.[43]

    Bachya does not mention Nachmanides, but he states that *Onkelos* means "supports," as Rashi states.

---

39. *Exodus* 31:5, 28:17, 20, etc. are similar.
40. Jastrow, *Dictionary*.
41. *Leviticus* 19:36, *Deuteronomy* 25:14, etc.
42. Babylonian Talmud, *Menachot* 87a.
43. In Drazin, *Targum Onkelos to Exodus*, 34–35, we listed eleven examples where *Exodus* translations did not conform to rabbinic *halakhah*.

27. Scholars differ as to whether the head covering of the high and regular priests differed and, if so, how they differed. The type of hat worn by Aaron's sons is called *migba'ot* in *Exodus* 28:40, and *Onkelos* renders it *kov'in*.

    Nachmanides, in 28:31, states that both the Hebrew and Aramaic suggest a conical helmet where the folds rise up.[44] It is true that *migba'ot*, from the Hebrew root *gaba*, implies height; but the Aramaic *kov'in* simply means "head cover."

28. *Exodus* 30:9 is an example where Nachmanides failed to perceive a targumic pattern and read his own interpretation of the passage into the characteristic targumic change.

    Scripture forbids the bringing of *ktoret zarah*, strange incense, on the altar. *Onkelos* inserts *busmin*, "aromatic," after *ktoret*, and changes *zarah* to the plural form. Nachmanides maintains that *Onkelos* made the alterations to tell us that the priest may not add to the incense prescribed in the Torah.

    Leaving aside our frequent obvious question "how can these two changes suggest Nachmanides' interpretation?" we should note that it is a frequently used targumic style to place the clarifying adjective "aromatic" before "incense"[45] and since "aromatic" is plural, grammar required that "incense" be rendered in the plural as "incenses."

29. In *Exodus* 30:19, Nachmanides argues that the *Onkelos* translator had a kabalistic idea in mind when he rendered "Aaron and his sons should wash their hands and feet [before serving at the altar]" as "sanctify their hands and feet." He states that the uplifted hands and the priest's head resemble and represent the "human form" of the three upper elements of the ten *sefirot*, while the priest's feet are like the lower parts of the *sefirot*. The washing of the hands and feet, he continues, "directs one's thoughts to this matter," i.e. the *sefirot* and the act of washing is performed "for the sake of holiness."[46]

    Actually, the targumist generally renders "washing" literally when the

---

44. Whereas the high priest's hat was also wound around his head like a turban, but it did not rise up. Josephus describes the headdress in *Jewish Antiquities*, III, 151 ff. See also Georg Fohrer, "Kopfbedeckung," in *BHH* (Biblisch-historisches Handworterbuch) 2, cols. 985 f., and Maimonides, *Mishneh Torah, Kelei Hamikdash* 8:5, and Rabad and *Mishnah Lamelek*.

45. As in verses 1 and 8. It is in the Hebrew in verse 7.

46. This change occurs in 30:18, 19, 20, 21 and 40:30, 31; but not in 40:12 probably since "sanctify" is used in verse 13 (in regard to anointing).

Torah is speaking of simple cleaning, but uses "sanctify" when it is an act of consecration. He makes the distinction because he usually focuses on the goal or purpose of the act. Most importantly, there is nothing in the single word "sanctify" itself, a word that reoccurs frequently in various contexts, to suggest the elaborate kabbalistic ceremony.

Bachya ben Asher describes the kabbalistic ceremony in great detail and agrees with Nachmanides that "this is why *Onkelos* translates the word *verachatzu*, 'they shall wash' as 'they shall sanctify.'" This is the third time that Bachya agreed with Nachmanides.

30. *Exodus* 30:35 reads: "Make them [an assortment of herbs] into incense, a compound expertly blended, *memulach*, pure, holy." Our targumist renders *memulach*, which is literally "seasoned" or "salted,"[47] as "mixed together." Nachmanides contends that *memulach* means "rubbed out" and cites three verses as proof.[48]

Nachmanides again failed to realize that our translator was not defining the word, but paraphrasing it in accordance to one of his methods. He is focusing on the goal of the seasoning: it is not the seasoning that makes the spices holy, but the fact that the mixture is used for God.[49]

Bachya ben Asher did not agree with Nachmanides. He defined *memulach* as either "salted" or "thoroughly mixed" as *Onkelos* translates it.

31. Nachmanides states that *Onkelos* explains *Exodus*'s 32:25 description of Aaron's act with the golden calf. The Bible states that it made the Israelites "a derision among their enemies." *Onkelos* tones down and identifies the "derision" as getting them "a bad name," and "enemies" is replaced by "for generations"[50] to refer to the Israelites themselves, not non-Israelites as stated in the Hebrew. The Israelite descendants would know that their ancestors acted improperly.

This is correct as far as it goes. However, Nachmanides did not observe that by replacing "enemies," Onkelos was following one of its methods: protecting

---

47. Arnold Bogumil Ehrlich, *Mikra Kipheshuto* (The Bible According to Its Literal Meaning), (New York: Ktav, 1969), 197.
48. *Isaiah* 51:6 (vanish), *Jeremiah* 38:11 (rotten or worm), *Psalms* 107:34 (salt waste).
49. Pseudo-Jonathan is like Onkelos. Rashi states that *memulach* is "mixed." He cites *Jonah* 1:15 and *Ezekiel* 27:27.
50. As in *Deuteronomy* 29:21 and *Numbers* 32:13.

the honor of Israelite ancestors. While future Israelites will realize the error of Aaron's act, Israel's enemies would not do so.

32. *Exodus* 32:35 appears to be contradictory. It suggests that both the Israelites and Aaron made the golden calf: "because they made the calf which Aaron made."

    Onkelos and another Aramaic translation called the *Peshitta* render Scripture's "because they made" into *d'ishtabdu*, which can mean "made" or "because they served [or 'worshipped'] it."[51]

    Nachmanides[52] argued that the targumist altered the verse to inform us that those "who died in the punishing plague were individuals who embraced and kissed the calf, and were pleased with it." He is stating that the Aramaic word *abad*, "made" or "serve" includes those who did not worship the idol fully. He is attempting to have *Onkelos* reflect the rabbinical view in the Babylonian Talmud, *Yoma* 66b, that these were people who did not worship the calf or sacrifice to it.

    Actually, as stated, the *Targum's abad* means both "made" – a characteristic translation of the Hebrew *asah* – and would therefore be a literal translation, and "serve," and neither definition implies "embracing," "kissing," or being "pleased."[53]

33. *Exodus* 33:6 reads: "the Israelites were stripped of their *edyam* from Mount Horeb on." Nachmanides argues that *Onkelos's zaynei* for *edyam* denotes "armament." Thus, he contends, the targumist is in agreement with the rabbinical view that the Israelites were given weapons of armor,[54] when the Torah was presented to them, to save them from mishaps and the angel of death.[55]

    Both *adyam* and *zaynei* mean "ornaments,"[56] and thus *Onkelos* is translating the word literally without the midrashic *derash*.[57]

---

51. As in *Genesis* 12:5, *Deuteronomy* 1:1, and *Targum Jonathan* to I *Kings* 15:33 and II *Kings* 17:29. Pseudo-Jonathan is similar with "because they bowed," as in 22:19.
52. See Adler, *Netina La'ger* and S.B. Shefftel *Biure Onkelos* (Munich, 1888).
53. It means "made" in *Genesis* 1:31, 2:2, 3:1, 5:1, 6:6, 6:22, etc. Aruch and Jastrow translate *abad* as "serve." See also II *Kings* 17:35 and *Pirkei Avot* 1:2 where it has this meaning in Hebrew.
54. In *Exodus Rabbah* 45:1.
55. This "armor" was the knowledge of God's names that protected them from death.
56. See Jastrow, *Dictionary*, 395, and II *Samuel* 1:24 where *adanim* clearly means "ornament."
57. In the commentary to this verse, Nachmanides adds the remarkable idea that the Israelites

Nevertheless, Bachya ben Asher agrees – now it is four times in *Exodus* – with Nachmanides on this point.

34. Nachmanides states that one cannot possibly understand *Exodus* 33:13 unless one knows *Kabbalah*. Moses said to God: "Now, if I found grace in Your eyes, please show me Your ways, so that I may know you, so that I will find grace in Your eyes. See this people is Your people." Nachmanides contends that the verse reflects a discourse between Moses and God concerning the mystical divine attributes of "justice" and "mercy."

He says that this is what our targumist intended with the rewordings that he incorporated into his translation. Actually, the targumist has eight alterations in this verse and they were made to enhance its clarity and to remove anthropomorphisms, and none suggest the mystical idea. He changes the abstract Hebrew "grace" to the more specific "mercy" twice.[58] This is a characteristic clarifying substitution. "In Your eyes," which is anthropomorphic, is replaced twice by "before You." "Good" is inserted before "ways,"[59] which is implied. "That I may know You" is changed to "know Your mercy" to preclude the impossible idea that humans possess the ability to comprehend God. "That" is inserted for grammatical reasons.[60] Finally, the anthropomorphic "see" is altered to "revealed" before You.[61]

Nachmanides saw the mystical interpretation in *Onkelos* not only because he felt that this "holy translation" must incorporate "holy *Kabbalah*," but because he was convinced, as discussed previously, that *Onkelos* never changed the text to remove a corporeal depiction of the deity.

Bachya not only agreed with the Gerona sage on this reading of *Onkelos*, but adds about a half dozen readings of his own into the *Onkelos* wording. He states that *Onkelos* is saying: (1) There exist "supernatural beings" that have no bodies that cannot be fully understood by people. (2) God caused

---

could have lived forever because of the "armor" but they gave up this benefit as an atonement for the sin of the golden calf.

58. As do *Pseudo-Jonathan*, the *Peshitta* and the *Samaritan Targums*. It is highly unlikely that the latter two non-Jewish sources changed the text to reflect Jewish *Kabbalah*.

59. Also by *Pseudo-Jonathan*.

60. "That I may know mercy."

61. "Let it be revealed before You that this people is Your people."

his *Shekhinah* to pass by Moses. (3) The *Shekhinah* is an attribute – that is, a part of – God, which is also called the angel Metatron and *khavod*, "glory." (4) Moses could not see the front of the *Shekhinah*, but "Moses would be able to see" the "western end of the *Shekhinah*," meaning Moses could "comprehend" some things about God. (5) Moses was speaking to the *Shekhinah*, not to all the aspects of God. (6) Moses prayed that God show the people divine mercy because the Israelites, who were stiffed necked, could not last if they were judged with "justice." This elaborate depiction of events is, as previously stated, not even hinted in the *Targum*, although Bachya argues differently.

– CHAPTER 11 –

Leviticus

> Nachmanides mentions *Targum Onkelos* thirty-three times in his commentary to *Leviticus*. His comments are not unreasonable in ten instances, which is thirty percent of the occasions that the *Targum* is mentioned. In eight of these ten events, he simply quotes the targumist. In the two remaining instances his interpretation goes beyond what is clearly stated by the Aramaic rendering, but his interpretation, while not certain, is reasonable.

PROBLEMATICAL INTERPRETATIONS

The remaining twenty-three references to the *Targum* in *Leviticus*, seventy percent of the total, are problematical. These include seven passages where Nachmanides appears to translate the targumic Aramaic incorrectly, six in which he is seeking rabbinic *halakhah* in the *Targum*, five places when he reads his own ideas into the translation, and five other times that he draws other unwarranted conclusions from *Onkelos*.

There are three commentaries among the twenty-three where Nachmanides tries to find support for his mystical notions in the Aramaic words of the *Onkelos* translation. In two instances, he mentions his belief in near-corporeal demons who affect human life and who must be bribed with a sacrifice for protection (items twelve and thirteen). In item nineteen, Nachmanides states that the sinful action of a single Jew causes the entire community to be in a state of sin even when the community does not sanction the behavior.

THE TWENTY-THREE PROBLEMATICAL NACHMANIDES
INTERPRETATIONS IN LEVITICUS

1. *Leviticus* 1:16 reads: "he removes its *murato* with its *b'notzata*." *Onkelos* renders "[bird's] crop" for the first noun, the same word in *Sifra*, the Babylonian Talmud,

Zevachim 68a, and *Pseudo-Jonathan*, and the root for the word in *Neophyti*. *Onkelos* renders the second as "excrement," which is discussed below.

Nachmanides recognizes that the Aramaic translation of *murato* is the minority view of the *Midrash* and Talmud. Feeling the need to find the *halakhah* in the *Targum*, he suggests that the targumist reversed the order of the words. He argues that the inverted word order is appropriate because the consumed food (*murato*) can only be removed by taking away the crop. He cites *Exodus* 23:21 and 28:25 as two other examples where the targumist reversed the biblical word order.

M. Lowenstein observes that Aramaic grammar does not indicate that the order was reversed.[1] More importantly, the Nachmanidean premise that *Onkelos* contains *halakhah* is not correct, as we have frequently shown.

2. The second noun in *Leviticus* 1:16 occurs only here in Hebrew Scripture, and its meaning is uncertain. Rashi here and in *Zevachim* 65a states that it denotes a loathsome thing, as in *Lamentations* 4:15. *Onkelos*'s word, which means "contents" or "excrement," reflects the interpretation in the *Mishnah* of *Zevachim* 6:5. It is used by the targumist in 4:11 in place of Scripture's *parshu*, "depart." Thus Nachmanides is probably incorrect when he states that the targumist derived its interpretation from *Deuteronomy* 25:11, "when men *yinatzu* [strive] together." The targumist more likely traced its meaning from *yatza*, "depart."[2]

3. The term *mido* in *Leviticus* 6:3 literally means "his measurement." Relying on the Babylonian Talmud, *Yoma* 23b, and *Sifra* ("What is *mido*? It is *k'mido*, like his measurement."), Rashi and ibn Ezra state that the singular form of *mido* signifies the priest's shirt, which must be fitted to his measurement.

The *Targums*, the Samaritan Bible, and its *Targums* treat *mido* as an inclusive term for all of the priest's "garments" and pluralize it, as "garments" as written in verse 4 and in *Exodus* 28:42. The singular *mido* appears once more in Hebrew Scriptures, in *II Samuel* 20:8, where it also implies the plural "garments" and is so interpreted by *Targum Jonathan*. It appears a third time as *k'mido* in *Psalms* 109:18, in a context that requires the singular and is so rendered by the *Targum*.

---

1. Lowenstein, *Nefesh Hager*.
2. *Neophyti*, *Pseudo-Jonathan*, the *Fragmented Targums* and the *Peshitta* are like our *Targum*, but the Septuagint, the Vulgate, ibn Ezra, Radak, Nachmanides, etc., translate "feathers," as in *Lamentations* 4:15 and *Jeremiah* 48:9. Saadiah has "gizzard," and the *Samaritan Targums* "with its parts."

Since *Targum Onkelos* reads "the priest puts on his garments of linen," Nachmanides concludes that our targumist is saying that the only material used in the common priests' garments was linen. This, he contends, reflects R. Dosa's opinion in the Babylonian Talmud, *Yoma* 12b, and *Sifra* that the common priest's belt was made of linen and was unlike the high priest's belt, which was of blue, purple, and scarlet wool, and twined linen.

Nachmanides is again drawing a broad conclusion from the targumic renderings of a single word and attempts to find *halakhah* in the *Targum*. All that the targumist did was interpret "his measurement" as a figure of speech for a garment. The word "linen" was already in Scripture, and he left it unchanged. Neither the biblical text nor *Onkelos*'s rendering suggest that every single priestly garment was made exclusively of linen.

4. Nachmanides contends that the *Onkelos* rendering of *Leviticus*'s 11:9 *kasheses*, "scales," as *kalfin* shows that the targumist was teaching the *halakhah* that the fish's scales do not have to be inflexibly fixed to the fish's body, a fish is kosher if it once had scales, even if they came off. He defines the Aramaic *kalfin* as "shells" that can, like all coverings, be removed.

Actually, *kalfin* means both "shells" and "scales," as well as other meanings, and nothing can be proven by its use in the Aramaic translation.[3] More significantly, all the *Targums* as well as the Samaritan *Targums* pluralize Scripture's singular "fin and scale" for this is what the text implies. This is contrary to the halakhic position in the Babylonian Talmud, *Chullin* 59a, and *Sifra*. They state that the biblical singular teaches that a fish is kosher even when it has a single fin and scale. Thus, apparently unnoticed by Nachmanides, who attempted to read *halakhah* in the targumic words, our targumist is clearly not reflecting the *halakhah*.

5. *Leviticus* 12:2 states *ishah ki tazria*, which literally means "if a woman caused fructification of seed." *Onkelos* explains it as "become pregnant" because the Aramaic *zera* lacks the connotation of "growth" that it has in the Hebrew,[4] and so forced this customary clarification.[5] Furthermore, as previously stated, our

---

3. Jastrow, *Dictionary*.
4. As well as the other Jewish Aramaic *Targums*, the Syropalestinian Version, Rashi, ibn Ezra, Abravanel, etc.
5. Simon Baruch Schefftel, *Biure Onkelos* (Munich, 1888).

targumist frequently renders words in an end-oriented manner and therefore he speaks of the pregnancy here rather than the conception.

Nachmanides reads more into this typical targumic change than is warranted. He states that the philosophers teach that a child is formed entirely from the mother's blood, whereas the rabbis and physicians know that a child is formed from both of its parents.[6] He argues that *Onkelos*'s wording "when a woman becomes pregnant" reflects the mistaken philosophical view.

Nachmanides' interpretation is problematical because: (1) The original Hebrew is the source that speaks about "seed" – which is the issue in Nachmanides' statement – while the Aramaic paraphrase has "pregnancy," which is totally irrelevant to his discussion. (2) The Aramaic is only explaining the metaphor "seed" and the explanation of the metaphor "seed" occurs frequently. (3) Nachmanides' discussion about who causes the fructification of the seed does not exist in the word "pregnant." (4) Neither the Hebrew nor the Aramaic speak about the sex of the unborn child.

6. In *Leviticus* 14:43, Nachmanides refers to *Onkelos* and states that it is possible that the correct interpretation of *pasah*, literally "spread," is to "increase," as the targumist states. However, he then takes an unjustified additional step and argues that the targumic verb *ysaph* denotes both growth and a fresh outbreak of the plague. Specifically, according to Nachmanides, *Onkelos* is informing us of the *halakhah* in the *Midrash Sifra* that the law applies even if the plague returned to a different part of the person's house or in a different color.

As usual, Nachmanides is reading too much into a typical targumic paraphrase. *Onkelos*'s *ysaph*, "increase," which appears many dozens of times in the Aramaic version of the Pentateuch and which is used to translate four different Hebrew words,[7] does not have a clear connotation of a new outburst in a different area or color.

7. Among other special priestly garments, the priest "should wind a winding of linen" (*Leviticus* 16:4). *Onkelos* uses the Hebrew root for "a winding" (which is a head covering called miter or turban in English) and adds the clarification

---

6. Babylonian Talmud, *Nidah* 31a.
7. *y-s-p, a-w-w, g-b-r, p-s-h*.

that the winding is placed on the priest's head. The *Targum* replaces the verb "wind," which is of the same root as "winding," with "place."

Nachmanides contends that the *Targum* had to use "place" because there is no Aramaic word for "winding." Thus our targumist and *Targum Jonathan* to *Isaiah* 3:23, had to select a close approximation and chose the Hebrew root in *Exodus* 28:4.[8]

It seems strange, however, that Aramaic should lack a word for "winding." Jastrow states that the Aramaic verb *savav* means "to place around,"[9] and it is utilized in this sense in more than several instances in rabbinic literature.[10] It may be that the *Targum*s used "place" because the turban could have been wound prior to being placed on the priest's head or to preclude the thought that the turban was wound around the entire head, hiding the priest's face, similar to the veil later worn by Moses.[11]

8. Arguably, no Nachmanidean interpretation of the Torah is a better example of his worldview, which is counter to modern thinking, than his view of *Leviticus* 16:8, which states: "Aaron places lots upon the two goats [selected as part of the Yom Hakippurim holiday tabernacle service]:[12] one lot [marked] for the Lord and one lot [marked] for *azazel*." The *azazel* goat is sent to the wilderness.

Nachmanides' reading of his understanding of the Yom Hakippurim ceremony into a single word in *Targum Onkelos* also serves as a paradigm both of his refusal to see that the targumist attempts to avoid even the possibility of an anthropomorphic depiction of the deity in his translation and his insistence that even the details of an elaborate ceremony can be suggested in a single Aramaic word, even when that same word means something else entirely when it appears in other verses. It is therefore worthwhile to elaborate in commenting on this passage.

A.B. Ehrlich warns us that the meaning of the Yom Hakippurim *azazel*

---

8. *Targums Pseudo-Jonathan* and *Neophyti* are similar with *yitkas*, "fit on." See Jastrow, *Dictionary*, *takas*, 535.
9. Jastrow, Dictionary, *savav*, 948.
10. *Onkelos* and *Pseudo-Jonathan* have *savav* in Exodus 27:5 and 38:4.
11. *Exodus* 34:29ff, especially 33.
12. The holiday was changed when the Temple was destroyed in 70 CE because sacrifices ceased, and was then called Yom Kippur. See Drazin, *Mysteries of Judaism*.

ceremony – the meaning of the word *azazel* and the purpose of the ceremony of dispatching a goat to the wilderness – is totally obscure, and what our sages tell us regarding it is pure imaginative guesswork based on myths and fables.[13] He cites as proof that the Babylonian Talmud, *Yoma* 67b, includes the *azazel* ceremony among the non-rational commandments.[14]

The Talmud defines *azazel* in several different ways.[15] It is defined as a "hard and rough" land, the understanding in the *Midrash Sifra*, and as a reference to the legend of fallen angels.[16] Others derive its meaning from *azal*, which means "distance" in Arabic, suggesting the removal or distancing of sin.[17] It was identified as a place name, the site to which the goat was sent.[18] It was interpreted as a contraction made up of *az*, "goat," and the Hebrew *azal*, "to go away," yielding "the goat that goes away."[19]

In view of the obscurity of *azazel* and its broad history in ancient Jewish myths, it would be unfair to criticize Nachmanides for his view of the scapegoat. However, his contention that *Onkelos* reflects his idea is another matter. It is improbable that *Onkelos* contains the Nachmanidean interpretation, as he contends, both because the thirteenth-century sage is reading more into the brief *Targum* paraphrase than is warranted and a different interpretation of the Aramaic is more reasonable.

Nachmanides bases his view of *Midrash Pirkei d'R. Eliezer* 46 and ibn Ezra's commentary to *Leviticus* 16:8. The *Midrash* states: "The reason why they [the

---

13. Ehrlich, *Mikra Ki-Pheschuto*, vol. 1, 227–28. See also David Zvi Hoffman, *Sefer Vayikra* (Jerusalem: Mossad HaRav Kook, 1976).
14. "Commandments to which Satan objects," meaning laws that are difficult, if not impossible to explain.
15. *Yoma* 67b.
16. Based on *Genesis* 6:1–4. Also *1 Enoch* 6:13.
17. F. Brown, S.R. Driver, and C.A. Briggs, *A Hebrew and English Lexicon of the Old Testament* (Oxford: Clarendon, 1907).
18. Baruch A. Levine, *The JPS Torah Commentary, Leviticus* (Philadelphia: Jewish Publication Society, 2001–2003), 102–3.
19. This interpretation is in the Greek Septuagint and the Latin Vulgate, and it may have been translated in the *Mishnah Yoma* 6:23 as *se'ir ha'mishtalleach*, "the goat that is sent away." Symmachus and the Latin Vulgate are similar with "to carry away sins." This is the basis of the term "scapegoat," and shortened version of "escape-goat." See C.L. Feinberg, "The Scapegoat of Leviticus 16," *Bibliotheca Sacra* 115 (1958): 320:33; and *Encyclopedia Judaica*, 16 volumes (Jerusalem: Macmillan, 1972).

Israelites] would give *Samael* [the Satan] a conciliatory gift on Yom Kippur was to deflect his ability to nullify [the effect of] their sacrifices."

He also supports his view with *Genesis Rabbah* 65:11 that equates *sair*, "goats" or "hairy," with *shay dan*, "demons":[20] Esau is *ish sair* (*Genesis* 27:11) means he is *givar shaydan*, demonic. He also refers to ibn Ezra.

In his Torah commentary to *Leviticus* 16:8, ibn Ezra quotes Saadiah that *Leviticus*'s 16 *azazel* is the name of a mountain, the composite of *az*, "might," and *el*, "God" and "mighty," yielding a very impressive (doubling of "mighty") mountain. The elevation was near the relatively modest Mount Sinai. Later, after leaving the desert, the Israelites reinterpreted the verse and led the scapegoat to some other location. The scapegoat was dispatched "to *azazel*, toward the wilderness," for the same reason that the bird of the person purifying himself of *tzara'at* was driven off into the fields, "so that the *tzara'at* would not spread" (14:7), suggesting that the bird is isolated as a symbolic riddance of sickness, impurity and sin. He rejects the view of the Gaon Shmuel ben Hofni, who contended that the scapegoat was for God, "because the scapegoat is not a sacrifice, since it is not slaughtered." The atonement, the purpose of the ceremony, is "accomplished by sending it away."

In his somewhat more philosophical *Yesod Mora V'sod Torah*, he compares the expelling of the scapegoat to the "*azazel* and the wilderness" to the *tzara'at* bird of 14:7, as well as the requirement to bring the she-calf to the non-fertile wadi in *Deuteronomy* 21:1–9. The latter being part of the expunging procedure when a homicide victim is found in the open country and the killer is unknown. In all three instances, the ceremony is designed to shift the sin and damaging illness to an isolated, non-fecund waste land.[21]

In the Torah Commentary, ibn Ezra adds cryptically: "If you can understand the mystery of the word *azazel*, you will know its mystery and the mystery of its name, for it has analogues in Scripture. I will disclose to you some of the mystery: When you are thirty-three, you will know it."

Ibn Ezra's brief obscure statement could be understood as follows: The

---

20. J. Theodor and Chanoch Albeck, *Bereschit Rabba*, (Jerusalem, 1965), 726.
21. J. Cohen and U. Simon, eds. *R. Abraham Ibn Ezra. Yesod Mora Ve-Sod Torah* (Ramat-Gan: Bar-Ilan University Press, 2002), *shaar* 9, 159.

scapegoat was not ceremoniously slaughtered as a sacrifice and it was dispatched to the wilderness to avoid the populace imagining that the scapegoat ceremony was a form of sacrifice to demons. However, most ibn Ezra commentators[22] and Nachmanides approve a more dramatic and exotic demon-laden solution.[23]

Nachmanides believed in near-corporeal demons. He states that humans were created out of the four basic elements (fire, water, earth, and air), but demons were created out of only fire and air. They have six characteristics. They eat and drink, procreate, die, have wings, fly, and know what will happen in the future. They know the future because when they fly, they hear about the future from the constellations.[24]

Nachmanides interprets *Exodus* 8:14 that demons performed the magic acts

---

22. See, for example, Bonfils, *Tzafanat Pane'ach*, the three commentaries in Isaac Dikordia, *Sefer Margoliot Tova* (Amsterdam, 5482), and D. Rosin, "Die Religions philosophie Abraham ibn Ezra's," *Monatschrift für Geschichte und Wissenchaft des Judentum* (1893), 242.

23. Nachmanides accepted many of ibn Ezra's interpretations, sometimes even when he appeared to disagree with them. R. Judah ibn Mosconi, in his *Even Ha-ezer*, ed. Abraham Berliner, in *OtzarTov* (1878), wrote: "Who knows whether Nachmanides followed this method [of concealing his true views], when he spoke of ibn Ezra.... Observe that at the beginning of his book he said of him, 'we will have open rebuke and hidden love with the scholar R. Abraham ibn Ezra.' Perhaps this way [of stating the opposite of what he believes] is the hidden love."

At the end of his commentary to *Leviticus* 16:8, Nachmanides rails against the rationalist Aristotle, whom Maimonides admired. He said he could not explain more for, if he did so, he would have to close the mouth of him and his wicked disciples who claim to understand the study of nature and who deny everything except for what they perceive through their senses and their reason. In his introduction to his commentary to *Job*, Nachmanides curses Aristotle and those who follow his views: "they should be destroyed, root and branch." There are many other similar Nachmanidean statements.

The rationalist Maimonides did not believe in demons. Indeed, he did not even believe in angels as they are commonly understood. In his *Guide of the Perplexed* 3:46, he points to many practices whose motive is to teach us not to believe in demons. In 2:6, he states: "every one that is entrusted with a certain mission is an angel.... The elements are also called angels... [as well as] a messenger sent by man... it is also used for ideals." Nachmanides, on the other hand, believed in demons and angels.

24. In post-biblical Jewish literature, Azazel is the name of a demon (*Enoch* 8:1, 9:6). Even in the Bible, the wilderness is looked at as the haunt of demons and similar creatures (*Leviticus* 17:7, *Isaiah* 13:21, 34:14; cf. *Matthew* 12:43, etc.).

Nachmanides also discusses his belief in demons in various places in his "The Law of the Eternal is Perfect," Chavel, *Ramban, Writings and Discourses*, vol. 1, 25–140. *Leviticus* 16:8 is examined on 104f.

for the magicians in their encounter with Moses before Pharaoh. He takes the Babylonian Talmud, *Sanhedrin* 67b literally and states that although they could copy the first miracles, the demons were unable to create gnats, as Moses did, because they are powerless to create anything smaller than a lentil.[25]

Nachmanides' interpretation of *Leviticus* 16:8 is based on ibn Ezra's comments on the verse, specifically the number thirty-three. Nachmanides understands the remark to refer to *Leviticus* 17:7, thirty-three verses away, "And they shall no longer sacrifice their sacrifices to the goats after whom they go astray."

In 16:8, Nachmanides contends, Scripture is mandating that the Israelites give a conciliatory gift to the demon Samael on the Day of Atonement as a bribe, so that the demon would not act maliciously to annul the good effect they wanted from their offering. Upon receipt of the bribe, Samael converts into a defense attorney for the Israelites and petitions God to grant them atonement.

Nachmanides tells us that the Israelites used to worship the demons.[26] However, when they received the Torah, they were forbidden to treat them as deities or to worship them in any fashion. Nevertheless, God allowed the Israelites to send a goat to the demon, "not as an offering, Heaven forbid! Rather our intention is only to fulfill God's wishes." It is as if we are making a feast for God, and God tells us "give a portion to one of my servants." It is God who wants us to bribe the demon to speak in our defense. This is why lots are cast. The Israelites did not choose the goat for the demon, God did so. This is also why the Israelites did not slaughter the demon's goat, but threw it to the demon from a high cliff, so as not to imply that this is a proper offering.

This teaching about the scapegoat being given to Satan as a bribe, Nachmanides contends, is contained in *Targum Onkelos*.

Leviticus 16:8 states: "Aaron places lots upon the two goats [selected as part of the Yom Hakippurim holiday tabernacle service]: one lot [marked] for the Lord and one lot [marked] for *azazel.*"

Onkelos places a single change in its rendering of the verse. In the Sperber

---

25. He criticizes Aristotle for his disbelief in demons, ibid., 49. He also expresses his belief in demons and ghosts and sorcery, ibid. 55, 59 and 123.
26. And the angels. He tells us that if we understood the sciences of astrology and necromancy we would understand how demons can be effected by gifts. See also his commentary to *Leviticus* 16:21.

edition of the *Targum*,²⁷ *Onkelos* introduces "the name" into verses 8 and 9 (where the phrase "lot for the Lord" is repeated). The Berliner edition of *Onkelos* also has "the name" in verse 8, but uses *qadam*, "before," in verse 9.²⁸ In any event, *Onkelos* made the change, as usual, to preclude the anthropomorphic notion that the lot was handed directly to God.²⁹

Nachmanides contends that his explanation of *azazel* is suggested by the *Onkelos* rendering. The targumist was careful, he insists, not to translate "and one lot for the name of *azazel*" because he wanted to tell us that the first goat was a sacrifice but the second was only a bribe.

Actually, a more reasonable explanation for the targumic deviation from the Hebrew text is that the targumist was focusing on the first phrase. He added "for the name of" to preclude an anthropomorphic notion.³⁰ Further, there is nothing in the added words, or in any *Onkelos* targumic rendering in the Pentateuch for that matter, that even remotely suggest that our targumist believed, as Nachmanides, that demons exist and that God would instruct us of a need to bribe them.

The *azazel* goat, we should note, is not the only instance where Nachmanides believed that demons must be bribed. In his commentary to *Leviticus* 14:4, he states that the reason why the leper's bird is let go into an open field "is like the secret of the goat sent to *azazel*." *Leviticus* 14 describes a very similar ceremony to the *azazel* ceremony. It mandates that a leper is cleansed, among other things, by the taking of two birds, one of whom is slaughtered and the second is sent into the open field. Bachya explains that the bird is sent to a species of destructive beings that are even "lower than the level of the prince of the desert who receives the bribe on Yom Kippur." ³¹

---

27. Alexander Sperber, *The Bible in Aramaic* (Leiden: E.J. Brill, 1959). *Targum Pseudo-Jonathan* is like *Targum Onkelos* in both verses. *Targum Neophyti* has "to the name of the *memra* ("word") of the Lord" in the two places. *Sifra*, from whom our targumist drew material, uses "name" as a substitute for "Lord."
28. Abraham Berliner, *Targum Onkelos* (Berlin, 1884).
29. As well as the other *Targums*.
30. Nachmanides, as we noted in the discussion of *Genesis* 46:1, was convinced that our *Targum* did not deviate to remove anthropomorphisms.
31. C.B. Chavel, *Kitvei Rabbeinu Bachya* (Jerusalem: Mossad Harav Kook, 1981), vol. 2, 483, on *Leviticus* 14:7.

Nor are these two the sole examples of bribes given to demons. Nachmanides notes that his predecessor, the rationalist Maimonides, gives a practical reason why a heifer is killed in a rough valley which has not been plowed or sown when a person is killed in the field. The reason is to have the incident become public knowledge so that witness will hear about it and come forward. "In my opinion," Nachmanides states in his commentary to *Deuteronomy* 21:4, "the reason for it is similar to the offerings performed outside [the Tabernacle], such as the goat sent [to *azazel*)] and the red heifer [of *Numbers* 19:3]." Bachya[32] explains that the heifer is left for the prince of the rough valley [desert] Samael.

The fourth instance when Nachmanides believed that a bribe was given to demons is mentioned in his commentary to *Deuteronomy* 21:4. *Numbers* 19 states that a red heifer was slaughtered outside the Tabernacle. Nachmanides obfuscates his view in his commentary to *Numbers* 19:2 where he states that "since [the procedure of the red heifer] is performed outside [the Sanctuary], it appears to the nations that it is slaughtered *to the satyrs* which are in the open field. But the truth is that [the red heifer] is brought to remove the spirit of impurity, and the burning thereof outside [the Sanctuary Court] is like the *sweet savor* [of the offerings brought within the Sanctuary Court]." While these words have been translated to deny the bribe to the demon, *Deuteronomy* 21:4 and the other two instances we mentioned, compels us to interpret that the slaughtering removes impurity because the demon outside is given a sweet savor, like the sweet savor given to God in the Tabernacle. Bachya is also obscure on this point, but he does state that part of the red heifer ceremony is holy and part is not, and the latter part makes the person involved in it impure.[33]

Our final point is worth mentioning. The reader will no doubt notice that in his interpretation of *Leviticus* 16:8, and in his interpretation of other verses, Nachmanides opted to understand the *aggadah* of the *Midrash* literally. This seems to contradict Nachmanides' statement in his 1263 disputation that *aggadot* are "sermons akin to the bishop standing and giving a sermon and one

---

32. To 21:1.
33. To 19:2.

of the auditors finding it favorable and writing it down. This book (*aggado*) – he who believes in it, well and good; but he who does not believe in it does no harm."[34]

Scholars resolved the apparent inconsistency in several ways. Some state that the 1263 statement, made in the midst of a rather difficult debate was a "ploy of desperation," and that Nachmanides actually accepted the *aggadot* literally. Others state the contrary view that Nachmanides did not accept the absolute authority of all *aggadot*.[35] This problem in understanding Nachmanides cannot be resolved with any degree of certainty. However, it is clear that he accepted at least certain *aggadot*, such as the one we just cited about demons, literally.

9. Nachmanides discusses *Deuteronomy* 32:17 in his commentary to *Leviticus* 17:7. *Deuteronomy* states, "They [the Israelites] sacrificed to demons who are not God." *Onkelos* renders "demons" literally and characteristically deviates at the end of the passage to remove even the remotest possible thought that there are other gods, and writes instead "for whom there is no need."[36] The targumist derived this idea from the *Midrash Sifrei*:[37] "Had they worshipped the sun and the moon...things the world needs and which produce delight, this would not have increased God's anger; but they worshipped things that do not benefit them, and which harm them."[38]

Nachmanides was persuaded that demons exist with six characteristics,[39] one being their ability to foretell the future from the placement and movements of the constellations.[40] However, they can only accurately predict the near future. This, he maintains, is the targumist's message when he states that there is "no need" for demons.

There are several problems with this interpretation of the *Targum*. First, our targumist, in hundreds of instances, drew non-*aggadic* material from the

---

34. R. Chazan, *Barcelona and Beyond, The Disputation of 1263 and Its Aftermath* (University of California Press, 1992), 149.
35. Ibid., 143–47.
36. Like the marginal notes in *Targum Neophyti* and some *Fragmented Targum* texts.
37. *Targum Neophyti* explains it as "idols of the demons" and *Targum Pseudo-Jonathan* "idols that are like demons."
38. Regarding *Onkelos*'s reliance on the tannaitic *Midrashim*, see chapter 1.
39. See our discussion on *Leviticus* 16:8.
40. He believed in astrology. See the discussion to *Leviticus* 16:8.

tannaitic *Midrashim*. It is clear that he did so here; and what is in the *Targum* does not even hint at what Nachmanides reads into the *Targum* text. Secondly, as we stated previously, there is absolutely no indication in any targumic rendering that our targumist believed in demons.

10. *Leviticus* 19:17 states, "Do not hate your neighbor in your heart, but still, admonish your neighbor, *v'lo tisa alav haeto*" ("and you should not carry [what is] on him [as a] sin"). The *Targum*'s second half is, "and you should not accept what is on him [as a] guilt." Nachmanides states that *Onkelos* is reflecting the Babylonian Talmud's lesson in *Shabbat* 54b, if you do not warn him you will be punished for his deed, as if you committed the improper act.[41] Actually, all that the *Targum* is doing is explaining the figurative "carry" with the prosaic "accept," and "sin" is replaced by "guilt," both characteristic renderings.[42] Thus, our targumist is only making typical changes to clarify the meaning of two words, and is not teaching theology as Nachmanides maintains.

11. In *Leviticus* 19:20, *bikoreth* occurs only in this verse and is obscure. Ibn Ezra suggests three possible definitions: "concubine," "valuable," and "seek." *Neophyti* and the *Fragmented Targum* paraphrase, "they have rebelled, they are guilty." *Pseudo-Jonathan*, the Septuagint, Rashi, *Sifra*, and the Babylonian Talmud, *Makkot* 22b have the *derash* "stripes," which is probably derived from *bakor*, "ox," suggesting an ox hide scourge. Ibn Janach and *Samaritan Targum A* use "she shall be disgraced. Speiser associates it with the Akkadian term for "damages."[43] Nachmanides relates *bikoreth* to the Aramaic *hephker*, "ownerless" or "loose." *Onkelos* and *Samaritan Targum J* do not define the term and only repeat the Hebrew root. Nevertheless, although Nachmanides sees that the biblical root is repeated in *Onkelos*, he cites our *Targum* to prove that his interpretation is correct.

12. *Leviticus* 19:32 states: "Rise before the hoary head, and give respect to the old." *Onkelos*[44] interprets the first metaphor ("hoary head") as "aged in Torah," and the second ("old") literally. This is contrary to the decisive view in *Sifra* and the

---

41. As well as Ehrlich, *Mikra Kipheshuto*, 231 and Benzion Judah Berkowitz *Chalifot Semalot* (Wilna, 1874).
42. As well as the *Samaritan Targums* which obviously do not intend to reflect the Talmud.
43. E. Speiser, *Oriental and Biblical Studies* (Philadelphia, 1967), 128–31.
44. As well as the other *Targums*.

Babylonian Talmud, *Kiddushin* 32b, that treats the first as any elderly person and the second as a scholar. Nachmanides, who preferred *Onkelos* to reflect the *halakhah*, decided that our targumist agreed that the second term denotes a scholar, but reversed the verse's order and stated the second clause first. It is more likely that since the first Hebrew term *saba*, "hoary head," and the Aramaic *sabar*, "aged [in Torah]," are close sounding this probably prompted the Aramaic rendering. As we noted frequently, our targumist does not try to match the simple overt meaning of the biblical text with rabbinic *halakhah*.[45] He also dislikes repetitions. Therefore, he paraphrases here to distinguish the two phrases.

13. *Leviticus* 20:2 commands that if anyone dwelling in Israel gives "any of his seed" (children) to the idol Molech, "people of the land" must kill him. *Onkelos* clarifies that "people of the land" means "the Israelite people," and not any inhabitant.[46] Nachmanides believed that if a single Jew sinned he defiled (*tetamei*) the entire nation: the single individual's act causes the *Shekhinah*, "God's presence," to depart from all Jews.[47] "Therefore *Onkelos* translated 'the Israelite people,'" for this expression tells us that all Jews in Israel, not only those in the area of the Molech worshiper are defiled, and involved in the death sentence. Nachmanides' theology is not explicit in the Aramaic words, *Onkelos* does not translate to teach theology, and, in any event, it is more reasonable to state that *Onkelos* is simply removing the possibility of a misunderstanding by clarifying that it is Israelites who administer the punishment.

14. Some *Onkelos* texts have *raba b'amei* in *Leviticus* 21:4, but the more correct Berliner and Sperber texts have *b'raba b'amei*.[48] The first could refer to the priest, while the second seems to state that a priest may not defile himself even for (the meaning of *b*) a high-ranking person among his people. Nachmanides bases his interpretation upon the first text and states that *Onkelos* is teaching

---

45. See Drazin, *Targum Onkelos to Leviticus*, 28–30, for other examples where *Onkelos* is contrary to the halakhic interpretation.
46. Here and in v. 4. The rendering is also in *Pseudo-Jonathan* and *Sifra*. Nachmanides commentary is in verse 3.
47. Nachmanides in v. 3 and 18:21. He refers us to the Babylonian Talmud, *Berakhot* that states that one who eats without a blessing robs God and other Jews.
48. Berliner, Targum Onkelos; Sperber, The Bible in Aramaic.

us that a priest may not defile himself because he is a distinguished person and must not lower himself. There are two problems with this explanation. First, it appears to be based on an incorrect text. Second, *Onkelos* is virtually literal and is most likely not reflected in Nachmanides' idea. There are only two targumic changes: *b* is added, and "people" is plural in the Hebrew and in the singular in the Aramaic.

15. *Onkelos* to *Leviticus* 22:28 transforms "Concerning a cow or lamb, you shall not slaughter him and its young in one day" in two significant ways. The names of the two animals in Hebrew denote both males and females. They are turned into the feminine form. Secondly, "him" is replaced by "her." These changes forbid the murder of the dam with its young, but not the male parent. Nachmanides states that the targumist made this rendering to conform to the *halakhah*.[49] However, we have seen that *Onkelos* does not deviate to teach *halakhah*; indeed, there are times that it translates contrary to the rabbinical interpretation.[50] It is more likely that the targumist used the feminine because the "mother" is mentioned in the prior verse and the male parent is frequently unknown.

16. Scripture calls the Jewish holidays *mikraei kodesh*, an obscure term.[51] It could mean "call,"[52] "befall,"[53] or "event."[54] Nachmanides to *Leviticus* 23:2, leans toward the first, and defines it as "a holy convocation:" a time for all Israelites to gather together in God's house and proclaim its holiness publicly with prayer, praise to God, clean garments and feasting. He notes that *Onkelos* has "sacred event," and maintains that the targumist is stating that whenever the festival occurs one must distinguish it from other days with words and acts,

---

49. The *halakhah* is in the Babylonian Talmud, *Chullin* 78a–79a.
50. Ibn Ezra, for example, applies the biblical law also to a known male parent.
51. The phrase occurs 17 times in the Pentateuch; *Exodus* 12:16 (twice); *Leviticus* 23:2, 3, 4, 7, 8, 24, 35, 36, 37; *Numbers* 28:18, 25, 26; 29:1, 7, 12. *Mikra* appears alone five times; *Numbers* 10:2; *Isaiah* 1:13, 4:5; and *Nehemiah* 8:8 (twice). In latter instances, the word clearly means "call." See *Encyclopedia Mikra'it* (Jerusalem: Mosad Bialik, 1950, IV, cols 437–39. See also Saadiah's rendering in *Torat Chayim*, vol. 3, 135, h. 17, to *Exodus* 12:16.
52. From the verb *kara*, "call."
53. As in *Genesis* 49:1, "Gather around and I will tell you what will befall (*yikra*)."
54. This is the view of *Onkelos*, Rashbam, *Pseudo-Jonathan*, *Neophyti*, the Cairo Geniza *Targum Fragments*, and *Sifrei* and *Sifra* to *Exodus* 12:26 and *Numbers* 28:36, as well as the *Samaritan Targums*.

and make it holy with special food and drink and clean garments. While it is true that *Onkelos* is stating that the festival is "a sacred event," there is nothing in these words that suggest that it is the Israelite's obligation to make it sacred, nor is there even a hint of food, drink, and garments.

17. Nachmanides expresses surprise in his commentary to *Leviticus* 23:11 that *Onkelos* appears to be inconsistent. He declared that the noun *shabbath* means "weeks," that *Onkelos* was correct in the latter part of verse 15, but inconsistently substitutes "holiday" in the first part of verse 15 and in verse 11. He rejects ibn Ezra's explanation that *shabbath* is an expression with different meanings depending on the context: occasionally denoting "holiday" and sometimes "seventh period." He also fails to note that it is more reasonable to render "holiday" than "weeks" here, since the verse states "the priest will offer it [the sheaf of the first fruits] on the day after the *shabbath* [the holiday]." Additionally, the *Targum*'s "holiday" reflects the rabbinic understanding of the verse[55] and contrary to the hotly disputed Saducean position that the offering is made "after Sunday."[56]

18. *Leviticus* 23:28 states: "Do no work *b'etzem* of that day because it is the Day of Atonement." *B'etzem* means "strength" or "high point," as in *Job* 21:23, "first appearance [of the day]," as in Lamentations 4:8 "on the day itself,"[57] that is, during the entire period of the day,[58] and there are also other interpretations.[59] *Onkelos* has *qeren*, literally "horn," an oft-repeated biblical metaphor for "strength." Nachmanides mentions the *Targum* and explains it: "the strength [of an animal] is in its horns, therefore the substance of a thing is called 'its horn.'" Since "strength," in his opinion, adds no clarity to the verse, he contends[60] that *Onkelos* is describing the biblical prohibition against working during the "strength" of the day, that is, "on the day itself," from one appearance of the stars to the second appearance on the following night. The targumist, he opines, is

---

55. In *Sifra*, and the Babylonian Talmud, *Menachot* 65a, b.
56. *Neophyti, Pseudo-Jonathan,* and Cairo Geniza *Targum Fragments* are more explicit than *Onkelos*: "after the holiday, the first [day] of Passover." See *Encyclopedia Judaica* v, Cols. 50–53, "Fixing the Omer."
57. See Rashi to Babylonian Talmud, *Menachot* 68a, s.v. *Ad asham*.
58. *Sifra, Emos* 14:7.
59. Nachmanides mentions several others.
60. With reference to *Sifra, Emos* 14:7.

excluding the additional time that the rabbis added in the post-biblical period to the beginning and end of the holiday.

Since, as noted above, one literal definition of *b'etzem* is "strength," all that the targumist is doing is translating the word literally. Furthermore, "strength," by itself, does not suggest that the day in question is the biblical day from one appearance of stars to the next. Finally, the halakhic rule that night begins with the appearance of stars is not biblical, but rabbinic.[61]

19. Rashi and ibn Ezra state the generally accepted view that Leviticus's 23:40 *hadar* means "adorned" or "beautiful," and that the rabbis interpreted it to refer to the *ethrog*. Nachmanides believed that the Hebrew *hadar* means the same as the Aramaic *ethrog*. He attempts to prove that *ethrog* means "desire" from two targumic renderings, both of which are not in our *Onkelos* text.[62] There are two additional problems with Nachmanides' notion. First, "beautiful" and "desire," although related, are not the same, *hadar* is "beautiful" and not "desire." Second, and more importantly, it is questionable whether the Aramaic root *r-g-g*, "desire,"[63] is related to *ethrog*. They have only two letters in common.

20. After discussing the holiday, *Leviticus* 23:44 concludes: "Moses spoke about the *moadei* (set times) [of] the Lord to the Israelites." *Onkelos* has: "Moses spoke about the order of the fixed times of the Lord and he taught them to the Israelites." There are two technical and two substantive changes. The three full *Targums* and the Cairo Geniza *Targum Fragments* handle the construct *moadei* as *hamoadim shel* and add the implied "of." *Onkelos* inserts *seder*, meaning "order" or "arrangement," which is implied, to enhance the clarity and readability of the passage.[64] All of the *Targums* also supply "and he taught them," adding a subject and a verb, since the Bible's "to the Israelites" is usually preceded by a subject and verb, as in *Deuteronomy* 31:19 and *Sifra*.

Nachmanides contends that *Onkelos*'s "order" expresses *Sifra* and the Babylonian Talmud *Megillah*'s 32a's teaching that Moses conveyed the laws of

---

61. The sources are in Shamma Friedman, ed., *Chameish Sugyot min Hatalmud Bavli* [Hebrew], (Jerusalem: Haigud l'Parshanut Hatalmud, 2003).
62. *Genesis* 2:9 and *Exodus* 20:14.
63. Jastrow, *Dictionary*, 1447.
64. The other full *Targums* and Cairo Geniza *Targums* also add the word, but place it in its plural form, "orders," since there is a plurality of holidays.

the festivals to the Israelites at the "proper time" (that is, the laws of Passover were taught around the Passover season, etc.), and that its "and he taught them" infers that Moses taught the people that years are intercalated with an extra month.

Nachmanides does not perceive that "order" and "at its proper time" are not the same, and if our targumist wanted to instruct the latter lesson, he could have easily written it ("at its proper time" is one word in Aramaic), and the other *Targums*, by pluralizing "orders," clearly understood that they, as *Onkelos*, were speaking about the specific "arrangements" of each holiday, not the time when Moses spoke to the people.

Nachmanides also fails to observe that "and he taught them" is used in *Deuteronomy* 31:19 in the same general context and does not have the meaning he is reading into it. Saadiah uses it here without Nachmanides' meaning, and there is a simple explanation for the insertion, as we mentioned above.[65]

21. The Bible prohibits eating certain produce in *Leviticus* 25:5, including "the grapes of *n'zirecha*," the root being *n-z-r*. Nachmanides attempts to prove that *nazir* means "separated" by pointing to *Onkelos*, which uses "separated." He does not note that *nazir* has many meanings and our targumist simply chose the meaning that is most appropriate for the context, and the *Targum* is rendering the word literally. Jastrow defines *nazir* as "to surround," "to keep off," "to set apart," "to vow to be a Nazarite," "to abstain," "to dedicate one's self to," and "to renounce."[66] As a noun, it means "a crown." Saadiah states that by using *n'zirecha*, the verse is prohibiting even the best of the grapes.[67] Chazkuni[68] and ibn Ezra[69] state that it forbids even grapes that grew without human toil.

22. The noun "Jubilee" is a transliteration of the Hebrew *yobel*. The Greek Septuagint translated it as *aphesis*, "release," as does ibn Ezra. Philo uses the Greek

---

65. It is worth repeating; I am not criticizing or even commenting upon whether Nachmanides' understanding of Scripture is correct. I am merely stating that there is no reasonable basis for arguing that *Targum Onkelos* contains Nachmanides' interpretation.
66. Jastrow, *Dictionary*, 891–93.
67. Chavel, *Torat Chayim*, 256, N. 1.
68. Ibid., 256.
69. Ibid., 256, N. 13.

apokatastasis, "restitution."[70] The Babylonian Talmud[71] states that the Jubilee period is named after the ram's horn that is sounded at the beginning of the year.[72] Luzzatto feels that this is a rationalization:[73] the word was originally a holiday by Baal worshippers made up of *yo*, an exclamation of joy, and *bal*, a shortened form of the idol Baal. The Torah, he explains, adopted, transformed, and elevated the word to describe a period of time when people would recall that the land belongs to God, when the poor and slaves would be redeemed, and produce would belong to rich and poor alike. My uncle, Dr. Sidney B. Hoenig, suggested that the Jubilee year was a leap year of forty-nine days that brought the lunar calendar in harmony with the solar year.[74]

Nachmanides contends in Leviticus 25:10 that the year is called "Jubilee" because of "the liberty" that it brings to Israel. He refers to *Onkelos's Numbers* 17:11, where *yobel* translates a word meaning "carry," as proof. Thus, he concludes, *yobel* is a year that brings (or "carries") liberty. This is a non-sequitur. While among other meanings, *yobel* is defined as "carry" and "bring,"[75] yet "carry" and "bring" do not extend to denote that the thing brought is liberty. Furthermore, if the targumist wanted to suggest liberty in this verse, he could have said so explicitly when the Jubilee is mentioned. Instead, he retains the Hebrew and does not translate it.[76] Thus, while there is as much merit to Nachmanides' definition as the others, there is no reasonable basis for proving his view by referring to our *Targum*.

23. *Leviticus* 25:47f requires Israelites to redeem fellow Israelites who became impoverished, and are sold to non-Israelites or to an *eiker mishpachat ger*. The latter phrase is obscure. *Eiker* is probably based on a verb meaning "to uproot,"

---

70. Philo, *The Works of Philo*, trans. C.D. Yonge (Massachusetts: Hendrickson Publishers, 1993), 164.
71. Babylonian Talmud, *Rosh Hashanah*, 26a.
72. See *Onkelos* to *Exodus* 19:13 and *Pseudo-Jonathan* to *Joshua* 6:4. This is also Rashi's view in *Leviticus* 25:10.
73. Commentary, 431.
74. Sidney B. Hoenig, "A Jewish Reaction to Calendar Reform," *Tradition* 7 (1964), 5; "Sabbatical years and the year of Jubilee," *JQR* 59 (1969), 222–36.
75. Jastrow, *Dictionary*, 561, defines it as "to break through," "come forth," "flow," "lead," "carry," "bring," "cut," and "trim."
76. The other *Targums* also render the word literally.

according to Nachmanides, Abravanel, and others. It could denote an idol, being that which should be uprooted, or refer to one who is sold to minister to an idol with tasks such as drawing water and hewing stones.[77] Thus, the final three Hebrew words would either mean "an uprooted one of a stranger's family," or "an idol worshiper of a stranger's family." *Onkelos* paraphrases it as "an Aramean from the seed of a proselyte."[78] The noun "Aramean" almost certainly means a "deceitful person," such as Laban the Aramean, who deceived his son-in-law, the patriarch Jacob.[79]

Nachmanides contends that the *Targum*'s "Aramean" denotes a non-Israelite: "the Israelite "sold himself to a stranger who dwells among us, or who sold himself to the *eiker* the stock, of the stranger's family, who is himself a non-Israelite." There are several problems with this interpretation of the *Targum*. First, "Aramean," as we noted above, probably means "deceitful person," which could be an Israelite, as noted by Levy.[80] Second, "Aramean" is not used elsewhere to refer to all non-Israelites. Third, if *eiker* and its Aramaic equivalent "Aramean" is a non-Israelite, this would be superfluous since the prior phrase speaks about a non-Israelite. Finally, and most convincingly, one must read the entire phrase: "an Aramean from the seed of a proselyte." The seed or child of a proselyte, is an Israelite.[81]

---

77. *Sifra*, the Babylonian Talmud *Kiddushin* 20a, b and *Bava Kama* 13, Rashi, *Pseudo-Jonathan*, and others.
78. There are four changes; (1) *eiker* became "Aramean," (2) the preposition "from" is inserted for the sake of clarity, (3) "family" is "seed," indicating, more specifically an offspring, and (4) *ger* is rendered "proselyte" by *Onkelos* whenever the context of the verse allows it.
79. J. Levy, *Chaldäisches Wörterbuch über dir Targumim I* (Leipzig, 1867), 65, identifies the Aramaic "deceitful person" as a renegade who slanders fellow Israelites before the Romans.
80. See above note.
81. Except when a male proselyte remarries a non-Israelite, a situation which is not suggested in the verse.

– CHAPTER 12 –

Numbers

> In his commentary to *Numbers*, Nachmanides quotes the Aramaic of *Onkelos* twenty-nine times, frequently seeking support for his own understanding of the scriptural text from this rabbinically authoritative translation, which he esteemed. Sixteen of these instances, representing just over half of the twenty-nine references, are what most people would consider reasonable, many simply because he only mentions the *Targum* without any analysis. However there are also thirteen difficult, counterintuitive explanations of *Onkelos*. In twelve of these thirteen interpretations, Nachmanides derives a rather lengthy, imaginative, and complex meaning from a single Aramaic word that a simple definition of the word would not warrant. Thus, in every instance but two where Nachmanides analyzes *Onkelos* in *Numbers*, or eighty-seven percent, his explanation is problematical.[1]

THE THIRTEEN DIFFICULT COMMENTS BY NACHMANIDES IN NUMBERS

1. Does "sacred" mean a person can choose to whom he wants to give produce?

    Numbers 5:10 reads, "Every man's sacred (*kodashav*) shall be his. Whatever a man gives to the priest shall be his." What is the meaning of "sacred"? The plain import of the text and the rabbinic commentary in *Numbers Rabbah*

---

1. The thirteen instances where Nachmanides simply mentions *Onkelos* without any elaboration are: *Numbers* 4:20, 26; 12:6; 16:15 (twice); 21:18; 23:10, 24; 24:1, 3, 20; and 33:55. The two instances where he analyzes *Onkelos* and is reasonable is his second discussion about the *Targum* in 16:1 and 22:32.

Bachya ben Asher, as previously mentioned, was a mystic like Nachmanides, mentions both him and *Onkelos* frequently, and frequently elaborates upon Nachmanides' interpretations. Yet, interestingly, he does not cite a single one of the difficult Nachmanidean readings to *Numbers* in his commentary. It is possible, therefore, that he also recognized the difficulties that are shown below.

and the Babylonian Talmud, *Berachot* 63a, is that "sacred" includes every kind of gift that an Israelite gives to a priest; when the priest receives the gift, it belongs to the priest.

Nevertheless, *Onkelos* and *Pseudo-Jonathan* insert the technical term *ma'aser*, "[sacred] tenth," which is usually used for two gifts, thereby restricting the biblical command to *ma'aser*, the tenth of the produce that is given to the Levites or the tenth of the produce that must be eaten by the field owner in Jerusalem.[2]

This insertion is probably a scribal error. Not all *Onkelos* texts have the word, although it is in *Midrash Sifrei Zutta*. It does not appear in other verses where "sacred" is alone, such as verse 9 and *Leviticus* 22:12.

Nachmanides argues that the targumist added *ma'aser* to inform his readers that, as explained by C.B. Chavel, "although [tithes are] given away by the owner, [they] are still partially 'his' inasmuch as the choice to whom to give them and satisfaction in so choosing, is his."[3]

The issue of whether *ma'aser* is part of the original *Targum* aside, Nachmanides' reading into the word is hardly likely since the one word *ma'aser* does not indicate or even suggest the elaborate idea that Nachmanides sees in it. Additionally, if the targumist wanted to explain the verse as Nachmanides contends, he could have stated what he wanted explicitly. Furthermore, if all that the targumist wanted to say is that the owner of the produce has a choice to whom he gives part of the produce, doesn't the text itself imply this – when it states, "every man's sacred [items] shall be his" – without the addition of the term *ma'aser*?

2. Does "longing" mean heating and drying temperaments?

Numbers 11:6 describes the Israelites crying out and expressing their displeasure to Moses. They wanted meat because without the meat "our souls are dry."[4]

---

2. The word is also inappropriately inserted into the Aramaic of *Deuteronomy* 12:26 and 26:13. See the discussion in Drazin, *Targum Onkelos to Deuteronomy*, 149 and 230. There is also a *terumat ma'aser*, a gift that the Levites give to priests from the *ma'aser* they receive from Israelites.
3. Chavel, *Ramban*, 49, note 68. Unfortunately, without Chavel's explanation, Nachmanides' interpretation is even more problematic.
4. The biblical word *nefesh*, commonly translated "soul," actually means "person" or "life force" (see the introduction).

Onkelos explains the quoted metaphor as "our souls [or, spirits] have a longing."⁵

Nachmanides does not recognize this phrase as a metaphor, and takes it literally. He states that it either means that because of their many desires, the Israelites' temperaments heated and dried up, or it means that they lacked sufficient food and essential liquids to moisten their bodies and satisfy their souls.⁶

Nachmanides contends that *Onkelos*'s "longing" reflects his first interpretation. This is problematical because the phrase "our souls have longing" does not suggest "temperaments [have been] heated and dried up." Again, Nachmanides is reading too much into an expression that means no more than the Israelites longed to have meat.

3. Mixed metaphors.

Numbers 11:12 contains Moses's complaint to God: "Did I conceive (*hariti*) this entire people or did I give birth to it?" *Onkelos* transforms the Bible's feminine and motherly metaphor into a masculine and fatherly one: "Am I the father to this entire people? Are they my children?" to protect Moses's dignity – he isn't compared to a woman – to simplify the figure of speech, and to conform to the masculine form of "nurse" later in the verse.

Nachmanides recognizes in this instance that Moses is speaking metaphorically, but argues that the targumist is translating the first phrase literally since *hariti* not only means "conceive," but also "cause to become pregnant [the father's role]."

His view fails to note that the biblical statement is a single metaphor: Moses would not mix metaphors and speak about the male and female role in a single statement.

4. A person can delegate and not diminish his power.

Nachmanides believed that *Onkelos* was translating the Hebrew *v'atzalti* "take," in *Numbers* 11:17 literally. The Bible states that God told Moses to assemble seventy Israelite elders: "I will take (*v'atzalti*) from the spirit that is

---

5. *Midrash Sifrei* is similar.
6. As noted above, contrary to Nachmanides' opinion, *nefesh* in the Bible does not mean "soul." He seems to want to translate it as "temperament" here.

on you and put it on them." These elders would then assist Moses in leading the people.

Onkelos substitutes "increase" in place of "take": "I will increase from the spirit that is on you and put it on them." Thus, rather than suggesting a lessening of Moses's powers, the verse is addressing the result, that the elders' powers would increase.[7]

Nachmanides states that *Onkelos* is informing us that *v'atzalti* has two meanings or objectives: (1) a drawing forth by the giver for the benefit of the received (the meaning in this verse), or (2) a drawing forth in which a giver gives to himself so that the object remains with him.

Actually, the *Onkelos* translator had no need to tell his readers that something was taken from Moses and given to the elders; this is explicit in the verse, "I will take from the spirit that is on you and put it on them." Why then did he change "take" to "increase"? The *Onkelos* wording is a paraphrase to remove the implication that Moses was diminished in any way when he gave over the ability to prophesy.

5. Was our translator literal because he wanted to reflect *Sifrei*?

Nachmanides to *Numbers* 11:19 refers to verse 23 and states that there is a dispute in *Midrash Sifrei* whether the verse should be understood literally. He argues that the *Onkelos* translator took the side of the literalists in this case since he rendered the verse literally.

Onkelos is generally literal and no *halakhah* should be deduced from a customary literal rendering.

6. Does "rich" and "poor" suggest selling produce for lower and higher prices?

Numbers 13:20 describes Moses telling the twelve spies to explore Canaan and examine whether the land is "fat or thin." *Onkelos* explains the metaphor as "rich or poor," because "fat" and "thin" are obviously metaphors since land cannot be "fat" or "thin," and the targumist's explanatory replacement is Scripture's obvious intent. He did not select "good" or "bad" since these words were already used in verse 19 and he prefers to avoid repetitions.[8]

---

7. This is also the interpretation of the other *Targums*, *Sifrei*, *Sifrei Zutta*, and Rashi. Moses' powers would leave him like a flame kindling and increasing fire in another object without any diminishment on its part.

8. *Pseudo-Jonathan* and *Neophyti* and the *Fragmented Targum* (V) (P) explain the metaphors by

Nachmanides states that our targumist made the change to refer to the fact that there are countries that are rich because they charge low prices for their goods and are able to reap wealth from the quantity they sell. In contrast, other countries may have good land with a small produce, are dependent upon their neighbors for sustenance, and are not powerful.

This is unlikely because "rich" and "poor" do not, in and of themselves, imply these ideas.

7. Does "let go" mean a person's punishment is delayed?

In 14:19, Moses beseeches God, who was angered over the Israelite murmurings, "Now forgive [or, pardon] this people's iniquity." The Hebrew is *selach*, the word used frequently during the Yom Kippur service when the Jew seeks atonement.

Nachmanides argues that *selach* is not a full pardon, but only a "remittance of punishment." The person is punished, but the punishment is delayed. He attempts to prove his position by referring to the targumic rendering *shavak*.

Leaving aside the startling idea that Jews praying on Yom Kippur are asking to be punished at a later time, *Onkelos's shavak* means "leave," "let go," "forsake," "abandon," "leave behind," "bequeath," "divorce," and "let alone,"[9] none of which imply the Nachmanidean idea. In fact, *shavak* arguably suggests the total removal of the sin.

8. Can we read the targumist's mind?

Numbers 16:1 states that Korach, who mounted an ill-fated rebellion against Moses, started the rebellion when he "took," but the object of this verb, what he took, is not mentioned. This obscurity stimulated a host of widely different speculations. *Onkelos* opted to paraphrase the action with "he separated himself," making the verb a reflexive referring to Korach who took himself. This interpretation is not unique. It is given in Job 15:12, *Genesis* 14:15 and *Exodus* 14:10.

While the targumic version is somewhat less obscure, it is nevertheless not entirely clear. The question remains, separated from what? The "separation" could have been physical (moving to the side) or an inclination (having

---

inserting "fruits" and applying "fat" and "thin" to it.

9. Jastrow, *Dictionary* 1516–1517.

a separate idea). There is no way to determine exactly what our targumist intended.

Nevertheless, Nachmanides states that *Onkelos* is reflecting the idea contained in the later *Midrash Tanchuma*; Korach took himself to one side to separate himself from the other Israelites so that he could argue with Moses about the priesthood that Moses had just recently conferred on Aaron and his sons.[10]

This reading of *Onkelos* is reasonable in the sense that it may have been in the translator's mind. Yet, as stated above, there is no way of determining *exactly* what our translator intended.

9. Does the removal of "aromatic" suggest that the spices were not the sacred spices?

Moses created a test to show whether the rebel Korach and his cohorts were correct. He and his party were told in 16:7 to take censers with burning spices and offer them to God. If God accepted the gift, they would be proven right. The word for spice, *ketoret*, is generally rendered *ketoret busmin*, "aromatic spice," by *Onkelos*.[11]

Nachmanides had a faulty *Targum* text that lacked *busmin*. He argues that our targumist intentionally omitted the adjective "aromatic" to make it clear that this was not the customary spice used in the tabernacle or because he did not want to praise these spices since they were not being used to fulfill the commandments to burn the incense daily.[12]

It seems unlikely that the removal of "aromatic" implies that the spices did not contain the same ingredients as the customary spices used in the Tabernacle. Additionally, Nachmanides had a faulty text to *Leviticus* 10:1 without

---

10. For other interpretations of 16:1, see Drazin, *Targum Onkelos to Deuteronomy*, 176. It may be asked: don't I do the same when I interpret *Onkelos*? Yes, I also try to read the targumist's mind, but I only explain the *Targum* according to the targumic methodology and I do not read an imaginative interpretation into the *Targum* that is not suggested in the wording of the passage. Bachya ben Asher mentions Nachmanides interpretation and what *Onkelos* says, but does not read the Nachmanidean view into the *Targum*.
11. The adjective is occasionally used in the Bible itself, as in *Exodus* 30:7.
12. Isaiah B. Berlin, *Minei Targuma* (University of Michigan Library reprint. 1836), argues that Nachmanides had the correct text. It appears that he bought into Nachmanides' view and wanted to change the *Onkelos* text to reflect it.

busmin where two of Aaron's sons brought spices with an improper fire and Nachmanides himself recognizes there that the rabbis taught that this was the sacred incense. Also, if the spices used in *Leviticus* 10:1 were sacred spices and smelled as usual, the absence of the word "aromatic" does not imply that the spices were somehow inferior.

10. Does "caused the death" imply that God did not give the instruction?

    The Israelites gathered against Moses and accused him in *Numbers* 17:6 that "you killed the Lord's people [who rebelled against you]." *Onkelos*[13] softens the accusation with the indirect "you caused the death," since Moses did not actually kill the rebels, he only indirectly caused their death by requiring the test of the fire pans. When the rebels brought the fire pans before God, God killed them for their disobedience.

    Nachmanides quotes the *Targum* and explains that the translator altered the passage to inform us that the people accused Moses and Aaron of causing the people's death by telling Korach and his company to offer the strange incense to God on their own initiative, because God never instructed them to do so. This is certainly an interesting reading of the congregation's intent, but changing "killed" to "caused the death" does not suggest an argument that God did not instruct Moses what to do.

11. Can we develop a narrative from a single word?

    Nachmanides' commentary to *Numbers* 21:1 is another example where he develops a lengthy narrative based on the targumist's change of a single word from the Hebrew original. The Bible states: "The Canaanite king of Arad, who lived in the south, heard that Israel was traveling by way of *atarim*. He attacked Israel and took some captives." *Onkelos* reads *atarim* as if it lacked the letter *aleph*[14] and denoted "spies."[15]

    Nachmanides writes: "According to *Onkelos*, when the spies came and went up from the south and then returned, the inhabitants of the land noticed them. This Canaanite [the king of Arad] who dwelt in the south heard about them

---

13. Also *Pseudo-Jonathan*, but not *Neophyti* and the Samaritan Targums.
14. The Hebrew Bible frequently has superfluous *alephs*.
15. The other *Targums*, *Peshitta*, *Vulgate*, *Aquilas*, *Symmachus*, *Samaritan Targums*, Rashi, ibn Ezra, Kimchi, Rashbam, and others also give this interpretation. There are other explanations. See Drazin, *Targum Onkelos to Deuteronomy*, 208.

and followed the way they went until he reached the Israelite camp. And he [the targumist] explained it well."

12. Does "wife's" suggest the drama Nachmanides reads into it?

It is unclear why the Bible mentions "And Asher's daughter's name [was] Serah" in *Numbers* 26:46. The only other females named in this section are Zelophehad's daughters in verse 33. Rashi states that the daughters are named because they uniquely inherited land, which was generally only given to males. It is also possible that Serah is mentioned because she was a well-known person. Rashi, who goes beyond the plain meaning of the Bible and includes midrashic interpretations, adds as a second explanation that she was renowned because of her unique longevity; she was the only survivor of the close to seventy people who entered Egypt with Jacob 210 years earlier. *Pseudo-Jonathan* extends her life much longer: she ultimately entered Paradise alive.[16]

Nachmanides had an *Onkelos* text that read "Asher's wife's daughter's name [was] Serah." This is not in the accepted Sperber and Berliner *Onkelos* texts.

Nachmanides explains this *Onkelos* version by reading an extended family drama into the single word "wife's": he suggests that Asher, Jacob's son, married a young woman with a child when he was very old. Although Asher had sons, this wife only had a daughter from a prior husband, and the daughter inherited her father's land like Zelophehad's daughters. He contends that this is why *Onkelos* added "wife's": to remind us of these "facts" and to tell us that she, like Zelophehad's daughters, also inherited land in Canaan.

This Nachmanidean commentary shows the sage's tendency to invent narratives to explain his view of the biblical and targumic texts. But it raises the question, what did the scribe intend when he added "wife's"? It is certainly possible that the scribe had the same feeling as Nachmanides that it is legitimate to invent stories to fill out biblical narratives when – as often happens – the Bible does not reveal everything. But – and this is the point – Nachmanides' explanation of the scribe's additional word is only a possibility. The scribe may have had another reason in mind for his addition. For example, he may have never considered the issue of inheritance; he may have only addressed why

---

16. Compare the Babylonian Talmud, *Sotah* 13a; *Midrash Derekh Eretz Zuta*, end; and *Midrash Pirke d'R. Eliezer*, chapter 48.

she was still alive; although many years passed since Asher lived, Serah was not his child, but his wife, and was a baby when he died of old age.

It is fair to say that Nachmanides had a right to imagine what occurred and that his explanation is "possible." But it is problematical to insist, as Nachmanides tends to do, that the long generally highly unusual narrative that he uses to explain the verse in the Torah and is what *Onkelos* is saying or implying. This is especially difficult when another solution than Nachmanides' is more reasonable.

13. Does "sprinkling" mean only sprinkling with ashes of the red heifer?

Numbers Chapter 31 recalls the war that the Israelites fought against the Midianites. After the war, in verse 23, the Bible states, "whatever [gold, silver, brass, iron, tin, and lead] can withstand fire, pass it through the fire and it shall be clean; but it must be cleansed with the water of sprinkling; and anything that cannot withstand fire, pass [it] through water." *Onkelos* renders the verse literally, adding only the final "it" to enhance the passage's clarity.

Is this a purification rule applicable only to Midianite items acquired as war spoil, or does it apply to all vessels that a Jew acquires from non-Jews: a Jew cannot use a vessel until it is immersed?

Nachmanides[17] and many others contended that there is a vessel immersion requirement today when vessels are acquired from non-Jews, but it is not biblical in origin, only rabbinical. Thus, verse 23, which seems to be speaking of vessels that must be purified *bemei nidah*, "with water of sprinkling," is referring to water mixed with the ashes of the red heifer which was required to purify a person who had come into contact with a dead body.

Nachmanides seeks support for this view from the *Targum*: "and similarly *Onkelos* translated it the purification of sprinkling the ashes of the heifer." *Onkelos* does not use these words; Nachmanides is referring to the Aramaic, "but it must be cleansed with the water of sprinkling." The Hebrew has *nidah* and the Aramaic *adayuta*, "sprinkling." In essence, Nachmanides is stating that *adayuta* is not a literal rendering of *nidah* and he reads into *adayuta*, "sprinkling," that the sprinkling is done with the ashes of the red heifer.

---

17. Also Saadiah; Maimonides, *Mishneh Torah, Hilkhot Maachaloth Assuroth* 17:5; Rashbam; Rashi; ibn Ezra; and others. The contrary view is in Rashba's commentary on Maimonides.

There are two problems with Nachmanides' interpretation of the *Targum*. First, *adayuta* is a literal rendering of *nidah*. *Onkelos* is literal and adds nothing in the passage except "it."

Whenever the term *nidah* is used in Scripture for a person, our targumist renders it *rachok*, a term that literally means "distance" or "far," and suggests repugnance.[18] He also uses *rachok* for *arlah, to'eivah* and *pigul*. However, when *nidah* is connected with "water," which cleanses, *rachok* is inappropriate, and "sprinkling," fits the context and is used because it is more suitable.[19] Thus the use of the word "sprinkling" is a characteristic even necessary, rendering having no special significance, certainly not referring to the water of the red heifer. Second, Nachmanides is reading his interpretation into a single word and ignores the fact that if the targumist wanted to teach about the sprinkling of the red heifer ashes on people, he should have said this explicitly.[20]

---

18. See, for example, *Leviticus* 12:2 and 20:21.

19. As in *Numbers* 19:9, 13, 20 and 21. Admittedly, these verses refer to the sprinkling of the waters of the red heifer, but this, in and of itself, does not prove that *Onkelos* to 31:23 also concerns this water.

20. Bachya ben Asher has an extensive discourse on this verse, but totally ignores Nachmanides' comment, apparently because he disagreed with his logic. Bachya refers to the Babylonian Talmud, *Avodah Zarah*, and explains that the Midianite vessels that were forbidden were only those that the Midianites used during the prior 24-hour period because the residue in the vessel could still enhance food cooked in them if the residue is less than 24 hours old. He says that that the basis of the law is *Deuteronomy* 14:21 that prohibits eating carcasses, animals that were not properly slaughtered. This law, as Nachmanides states, is the biblical law, but the rabbis extended it considerably. Why was this law not issued after the battle with Sichon and Og in *Numbers* 21 and 22? Bachya states that the war with Sichon and Og was fought on land promised to the Israelites and, says Bachya, according to the Babylonian Talmud, *Chullin* 17, "even dried pork was allowed at that time for the soldiers to eat as booty." The war with Midian, in distinction, was fought on non-promised land. Bachya does not explain why this eating distinction was made.

– CHAPTER 13 –

Deuteronomy

> Nachmanides mentions *Onkelos* twenty-eight times in his commentary to *Deuteronomy*. Only ten of these twenty-eight comments appear to be reasonable; however seven of the ten are really not analyses; they simply mention the *Targum* without any discussion.[1]

DIFFICULT INTERPRETATIONS

Eighteen of the twenty-eight Nachmanidean comments where he offers an analysis, or ninety percent, are difficult. In six instances Nachmanides did not recognize that the targumic deviation is a characteristic translation device and that it was not done for the purpose he imagines. Five times he read into the targumic paraphrase an interpretation or teaching that a reasonable reading of the words does not suggest. In three verses he failed to see that *Onkelos* is reflecting the word's plain meaning that is in a Tannaitic *Midrash*. He does not see that our targumist avoids an anthropomorphism twice. He appears to mistranslate the Aramaic in two verses.

EIGHTEEN DIFFICULT NACHMANIDEAN COMMENTS
ON ONKELOS IN DEUTERONOMY

1. Does the Torah only identify borders that are necessary to know when buying the land?

    Deuteronomy 1:1 states that Moses spoke to the Israelites "beyond the Jordan; in the wilderness, in the Arabah, over against Suph, between Paran and Tophel, and Laban, and Hazerot, and Di-zahab."

---

1. The seven instances where Nachmanides only mentions *Onkelos* without any elaboration are: 1:4, 15:1, 21:14, 21:16, 28:42, 29:25, and 33:7. The three times that he treats *Onkelos* at some length and is reasonable are 3:9, 3:11, and 33:6.

In his commentary to this passage, Nachmanides states that *Onkelos* had to interpret these apparent place names not as places but as allusions to various Israelite misdeeds because the Israelites were presently not in the wilderness as the verse seems to say, and had already entered the land of Moab.[2] Besides, he adds, Scripture does not "specify signs and borders more than [would be required] in selling a field."

Nachmanides is correct in regard to his first reason. Additionally, Tophel and Laban, mentioned in verse 1, are not cited elsewhere in the Bible, and it is reasonable to assume that they are not real places.[3] In fact, none of the six sites can be identified with certainty. However, Nachmanides' second explanation is obscure. Why would one think it is unreasonable to list how the Israelites traveled in the desert? Indeed, the Bible has such a list in *Numbers* 33. Furthermore, what is the relevance of "selling a field?" When Abraham purchased the double cave in *Genesis* 23, "signs and borders" were not mentioned.

2. Does the one word "cease" imply three interpretations?

Onkelos renders the end of *Deuteronomy's* 5:19, "the Lord spoke with your whole congregation… with a mighty voice, and He added no more," as "He did not cease [or, pause]."

The targumic language parallels various rabbinic interpretations. The Babylonian Talmud, *Sanhedrin* 17a, states: "Because it is characteristic of human beings that they are unable to utter all their words in one breath, but must make pauses, and it is characteristic of the Holy One, blessed be He, that this is not so, therefore He did not pause, and since He did not pause, He did not have to resume – for His voice is strong and goes on continuously."[4]

The Jerusalem Talmud, *Megillah* 70:4, states that R. Yohanan understood that the Bible means "cease" and said: "The Prophets and Writings will be suspended in the future, but the Five Books of the Torah will not, because it says 'did not cease.'"[5]

---

2. As indicated in *Numbers* 36:13 and infra verse 5.
3. Cf. Babylonian Talmud, *Arachin* 15a.
4. The Jerusalem Talmud, *Megillah* 1:5, is similar.
5. Géza Vermes, "The Decalogue and the Minim," in *In Memoriam Paul Kahle*, ed. Black, Matthew, Fohrer (Berlin: Topelmann, 1968), 236ff, notes that the interpretation is not derived from Scripture's *y-s-p* but from a variation of the word, the root *s-w-p*. This does not mean that our

Nachmanides reads three possible interpretations into the *Targum* wording "He did not cease," none of which are implied in the targumist's words. First, that God's "greatness and power were not withdrawn until He finished all the commandments." Second, that "there will never again be so great [a voice]." Third, "by way of the Truth (the mystic teachings of the *Kabbalah*), the verse is stating that they [the Israelites] heard all these words [proclaimed by] the voice of the Great One, and he did not add anything [perceivable] to all your assembly, except for this one voice, for it was only that voice that they grasped."[6]

3. Does *eikev* mean "roundabout"?

Deuteronomy 7:12 states "and it shall come to pass [Hebrew, *eikev*] because you listened to these ordinances" God will treat the Israelites well.

The term *eikev*, which usually means "heel," means, by extension, "a consequence." Relying on *Midrash Tanchuma*, Rashi translates it "heel." Chazkuni has "because." Ibn Ezra uses "end." Saadiah is similar with "reward."

The *Targums* clarify the plain meaning of the text with *chalaf*, "as a consequence," as in *Numbers* 14:24. Nachmanides notes the *Onkelos* rendering and praises it. However, he fails to note that both *eikev* and *chalaf* mean "as a consequence," and translates them "roundabout" or "circular."

4. Nachmanides fails to see that Onkelos is avoiding an anthropomorphism.

Onkelos (and *Pseudo-Jonathan*, but not *Neophyti*) changes the biblical reference to God "who favors no person and takes no bribe" (*Deuteronomy* 10:17).[7] The *Targum* reads, "there is not before Him the favoring of persons, nor the taking of a bribe." The paraphrase softens the anthropomorphism of God favoring and taking by distancing God with the addition of "before" and using the passive form. Also, it would be presumptuous even to say that God does

---

sources used a pre-Masoretic text. It is a well-known targumic (as well as midrashic) technique to base interpretations on such things as change of letters, sound changes, letter metathesis, and acronyms, as well as on reading the Hebrew as if it were Aramaic or another language. Compare 31:7; 32:2; 33:19, and 22. See, for example, Yitzchak Heinemann, *Darkei ha-Aggadah* (Jerusalem, 1954), 96 ff.

6. The quotes and emphases are from Chavel, *Ramban, Commentary on the Torah, Deuteronomy,* 70–71. Chavel explains the third point as an illusion to the idea that the Israelites heard only the first two commandments from God. Regarding the remaining eight commandments, the Israelites heard a divine voice (sound), but Moses had to explain the words to them.

7. Cf. *Deuteronomy* 1:16–17, 16:19.

not show favoritism or take bribes. The very association of such wrongdoing with God is inadmissible, even for the purpose of denying it.

Nachmanides, who rejected the idea that *Onkelos* avoids, or at least softens anthropomorphisms, states that the targumist is teaching a basic tenet of Maimonides (*Guide of the Perplexed* 1:58–60) that God's essence and attributes can only be expressed in negations. Furthermore, he does not explain why the targumist expresses this philosophy here and fails to incorporate the idea in other verses. [8]

5. Nachmanides quotes Rashi's interpretation of *Deuteronomy* 11:29, "put the blessing on Mount Gerizim" and the curse on Mount Ebal." Rashi states that he accepts the understanding of *Onkelos* that God is instructing the Israelites to "put those [people] who bless" and "those who curse," and not to put the blessing and curse on the mountain. Nachmanides rejects this interpretation stating that our verse could not refer to "those who bless" since Moses was not charged to select the people who would stand on Mount Gerizim until 27:11ff. [9] He contends that our verse "clearly does not pertain to the Mount Gerizim and Mount Ebal setting," but is teaching the lesson of 30:15 that one will be blessed if one performs the divine commandments. He ignores the plain meaning of the verse which mentions the placing of something on Mount Gerizim and Mount Ebal. He also fails to note that our targumist, as usual, is paralleling *Midrash Sifrei*, which speaks about the people who bless and curse. *Onkelos* is explaining 11:29 by what is clarified in 27:11ff, and is removing the problem that one cannot "put" an intangible object like a blessing and curse on a mountain. Further, Rashi's super commentator Mizrachi explains Rashi, and thereby *Onkelos*, that when one states he is placing a blessing, he is implying that he who gives the blessing is present.

6. Nachmanides quarrels with Rashi over the interpretation of *Deuteronomy*'s 13:9 *thoveh*. Rashi, quoting *Sifrei*, defines it as "longing." Nachmanides, quoting the Babylonian Talmud, *Sanhedrin* 61b states it is "willingness." Nachmanides supports his definition by referring to our targumist's rendering of the following

---

8. See our discussion of *Genesis* 46:1.
9. Unlike Rashi, Nachmanides generally rejected the interpretive principle *ein mukdam u'me'uchar ba'Torah*, that Scripture frequently records incidents out of chronological order. This view led him to develop his problematical interpretation.

word "hear" as "accept" arguing that this shows that the targumist understood the prior word as "willingness." As the commentator Mizrachi points out, Nachmanides fails to recognize that *Onkelos* frequently explains biblical metaphors and that whenever Scripture's "hear" is a figurative term for "listen," which occurs dozens of times, the targumist inserts the latter clearer term. Thus the rendering was nothing more than a characteristic stylistic deviation.[10]

7. *Sifrei*, Jerusalem Talmud, *Pessachim* 6:1, Babylonian Talmud, *Pessachim* 69b–70b, Saadiah, Rashi, Rashbam, Sforno, etc. explain *Deuteronomy* 16:2 "You shall sacrifice the Passover [sacrifice] to the Lord your God, lamb and herd" as *Targum Onkelos*: the lamb is for the paschal sacrifice "and sacred sacrifices [that is the *hagigah* sacrifice is] from your herd." The explanatory gloss is a necessary addition because the Passover offering is not brought from the herd, as indicated in *Exodus* 12:5. Nachmanides states that he disagrees with our targumist because he feels that the biblical conjuncture "and [herd]" indicates that both the flock and herd are for the *hagigah*. He criticizes Onkelos for the failure to use the "and" properly, since "'and' indicates that both were used for the same offerings." He fails to note that (1) the *Targum* is following the generally accepted interpretation of the verse, (2) it is reflecting *Sifrei* as it usually does when the *Midrash* offers the word's plain meaning, (3) the word "and" does not necessarily mean that both were the same offering.[11]

8. *Deuteronomy* 17:8 states "matters of controversy within your settlements." *Onkelos* adds a single word "legal [controversy]." Rashi explains the biblical text, "The wise of the city [judges] will have different opinions regarding the matter." Nachmanides mistakenly mentions that Rashi reflects the view of the *Targum*. Actually, unlike ibn Ezra who states that the "controversy" is between the litigants, Rashi contends that it is between the judges.[12] Nachmanides fails to notice that *Onkelos*'s single additional word "legal" could be understood

---

10. Rashi's super commentary Mizrachi was also puzzled over Nachmanides' reliance on *Onkelos*.
11. *II Chronicles* 35:7 mentions that the bovines were used for "sacred sacrifices." See Menachem Haran, *Templar and Temple Service in Ancient Israel* (Oxford: Clarendon Press, 1978) 322, h. 11. See also Drazin, *Targum Onkelos to Deuteronomy*, 167–68, for more details and sources, as well as the different renderings of *Pseudo-Jonathan* and *Neophyti*.
12. See Rashi's super commentators Mizrachi, Gur Aryeh, etc. who defend Rashi against Nachmanides.

as either the judges or the litigants disagree. The targumist added the word because he deviates frequently from the biblical text by adding a word or two so that the people would realize they must use the courts and not take justice into their own hand.[13] Nachmanides does not see that in this chapter itself the targumist adds "court" and "testimony" in verses 5 and 6 for this reason.

9. *Onkelos* and *Pseudo-Jonathan* add "in the fear" into *Deuteronomy* 18:13, "You must be wholehearted in the fear of the Lord your God." The characteristic and frequent addition removes the improper impression that humans can have a physical attachment to God. The *Targums* inform us that the connection is with the "fear" of the Lord and not with a corporeal divinity.[14] Ignoring that this is a consistent targumic style,[15] Nachmanides (Patshegan, Shefftel and others) seeking a halakhic implication contend that the gloss "fear" refers to a positive commandment: we should not be deficient in fearing God, but should direct our hearts to the Lord alone, and not try to predict future events through astrology, magic, or similar means, even though we could secure the information from these souces.[16]

10. *Deuteronomy* 21:12 has a seemingly obscure phrase: the captured beautiful woman should "make her nails." *Onkelos* explains it as "let her nails grow long." The paraphrase parallels R. Akiva's view in the Babylonian Talmud, *Yevamot* 48a and *Sifrei* as well as the commentaries of Rashi, ibn Ezra, Maimonides and others. Nachmanides, *Pseudo-Jonathan*, *Neophyti*, its marginal note, and the Septuagint have "cut her nails," which is R. Eliezer's opinion in the *Midrash* and Talmud. Rashi explains the view of the former interpreters: "She must let her nails grow long so that she will become unattractive." Nachmanides, curiously, states that she has to cut her nails to mourn the loss of her gods since

---

13. See, for example, 17:5, 21:19, 22:15 and 25:7 where *Onkelos* adds "court." All of the *Targums* do this. See, for example *Pseudo-Jonathan* to this verse and the *Targums* to *Esther* 23:21, *Ruth* 3:11 4:10ff, *Amos* 5:10, and *Lamentations* 5:14.
14. *Targum Neophyti* and its marginal notes have similar additions for the same reason: "good deeds" and "before," respectively.
15. *Targum Onkelos* inserts "fear" forty-five times into its translation of the Bible to remove an anthropomorphism or as a substitute for the biblical "idol."
16. *Targum Neophyti* and its marginal notes have similar additions for the same reason: "good deeds" and "before," respectively.

she will now become Jewish. This is contrary to the *halakhah* which prohibits the cutting of nails during mourning.[17]

Nachmanides contends that our targumist is relying on *Leviticus* 25:21, where *asa* means "growth," but considers that *II Samuel* 19:25, which suggest a translation of "cutting [the nails]," to be a better proof of the meaning here.[18] Actually, as pointed out by B.Z.J. Berkowitz,[19] the targumist is not relying on any verse. The Hebrew *asa* simply means "fix," as Rashi explains in his commentary to *Genesis* 1:7, and as *Onkelos* translates *Leviticus* 25:21.

11. While discussing *Deuteronomy* 21:14, Nachmanides mentions the targumic rendering of *Genesis* 3:24, and states that *Onkelos* renders *kervim*, "cherubim," as *k'rwoaya*, which he translates "like children." Actually, the *Targum* is literal and it is unlikely that the Bible is telling us that children guarded the Garden of Eden.

12. *Deuteronomy* 23:18 states: "There shall be no *qedeshah* of the daughters of Israel and no *qadesh* of the sons of Israel." *Onkelos* paraphrases: "A woman of the daughter of Israel shall not become the wife of a slave, and no man of Israel shall marry a bondwoman." The biblical text is subject to several interpretations.[20] The Bible's *qedeshah* could mean "harlot."[21] It could also express readiness as explained by ibn Ezra, Radak and other commentaries.[22] Since *Onkelos* was written for popular consumption, it has a reading that would be meaningful to its readers.

Nachmanides' interpretation of *Onkelos* is totally absent from its wording. He reads the first part of the targumic statement to admonish the Israelite court [which is not mentioned] to prohibit an Israelite female from sitting in

---

17. See Chavel, *Torat Chayim*, 181, note 7, regarding the anti-halakhic problem and note 11 for sources as to whether her conversion is forced upon her. See also Drazin, *Targum Onkelos to Deuteronomy*, 199, for additional details concerning why *Onkelos* chose its interpretation. For the views of Josephus, Abravanel and others, see J.H. Tigay, *The JPS Torah Commentary* (Jewish Publication Society, 2001–2003), 194 and 381.
18. See also *Job* 1:20 and *Jeremiah* 7:29.
19. Benzion Judah Berkowitz, *Lechem Vesimla* (Wilna, 1843).
20. See, e.g., Samson Raphael Hirsch, *The Pentateuch* (The Judaica Press, 1971), 465, and Schefftel, *Biure Onkelos*.
21. Maimonides, *The Commandments*, negative command, p. 332. Also *Mishneh Torah, Hilkhot Sanhedrin* 9:4. Rashbam to *Genesis* 28:21 is similar.
22. Compare *Isaiah* 13:3 and *Zephaniah* 1:7.

public [not mentioned] soliciting illicit sexual intercourse [also not in or even suggested by the Aramaic words].

13. *Onkelos* and the other Aramaic translations generally add *qadam* "before," as an evasive respectful technique to avoid an anthropomorphic portrayal of a close proximity between a human and a corporeal God. It corresponds to the typical biblical *lifnei*. There are over five hundred such additions in *Onkelos* and many more in *Pseudo-Jonathan* and *Neophyti*. Thus in *Deuteronomy* 29:28, for example, our *Targum* typically separates "things" from God by rendering the Bible's "Secret things are the Lord's" as "Secret things are *qadam*, before, the Lord." Unmindful of the characteristic nature of *qadam*, Nachmanides argues that the targumist inserted it here to teach a theological lesson: people are not punished for sins committed unknowingly, as the targumist teaches; secret things (unconscious acts) belong before God and humans bear no guilt for them.

14. *Deuteronomy* 32:6 has *naval*, "a foolish [people]" that *Targum Onkelos* paraphrases as "[people] who have received the Torah [but have not become wise]." Thus, our targumist understands *naval* as "foolish" and explains to its audience why the people were so: as *Sifrei* states, "who but yourself caused you to be so foolish as to fail to study and become wise from the Torah?"[23] *Pseudo-Jonathan*, Saadiah and Rashi understand *naval* like *Onkelos*, while ibn Ezra and Sforno take it to mean "villainous."

Nachmanides here and in verse 21, argues that it means "weak" as in *Exodus* 18:18. He contends that our *Targum* should be interpreted as saying that the people were apathetic in performing the Torah requirements. Needless to say, the *Targum*'s "who have received the Torah" does not address or even hint at the people's weariness. Again, had Nachmanides recognized that *Onkelos*

---

23. Baruch HaLevi Epstein, *Tosefet Berakha*, Hebrew (Israel: Moreshet Publishing House, 1999), 253, 4, quotes the Babylonian Talmud, *Megillah* 28b and explains *Onkelos* as saying: The Israelites are like a bushel (shelf) filled with books (which they received from Moses) but do not understand what is in them. Leibowitz, *Seven Years of Discourses on the Weekly Torah Reading*, 931, cites N.Z.Y. Berlin (Netziv, 1817–1893) that his is a criticism against students and rabbis who study to become righteous but never seem to become wise enough to behave properly. It was because of righteous idiots like this that the Second Temple was destroyed.

generally incorporates the *peshat* interpretations of the tannaitic *Midrashim*, he would not have misread the *Targum*.[24]

15. Nachmanides recognizes that in *Deuteronomy* 33:8 *t'riveihu* means "strived," as it is translated in *Psalms* 35:1. He quotes *Sifrei* and *Onkelos*'s "put to the test," and states that the *Targum* is informing us that 33:8 is referring to *Numbers* 20:13 where the Israelites "strived" with the Lord at the waters of Meribah.[25] He is correct that *Deuteronomy* 33:8 is referring to *Numbers* 20:13, but our *Targum*[26] did not use the words "put to the test" to inform us of this fact because the Aramaic paraphrase does not suggest the *Numbers* incident more than the biblical Hebrew. Our targumist used "put to the test" to avoid the unseemly anthropomorphic portrayal of humans striving (i.e., wrestling) with God. Nachmanides, as we noted in our discussion of *Genesis* 46:1, did not feel that *Onkelos* avoided anthropomorphisms.[27]

16. In hundreds of verses the *Onkelos* targumist inserts a word that the Bible only implies, and which is unnecessary in Hebrew, to enhance the clarity of the verse, and for no other reason. For example, in *Deuteronomy* 4:43, the *Targum* adds "the tribe" into the phrase "belonging to [the tribe of] Manasseh." In 4:34, it is "performed" in "or has the Lord [performed] miracles." In 4:3, "the worship of" is placed in "what the Lord did in regard to [the worship of] Baal-peor." So, too, the *Targum* inserts "worthy" into *Deuteronomy*'s 33:10 "These [are worthy to] teach Your laws to Jacob." However, Nachmanides states that "the entire tribe [of Levi] that He [God] tested in the affair of the [golden] calf, in Egypt, and in the wilderness; and, therefore they will teach His laws to Jacob. This is also the opinion of *Onkelos* who rendered the verse: These are worthy to each Your laws to Jacob." Actually, Nachmanides' interpretation, which is also in *Sifrei*, can be read into the passage without the implied word "worthy" being made explicit.

17. Our targumist translates *Deuteronomy*'s 33:11 *cheilo* as "his possessions," as he does in *Genesis* 34:29, *Numbers* 24:18, 31:9, and *Deuteronomy* 8:17, 18. This

---

24. Nachmanides is, of course, correct that *naval* also means weak. He is, however, incorrect in reading what he does into the Targum.
25. Scripture uses the same Hebrew root in *Numbers* as in *Deuteronomy*.
26. As well as *Pseudo-Jonathan* and *Neophyti*.
27. *Onkelos* removes the anthropomorphism in *Numbers* 20:13 by retaining the verb, but adding *qadam*, "before," thereby distancing the struggle from the divine.

definition is also in the Babylonian Talmud, *Yoma* 26a; *Sifrei*; *Pseudo-Jonathan*, ibn Ezra, Sforno and elsewhere. However, Nachmanides reads into the targumic rendering, which is only a literal translation: "He means what our rabbis[28] have said about the incense:[29] it bestows a blessing."

18. *Onkelos* clarifies *Deuteronomy*'s 33:24 obscure "blessed be Asher among sons" with "blessed be Asher with the blessings of children." The clarification is accomplished by disassociating the letter *mem*, "among," from "sons" and attaching it to "blessings," which the targumist adds and which yields "with the blessings." The *Targum* appears to reflect *Sifrei*, the tannaitic *Midrash*, from which it draws material: "You will find more of the tribes who was so blessed with children as Asher." It is also likely that "blessings" was added simply because it is implied in the text. It is also remotely possible that *Onkelos* has the idea contained in the later *Midrash Tanchuma* that no tribe was so blessed by the men of Israel as Asher because of the beauty of its women. However, Nachmanides' reading of *Onkelos* is not suggested by the Aramaic wording: "all the tribes will travel to Asher to purchase oil."

---

28. The term *cheilo* has other possible meanings. The Septuagint, Vulgate and others have "strength." Nachmanides, Saadiah, *Neophyti* and others have "hosts." However, what is significant for our purposes is what Nachmanides is reading into the *Targum*. See 18:1ff regarding the Levite's possessions.
29. Babylonian Talmud, *Yoma* 26a.

– APPENDIX –

Bachya ben Asher

> A review of the Torah commentary of Bachya ben Asher adds support to the conclusions reached in this study.

WHO WAS BACHYA?

Bachya was born in Saragossa, Spain on 1255, and died in 1340. He was a pupil of Rabbi Solomon ben Adret, known by the acronym of his name Rashba, who was a student of Nachmanides. He mentions Rashba and Nachmanides in his Torah commentary frequently, and while he does not always accept Nachmanides' interpretation of passages, he agrees with his mystical teachings and those of the *Zohar* that appeared after Nachmanides but during Bachya's lifetime.

SOME STATISTICS

There are a total of fifteen times that Bachya mentions *Onkelos* in his Torah commentary to *Genesis* when Nachmanides also does so. Remarkably, seven of these fifteen are instances where Nachmanides gives what we called a reasonable interpretation; thus he generally avoids the problematical interpretations of Nachmanides. He does address these difficult comments about *Onkelos* in eight instances and he only agrees with Nachmanides twice, in 36:24 and 48:6. Put differently, Bachya only agrees with Nachmanides in two of the twenty-four instances where we found problematical interpretations. Thus, Bachya seems to support our contention that Nachmanides' understanding of *Onkelos* is difficult and enigmatic.

The fifteen instances out of the eighty where Nachmanides mentions *Onkelos* in his commentary to *Genesis*, and where both Nachmanides and Bachya mention *Onkelos* are:

1. 12:8. Nachmanides presents a reasonable explanation of *Onkelos* and Bachya agrees.
2. 17:7. Bachya disagrees with Nachmanides and has a reasonable explanation of the *Targum*.
3. 21:33. Mentions Nachmanides and disagrees with his interpretation of *Onkelos*.
4. 22:2. Rejects Nachmanides' understanding of *Onkelos*.
5. 23:15. Mentions *Onkelos* but ignores Nachmanides' understanding of it.
6. 24:64. Explains *Onkelos* contrary to Nachmanides.
7. 31:42. Same as 12:8.
8. 32:11. Same as 12:8.
9. 36:24. Accepts Nachmanides' problematical interpretation of *Onkelos*.
10. 38:2. Same as 12:8.
11. 41:1. Same as 12:8.
12. 43:18. Same as 12:8.
13. 46:1. Rejects Nachmanides contention that *Onkelos* does not avoid anthropomorphisms.
14. 48:6. Same as 36:24.
15. 49:12. Same as 12:8.

BACHYA MISUSES *ONKELOS*

It appears that Bachya followed Nachmanides' practice of reading mysticism into the targumic wording, but did not always do it in as puzzling a manner as Nachmanides. The following are some examples in *Genesis* where Bachya sought to prove the truthfulness of his interpretation by reference to the Aramaic wording where Nachmanides did not make the comment:

1. In *Genesis* 1:10, he writes, "The term 'oceans' [in the Bible] does signify the water but the hollow of the globe within which it is situated. This is why *Onkelos* translates these words (*u'lemakom hamayim*, "and the place of the water") as *u'l'beit kh'neshut mei'at*, "and the place of the gathering of the water" by adding "gathering." Actually the translator's addition of "gathering" lacks any connotation of "hollow," and the translator only inserted it to clarify that the scriptural passage does call the "place of the water," the dry ground, "ocean," but the water itself; the "gathering of the water" is the "ocean."

2. Bachya was convinced that the fruit of the tree of good and evil was an *ethrog*. He attempted to prove this by noting that *Onkelos* renders Scripture's *v'nechmad* as *u'mirgag*, a word that has two of the letters of *ethrog*, a *reish* and a *gimmel*. Needless to say, the correspondence of two letters proves nothing, especially when both the Hebrew and its Aramaic translation mean "beautiful." *Onkelos* is nothing more than a literal translation in *Genesis* 3:6.

Bachya also mentions *Onkelos* without seeking a mystic teaching in the translation, as in *Genesis* 1:1, 2, 21, 2:9, 3:5, 3:21, 5:24 (mentioning a faulty text), 6:2, 6:14, 9:6, 9:13, 9:27, 12:8 (twice), 13:9 (mentioning a faulty text), 15:17, 15:18, 17:17, 18:21, 21:33, 22:1, 22:13.

– BIBLIOGRAPHY –

Adler, Nathan. *Netina La'ger.* Vilna, 1886.

al-Fayyumi, Saadiah ben Joseph (Saadiah Gaon). *The Book of Beliefs and Opinions.* Edited by D. Sluzki. Leipzig, 1864. Translated by S. Rosenblatt. New Haven: Yale University Press, 1948.

———. *Perushei Rabbenu Saadia Gaon al haTorah.* Edited by Joseph Kafih. Jerusalem: Mossad Harav Kook, 1963.

———. "Perushei Rav Saadiah Gaon," in *Torat Chayim.* Jerusalem: Daf-Chen Press, 1984 and Mossad Harav Kook, 1986.

Babylonian Talmud tractates: *Avodah Zarah, Bava Batra, Bava Kama, Berakhot, Chullin, Horayoth, Keritut, Ketubot, Kiddushin, Makkot, Megillah, Menachot, Nedarim, Nidah, Pesachim, Rosh Hashanah, Sanhedrin, Shabbat, Sotah, Yevamot, Yoma, Zevachim.*

Banitt, M. *Rashi, Interpreter of the Biblical Letter.* Tel Aviv: Tel Aviv University, 1985.

ben Asher, Bachya. *Torah Commentary.* Jerusalem: Urim Publications, 1998.

ben Hofni Gaon, Samuel. *Peirush Hatorah L'Rav Shmuel ben Hofni Gaon.* Jerusalem: Mossad Harav Kook, 1978.

ben Maimon, Moshe (Maimonides). *Guide of the Perplexed.* Translated into English by M. Friedlander. New York: Dover, 1956.

———. *Introduction to the Mishneh,* Chelek.

———. *Letters of Maimonides.* Leon D. Stitskin, New York: Yeshiva University Press, 1977.

———. *Moreh Nevuchim (Guide of the Perplexed).* Translated into Hebrew by Shemuel ibn Tibbon with four ebrew commentaries of Efudi, Shemtov, Karshekesh, and Abarbanel. Jerusalem: Isaac Goldman, 1960.

———. *Moreh Nevuchim (Guide of the Perplexed).* Translated into Hebrew by Samuel ibn Tibbon with commentary by Shemuel ibn Shemuel. Jerusalem: Mossad Harav Kook, 2000.

———. *Moreh Nevuchim (Guide of the Perplexed)*. Translated into Hebrew by David Kafiah. Jerusalem: Mossad Harav Kook, 1977

———. *Mishneh Torah* (Code of Law and Ethics). *Hilkhot Tefillah* 1:1–3.

———. *Sefer Hamitzvot La'Rambam im Hasagot Haramban (Book of Commandments)*. Jerusalem: Mossad Harav Kook, 1981.

———. *The Commandments*. Translated by Charles B. Chavel. London and New York: Soncino Press, 1967.

———. *The Guide of the Perplexed*, translation and introduction by Shlomo Pines. Chicago: University of Chicago Press, 1963.

ben Meir, R. Samuel (Rashbam). *The Commentary of R. Samuel ben Meir on Qohelet*. Edited by Sara Japhet and Robert B. Salters. Translated by Robert B. Salters. The Magnes Press, Jerusalem, 1985.

ben Nachman (Nachmanides). *Asifat Zekenim to Ketubot*. Warsaw, 1861.

———. *Commentary on the Torah, Genesis, Exodus, Numbers, Leviticus, Deuteronomy*. Translated with commentary by Charles B. Chavel. New York: Shilo Publishing House, 1971.

———. *Kitvei Ramban*. Edited by Charles Ber Chavel. Jerusalem: Mossad Harav Kook, 1964.

———. *Hasagot Haramban on Maimonides' Sefer Hamitzvot*. Jerusalem: Mossad Harav Kook, 1981.

ben Uziel, Jonathan. *Targum of the Prophets*.

ben-Meir, Ruth. "Avraham in Nachmanides' Thought" [Hebrew]. In *Avraham Avi ha-Ma'aminim* [The faith of Abraham in the light of interpretation throughout the ages). Edited by Moshe Halamish, Hannaha Kasher, and Yohanan Silman. Ramat Gan: Bar-Ilan University Press, 2002.

Berkowitz, Benzion Judah. *Chalifot Semalot*. Wilna, 1874.

———. *Lechem Vesimla*. Wilna, 1843.

Berlin, Isaiah B. *Minei Targuma*. University of Michigan Library reprint. 1836.

Berliner, Abraham. *Die Masorah zum Targum Onkelos*. Leipzig, 1877.

———. *Targum Onkelos*. 2 vols. Berlin, 1884.

Blau, Y. *Responsa Haramban*. Jerusalem, 1960.

Bonfils, Joseph. *Tzafanat Pane'ach*. Edited by D. Herzog. Heidelberg, 1930.

Bromberg, A.I. *Perush HaTorah l'Rashbam*. Tel Aviv, 1964.

Brown, D., S.R. Driver, and C.A. Briggs. *A Hebrew and English Lexicon of the Old Testament*. Oxford: Clarendon, 1907.

Buber, Martin. *On Judaism*. New York: Schocken Books, 1967.

Cahill, Thomas. *Sailing the Wine-Dark Sea*. New York: Doubleday, 2003.

Chacham, Amos. *Sefer Shemot*. Jerusalem: Mossad Harav Kook, 1991.

Chavel, Charles Ber. *Kitvei Rabbeinu Bachya*. Jerusalem: Mossad Harav Kook, 1981.

———. *Maimonides, The Book of Divine Commandments*. New York: The Soncino Press, 1967.

———. *Perushei Rashi al Hatorah*. Jerusalem: Mossad Harav Kook, 1982.

———. *Ramban, Commentary on the Torah. Genesis*. Translated and annotated. New York: Shilo Publishing House, 1971–1976.

———. *Ramban: His Life and Teachings*. New York: Feldheim, 1960.

———. *Sefer Hamitzvot La'Rambam im Hasagot Haramban*. Jerusalem: Mossad HaRav Kook, 1981.

———. *The Disputation at Barcelona*. New York: Shilo Publication House, 1983.

———. "The Gate of Reward," in *Ramban: Writings and Discourses*. New York: Shilo Publishing House, 1978.

———. "The Law of the Eternal is Perfect," in *Kitvei Haramban*. Jerusalem: Mossad Harav Kook, 1983.

———. *Torat Chayim*. Jerusalem: Mossad Harav Kook, 1993.

———. *Writings of the Ramban/Nachmanides*. New York: Judaica Press, 2010.

Chazan, Robert. *Barcelona and Beyond: The Disputation of 1263 and Its Aftermath*. Berkeley: University of California Press, 1992.

Cohen, Hermann. *Religion der Vernunft aus den Quellen des Judentums*. Wiesbaden: Fourier 1978.

Cohen, J. and U. Simon, eds. *R. Abraham Ibn Ezra: Yesod Mora V'sod Torah*. Israel, Ramat-Gan: Bar-Ilan University Press, 2002.

Creskas, Chasdai ben Judah. *Sefer Or Hashem*. South Carolina: Nabu Press, 2010.

Dalman, Gustaf. *Grammatik des Jüdisch-Palästinischen Aramäisch*. Leipzig, 1905.

Drazin, Rabbi Dr. Israel. "Dating Targum Onkelos by means of the Tannaitic Midrashim," *Journal of Jewish Studies* 50, no. 2 (autumn 1999).

———. *Maimonides and the Biblical Prophets*. Jerusalem: Gefen Publishing House, 2009.

———. *Targum Onkelos to Deuteronomy*. New York: Ktav, 1982.

———. *Targum Onkelos to Numbers*. New York: Ktav, 1998.

———. *Targumic Studies*. Ann Arbor: University Microfilm International, 1980.

Drazin, Rabbi Dr. Israel, and Rabbi Dr. Stanley Wagner. *Onkelos on the Torah*. Jerusalem: Gefen Publishing House, 2008.

Ehrlich, Arnold Bogumil. *Mikra Kipheshuto*. (The Bible According to Its Literal Meaning). New York: Ktav, 1969.

Encyclopedia Judaica, 16 volumes. Jerusalem: Macmillan, 1972.

Encyclopedia Mikra'it. Jerusalem: Mosad Bialik, 1950.

Epstein, Baruch HaLevi, Rabbi. *Tosefet Berakha* (Hebrew). Israel: Moreshet Publishing House, 1999.

Even-Shoshan, Abraham. *Dictionary. Hamilon Hechadash*. Jerusalem: Kiryat Sefer, 1974.

Feinberg, C.L. "The Scapegoat of Leviticus 16." *Bibleotheca Sacra*, 115. 1958.

Festinger, Leon. *The Theory of Cognitive Dissonance*. California: Stanford University Press, 1973.

Fohrer, Georg. "Kopfbedeckung," *BHH* (Biblisch-historisches Handworterbuch) 2.

Friedman, Shamma, ed. *Chameish Sugyot min Hatalmud Bavli*. Jerusalem: Haigud l'Parshanut Hatalmud. Jerusalem, 2003.

Friedmann, Meir, ed. *Nispahim l'Seder Eliyahu Zuta*. Second edition. Jerusalem, 1960.

Green, Arthur. "Shekhinah, the Virgin Mary and the Song of Songs." *AJS Review* 26:1 (2002).

Grossfeld, Bernard, "Targum Onkelos, Halakha and the Halakhic Midrashim," in *The Aramaic Bible*, edited by M. McNamara. and D.R.G. Beattie. Sheffield: Sheffield Academic Press, 1994.

Halevi, Judah. *Kuzari*. New York: Schocken Books, 1987.

Haran, Menachem. *Templar and Temple Service in Ancient Israel*. Oxford: Claredon Press, 1978.

Heinemann, Yitzchak. *Darkey ha-Aggadah*. Jerusalem, 1954.

Heller, Chayim. *A Critical Essay on the Palestinian Targum to the Pentateuch*. New York, 1921.

———. *Maimonides, Sefer Hamitzvot L'harambam.* Mossad Harav Kook, 1995.

Henoch, C.J. *Nachmanides: Philosopher and Kabbalist.* Jerusalem: Torah Laam Publications, 1998.

Hirsch, Samson Raphael. *The Pentateuch.* The Judaic Press, 1971.

Hoenig, Sidney B. "A Jewish Reaction to Calendar Reform, *Tradition* 7 (1964)

———. "Sabbatical Years and the year of Jubilee." *JQR* 59, 1969.

Hoffman, David Zvi. *Sefer Vayikra.* Jerusalem: Mossad HaRav Kook, 1976.

ibn Ezra, Abraham. *Yesod Mora Ve-Sod Torah.* Edited by J. Cohen. and U. Simon. Ramat Gan: Bar Ilan University Press, 2002.

ibn Mosconi, Yehuda Leon. *Even Ha'ezer.* Edited by Abraham Berliner, in *OtzarTov*, 1878.

ibn Saruq, Menachem. *Sefer Machberet Menahem.* Edited by H. Filipowski. London and Edinburgh, 1854.

ibn Shaprut, Chasdai. *Tzafanat Pane'ach.* Ms. Oxford: Bodley Opp. Add, Neubauer 2350.

Jastrow, Marcus. *A Dictionary of the Targumim, the Talmud Babli and Yerushalmi, and the Midrashic Literature.* 2 vols. Philadelphia, 1886–1903.

Jerusalem Talmud: *Berakhot, Megillah, Sotah.*

Kamin, Sarah. *Rashi's Exegetical Categorization with Respect to the Distinction Between Peshat and Derash* (Doctorial Thesis). Jerusalem, 1978.

———. *Rashi's Exegetical Categorization* (Hebrew). Jerusalem: The Magnes Press, Jerusalem,1986.

———. *The Bible in the Light of its Interpreters: Sarah Kamin Memorial Volume.* Edited by Sara Japhet. Jerusalem: The Magnes Press, 1994.

Karo, Joseph. *Shulchan Aruch, Orach Chayim.*

Kasher, Menachem Mendel. *Torah Shelemah.* Jerusalem, 1974.

Kugel, J.L. *The God of Old.* The Free Press, 2003.

Landauer, Samuel. *Die Masorah zum Targum Onkelos.* Amsterdam, 1896.

Lauterbach, Jacob Z., trans. *Mekhilta d'Rabbi Ishmael.* Philadelphia: Jewish Publication Society, 1933.

Leibowitz, Yeshayahu. *Conversations with Yeshayahu Leibowitz on the Moreh Nevukhim of Maimonides* (Hebrew), Jerusalem: Mira Ofran, 2003.

———. *Seven Years of Discourses on the Weekly Torah Reading* (Hebrew). Jerusalem, Keter Publishing House, Israel, 2000.

Lerner, Ralph. *Maimonides' Empire of Light*. Chicago: University of Chicago Press, 2000.

Levine, Baruch A. *The JPS Torah Commentary, Leviticus*. Philadelphia: Jewish Publication Society, 2001–2003.

Levy, J. *Chaldäisches Wörterbuch über dir Targumim*. Leipzig, 1867.

Licht, Jacob. *Story Telling in the Bible*. The Magnes Press, 1986.

Lippmann G. ed. *Safah Berurah*. Furth: Fulda and Zumfdorffer, 1839.

Lockshin, M.I. *Rabbi Samuel ben Meir's Commentary on Genesis*. Jewish Studies, The Edwin Mellen Press, 1989.

Lowenstein, M. *Nefesh Hager*. Pietrokov, 1906.

Maccoby, Hyam, trans. and ed. *Judaism on Trial: Jewish-Christian Disputations in the Middle Ages*. Littman Library of Jewish Civilization in association with Liverpool University Press, 1993.

Margolith, David. "Ramban as Doctor." *Sinai*, year 2, Vol. 40, Booklet 3, (Kislev 1957).

Maybaum, Siegmund. *Die Anthropomorphism und Anthropopathien bei Onkelos und spateren Targumim*. Breslau, 1870.

Midrashim: *Canticles Rabbah, Derekh Eretz Zuta, Exodus Rabbah, Genesis Rabbah, Keilim, Mekhilta, Numbers Rabbah, Pesikta, Pirkei d'Rabbi Eliezer, Psalms, Sifra, Sifrei, Socher Tov, Tanchuma*.

Milgrom, J. *The JPS Torah Commentary, Numbers*. Philadelphia: Jewish Publication Society, 2001–2003.

Mishnaot: *Avodah Zarah, Avot, Lamelek, Makkot, Mekhilta, Pessachim, Sanhedrin, Zevachim*.

Mizrachi, Eliyahu. "Sefer ha-Mizrachi" in *Hameorot Hagedolim, Eleven Commentaries on Rashi*. Hebrew. Edited by Avraham Krishewsky. Jerusalem: Mifal Toroh Mefoyreshes, 1992.

Nebo, Jehoshapat, Dr. *Perushei Rabbi Josef Bechor Shor al Hatorah*. Jerusalem: Mossad Harav Kook, 1994.

Novak, David. *The Theology of Nachmanides Systematically Presented*. Atlanta: Scholars Press, 1992.

Patshegen. In Nathan Adler, *Netina La'ger.* Wilna, 1886.

Philo, *The Works of Philo.* Translated by C.D. Yonge. Massachusetts: Hendrickson Publishers, 1993.

Rachman, Y. *Igeret Rashi.* Mizrachi, 1991.

Ratzhavi, Yehuda, *M'Pirushei Rav Saadyah Gaon Lamikra.* Jerusalem, Mossad Harav Kook, 2004.

Reifman, Jacob. *Sedeh Aram.* Berlin, 1875.

Revel, Dov. *Targum Yonathan al Hatorah.* New York, 1924–1925.

Rosenthal, Erwin, I.J. "The Study of the Bible in Medieval Judaism," *Studia Semitica.* Cambridge: Cambridge University Press, 1971.

Rosin, D. "Die Religions philosophie Abraham ibn Ezra's." *Monatschrift für Geschichte und Wissenchaft des Judentum,* 1893.

Rosner, Fred. *Maimonides' Commentary on the Mishnah, Tractate Sanhedrin.* New York: Sepher-Hermon Press, Inc.,1981.

Ruderman, David B. *A Valley of Vision: The Heavenly Journey of Abraham ben Hananiah Yagel.* University of Pennsylvania Press, 1990.

Sarna, N.M. *The JPS Torah Commentary: Genesis.* Philadelphia: The Jewish Publication Society, 2001–2003.

———. *The JPS Torah Commentary: Exodus.* Philadelphia: The Jewish Publication Society, 2001–2003.

Schechter, Solomon. *Studies in Judaism, First Series, The Dogmas of Judaism.* Philadelphia: Jewish Publication Society of America, 1896.

Schefftel, Simon Baruch. *Biure Onkelos.* Munich, 1888.

Scriptural sources (Pentateuch/Prophets/Writings): Aquilas, *Amos, I/II Chronicles, Daniel, 1 Enoch, Ezekiel, Hosea, Isaiah, Jeremiah, Job, Joshua, I/II Kings, Lamentations,* Latin Vulgate, *Matthew, Nehemiah,* Pentateuch, *Peshitta, Pirkei Avot, Psalms, Proverbs, I/II Samuel,* Septuagint, *Song of Songs, Zechariah, Zephaniah.*

Septimus, Bernard. "'Open Rebuke and Concealed Love': Nachmanides and the Andalusian Tradition," in *Rabbi Moses Nachmanides (Ramban): Explorations in His Religious and Literary Virtuosity.* Edited by I. Twersky. Cambridge, Mass.: Harvard University Press, 1983.

Shulman, Yaacov Dovid. *The Ramban.* New York: CIS, 1993.

Simon, Maurice, ed. *The Zohar*. London: The Soncino Press, 1984.

Sokoloff, Michael. *A Dictionary of Jewish Palestinian Aramaic of the Byzantine Period*. Ramat Gan, 1990.

Speiser, Ephraim Avigdor. *Oriental and Biblical Studies*. Philadelphia, 1967.

Sperber, Alexander, ed. *The Bible in Aramaic*. 5 vols. Leiden: E.J. Brill, 1959.

Sperber, Daniel, Rabbi, Dr. *Minhagei Yisrael*. Jerusalem: Mossad Harav Kook, 1989.

Stern, Joseph. *Problems and Parables of Law: Maimonides and Nachmanides on the reasons for the Commandments*. Albany: State of New York University Press, 1998.

Targumim: *Cairo Geniza Targum Fragments, Other Fragmented Targums, Neophyti, Onkelos, Pseudo-Jonathan, Samaritan, Syropalestinian*.

Theodor, J. and Chanoch Albeck. *Bereschit Rabbah*. Jerusalem, 1965.

Tigay, Jeffrey H. *The JPS Torah Commentary*. Jewish Publication Society, 2001–2003.

Tishby, Isaiah. *Mishnat Hazohar*, 2 volumes. Jerusalem, 1957.

Tosaphot: *Berakhot, Kiddushin, Makkot, Sotah*.

Trachtenberg, Joshua. *Jewish Magic and Superstition*. New York: Behrman's Jewish Book House, 1939.

Twersky, Isadore. ed. *Rabbi Moses Nachmanides (Ramban): Explorations in his Religious and Literary Virtuosity*. Cambridge, MA: Harvard University Press, 1983.

Twersky, Isadore. *Rabad of Posquieres*. Philadelphia: Jewish Publication Society, 1980.

Unna, Isaac. *R. Moses Ben Nahman: His Life and Activity*. Jerusalem, 1942.

Vermes, Géza. "The Decalogue and the Minim," in *In Memoriam Paul Kahle*. Edited by Black, Matthew, Fohrer. Berlin: Topelmann, 1968

Weiser, Asher *Ibn Ezra, Perushei Hatorah*. Jerusalem: Mossad Harav Kook, 1977.

Winston, David, "The Wisdom of Solomon." *Anchor Bible*. New York: Doubleday, 1979.

INDEX

A

Abel 25, 97
Abihu 129
Abimelech 81
Abravanel, Isaac 28, 37, 155
Adam 25–26, 97, 114
adayuta 164–65
Adler, Nathan 102, 124
aggadah xx, 146–47
Amalek 45
amtachat 108
Anah 103
Aquilas 87
Arabah 166
Aristotle xvii, xix, 33, 65, 143
ashlamuta 130
Asshurim 101
azazel 140–42, 144–46

B

Baal-peor 174
Babylonian Talmud
    Berakhot 84
    Chullin 44, 49–50, 138
    Exodus Rabbah 22
    Kiddushin 94, 149
    Makkot 11, 148
    Megillah 113, 152, 167
    Menachot 10
    Nedarim 37
    Rosh Hashanah 45
    Sanhedrin 13, 35, 41, 48, 144, 167, 169
    Shabbat 12, 31, 148
    Sotah 29–30, 84
    Yevamot 171
    Yoma 133, 137–38, 141, 175
    Zevachim 137
Balaam xix, 10, 36
Balak 10
ben Adret, Rabbi Solomon . . .
    See Rashba 177
ben Asher, Bachya xviii, 25–26, 28,
    30–32, 78–80, 82–87, 89, 91, 93,
    95, 97, 99–100, 104, 107–108, 114,
    116, 118, 122, 124–25, 128, 130, 132,
    134, 145–46, 156, 165, 177–79
ben David, Rabbi Abraham (RaBad
    of Posquieres) 32, 112
ben Kalonymus, Eleazar ben Judah
    (Eleazar of Worms) 23
ben Meir, Rabbi Samuel . . .
    See Rashbam 61
ben Uziel, Jonathan 110
beriah 35–36
Berkowitz, Benzion Judah 172
bikoreth 148
Bilhah 27, 104

C

Cain 25, 78, 92, 97
Caleb 23
Canaan 11, 30, 43, 46–49, 82–83,
    86, 102, 115, 117, 128, 159, 163
chalaf 168
Chavel, Charles Ber 3–5, 40, 157

Chazkuni 84, 87, 95, 106, 153, 168
Christiani, Pablo xvii

D

dachal 69–70
Dan 87
Decalogue 22, 49–51
derash xx, 55–64, 133, 148
didan xx, 72
Dinah 87, 105, 128
Di-zahab 166
Drazin, Israel, Rabbi Dr. 192–94
dudaim 82

E

Eden 24, 26, 92–93, 114, 172
Eheyeh 118–19
eikev 168
eizer 22
Elohim 70
Ephraim 86, 115–16
Ephron 98
Epstein, Rabbi Baruch HaLevi xix
Esau 81–83, 101–103, 142
ethrog 152, 179
Eve 26, 38, 92, 114
Even-Shoshan, Abraham 94–95

F

Festinger, Leon xxi

G

Gad 46, 116–17
Gaon, Saadiah 59–60, 95, 142
Gilead 46
Green, Arthur 18
Guide of the Perplexed ... See Maimonides, Moses 14, 19, 68, 114, 169

H

halakhah 12, 18, 41, 55, 72, 119–120, 126–27, 130, 136–39, 149–150, 159, 172
Halevi, Judah 32
Ham 78
Hazerot 166
Heller, Chaim 64
hephker 148
Hoenig, Sidney B. 154, 194
Hofni, Shmuel ben, Gaon 60, 142

I

ibn Ezra, Abraham xix, xx, 4, 11, 22, 33, 36–37, 44–45, 50–51, 62, 64, 80, 82, 85, 87, 95, 108, 114, 123, 129, 137, 141–44, 151–53, 170–73, 175
ibn Janach, Jonah 148
Isaac 22, 81–82, 96–97, 99–100

J

Jacob 17, 27–28, 81–84, 86–87, 101–104, 108–109, 112, 114–16, 155, 163, 174
Jastrow, Marcus 94, 125, 130, 140, 153
Jethro 123
Joseph 13, 17, 31, 55, 57, 63, 71, 79, 83–86, 88, 104–105, 107–108, 115–16, 193–94
Joshua 23, 29–30, 43–44, 46–47, 86, 115

K

Kabbalah xviii, xxi, 3–4, 64, 82, 93, 110–11, 113, 115, 125, 128–29, 131–32, 134, 168
Karo, Joseph 13, 55, 57
King
    David 13, 105
    Nimrod 13
Korach 42, 160–62
Kugel, James L. 69

L

Laban 82, 155, 166–67
Letushim 101
Leummim 101
Levi 57, 87, 174

M

Maimonides, Moses (Rambam) xvii–xix, xxi, 4, 9, 11–12, 14–15, 17–20, 24, 27–29, 31–33, 38, 45–46, 49–51, 55, 62, 68, 91, 96, 102, 109, 111–12, 114, 125, 143, 146, 169, 171, 193
memra 68, 109–11, 129
Menasheh 86, 115–17
Meribah 174
Metatron 128, 135
mido 137
Midrash
  Exodus Rabbah 22
  Genesis Rabbah 13, 34, 57, 80, 87, 91, 94, 100, 114, 142
  Mekhilta 57, 110, 113, 124, 126–28
  Numbers Rabbah 7, 156
  Pesikta 28, 50
  Psalms 126
  Sifra 57, 136–39, 141, 148, 152
  Sifrei 8, 44–45, 57, 147, 157, 159, 169–71, 173–75
  Tanchuma 7, 10, 161, 168, 175
Mikdash 41
Mizrachi, Eliyahu (Re'em) 126, 169–170
Molech 149
Mount Ebal 169
Mount Gerizim 169
Mount Sinai xix, 3, 22, 51, 56, 114, 125, 142
murato 136–37

N

Nadab 129

Neophyti 70, 87, 111, 126, 137, 148, 168, 171, 173
nidah 164–65

P

pakad 42
Paran 79, 166
Patshegan 171
pelilim 126
Pentateuch xviii–xx, 5, 9, 57, 67–71, 73, 77, 91–92, 110, 139, 145, 150
peshat xx, 55–58, 61–62, 64, 127–28, 174
pilug 94
Pinchas 13
Plato xvii, 22, 91
Potiphar 79, 83
Proverbs 34
Pseudo-Jonathan 70, 80, 87, 111, 126, 128, 137, 148, 157, 163, 168, 171, 173, 175
psyche 91

Q

qadam 69–70, 92, 128, 145, 173–74
qatal 126

R

Rachel 16, 27–28, 82
Rashba 79, 91, 177
Rashbam 28, 44, 61–63, 84–85, 87, 106, 125, 170
Rashi xix, xx, 4, 6–11, 22, 28, 32–33, 35–38, 40–41, 44–45, 50–51, 56–57, 60–61, 79–87, 90, 92–93, 95, 97, 100, 105–109, 115, 119, 121–23, 127, 130, 137, 148, 152, 163, 168–73
Rebecca 99–101
Reuben 27, 46, 82, 117
Ruth 13

S

Samael 142, 144, 146
Samson 87
savav 140
sefirot xviii, 17, 26, 34, 113, 131
Segal, Rabbi David Ha-Levi 57
Serah 163–64
Sforno, Obadiah ben Jacob 28, 37, 106, 170, 173, 175
Shechem 87, 128
Shekhinah 69, 110, 112–15, 135, 149
sheretz 90
Shor, Rabbi Joseph Bechor 63
shoshipakh 106
siddur xix
Sihon 48
Simeon 31, 87
Song of Songs 10, 50
Suph 166
Symmachus 87

T

tekheilet 10
tekiah 45
teruah 45
Tophel 166–67
Torah xviii–xxi, 3–6, 8–9, 11, 15–20, 22, 25, 27–29, 34–37, 40–42, 44–51, 55–59, 64–65, 70, 73, 90, 93, 95–97, 110, 114, 120–21, 123, 131–33, 140, 142, 144, 148, 154, 164, 166–67, 173, 177
Tosaphot 56
Transjordan 11, 46, 48
tzachak 95
tzitzit 9–10, 106

U

ulai 36

W

Wadi Jabbok 102

Y

yekara 69
Yitzchaki, Rabbi Shlomo … See Rashi 60

Z

zekhut avot 13, 42
zekhut banim 13
Zelophehad 47, 163
Zilpah 27, 104
Zohar 23, 28, 31, 177

– ABOUT THE AUTHOR –

Dr. Israel Drazin

EDUCATION: Dr. Drazin, born in 1935, received three rabbinical degrees in 1957, a B.A. in Theology in 1957, an M.Ed. In Psychology in 1966, a JD in Law in 1974, a M.A. in Hebrew Literature in 1978 and a Ph.D. with honors in Aramaic Literature in 1981. Thereafter, he completed two years of post-graduate study in both Philosophy and Mysticism and graduated the U.S. Army's Command and General Staff College and its War College for generals in 1985.

MILITARY: Brigadier General Drazin entered Army Active Duty, at age 21, as the youngest U.S. Chaplain ever to serve on active duty. He served on active duty from 1957 to 1960 in Louisiana and Germany, and then joined the active reserves and soldiered, in increasing grades, with half a dozen units. From 1978 until 1981, he lectured at the US Army Chaplains School on legal subjects. In March 1981, the Army requested that he take leave from civil service and return to active duty to handle special constitutional issues. He was responsible for preparing the defense in the trial challenging the constitutionality of the Army Chaplaincy; the military chaplaincies of all the uniformed services, active and reserve, as well as the Veteran's Administration, were attacked utilizing a constitutional rationale and could have been disbanded. The Government won the action in 1984 and Drazin was awarded the prestigious *Legion of Merit*. Drazin returned to civilian life and the active reserves in 1984 as Assistant Chief of Chaplains, the highest reserve officer position available in the Army Chaplaincy, with the rank of Brigadier General. He was the first Jewish person to serve in this capacity in the U.S. Army. During his military career, he revolutionized the role of military chaplains making them officers responsible for the free exercise rights of all military personnel; requiring them to provide for the needs of people of all faiths as well as atheists. General Drazin completed this four-year tour of duty with honors in March 1988, culminating a total of 31 years of military duty.

ATTORNEY: Israel Drazin graduated from law school in 1974 and immediately began a private practice. He handled virtually all manners of suits; including, domestic, criminal, bankruptcy, accident and contract cases. He joined with his son in 1993 and formed offices in Columbia and Dundalk, Maryland. Dr. Drazin stopped actively practicing law in 1997, after 23 years, and became "Of Counsel" to the Law Offices of Drazin and Drazin, P.A.

CIVIL SERVICE: Israel Drazin joined the U.S. Civil Service in 1962 and remained a civil service employee, with occasional leave for military duty, until retirement in 1990. At retirement he accumulated 28 years of creditable service. During his U.S. Civil Service career, he held many positions; including, being an Equal Opportunity Consultant in the 1960s (advising insurance company top executives regarding civil rights and equal employment) and the head of Medicare's Civil Litigation Staff (supervising a team of lawyers who handled suits filed by and against the government's Medicare program). He also served as the director for all Maryland's Federal Agencies' relationship with the United Fund.

RABBI: Dr. Drazin was ordained as a rabbi in 1957 at Ner Israel Rabbinical College in Baltimore, Maryland and subsequently received semichot from two other rabbis. He entered on Army active duty in 1957. He left active duty in 1960 and officiated as a weekend rabbi at several synagogues, including being the first rabbi in Columbia, Maryland. He continued the uninterrupted weekend rabbinical practice until 1974 and then officiated as a rabbi on an intermittent basis until 1987. His rabbinical career totaled 30 years.

PHILANTHROPY: Dr. Drazin served as the Executive Director of the Jim Joseph Foundation, a charitable foundation that gives money to support Jewish education, for just over four years, from September 2000 to November 2004.

AUTHOR: Israel Drazin is the author of thirty-eight books, more than 500 popular and scholarly articles, and close to 5,000 book and movie reviews. He wrote a book about the case he handled for the US Army, edited a book on legends, children's books, and scholarly books on the philosopher Maimonides and on the Aramaic translation of the Bible. His website is www.booksnthoughts.com. He places two essays on this site weekly.

LECTURES: Dr. Drazin delivered lectures at Howard Community College, Lynn University, and the US Army Chaplains School.

MEMBERSHIPS AND AWARDS: Brigadier General Drazin is admitted to practice law in Maryland, the Federal Court, and before the U.S. Supreme Court. He is a member of several attorney Bar Associations and the Rabbinical Council of America. He was honored with a number of military awards, the RCA 1985 Joseph Hoenig Memorial Award, and the Jewish Welfare Board 1986 Distinguished Service Award. Mayor Kurt Schmoke, of Baltimore, Maryland, named February 8, 1988 "Israel Drazin Day." A leading Baltimore Synagogue named him "Man of the Year" in 1990. He is included in the recent editions of *Who's Who in World Jewry*, *Who's Who in American Law*, *Who's Who in Biblical Studies and Archaeology*, and other *Who's Who* volumes.